An

ACTOR'S
LIFE

An
ACTOR'S
LIFE

From First Night to Final Curtain

A Theatrical Anthology
edited by

Philip Franks

PAVILION

First published in Great Britain in 1995 by

PAVILION BOOKS LIMITED
26 UPPER GROUND
LONDON SE1 9PD

Designed by Nigel Partridge
Typeset in Bembo

A CIP catalogue record for this book is available from the British Library.

ISBN 1-85793-416 4

Printed and bound in Great Britain by Hartnolls Ltd.

2 4 6 8 10 9 7 5 3 1

This book may be ordered by post direct from the publisher.
Please contact the Marketing Department.
But try your bookshop first.

CONTENTS

INTRODUCTION

Every so often, when news is thin on the ground, one of the Sunday papers will run a scary article about evolution. A new strain of rats, or bees, or antibodies will have been discovered, completely immune to the good efforts of doctors, exterminators, bee-keepers or hapless victims. We all shiver and flip on to the TV guide.

A disconcertingly similar evolutionary process is periodically visible in relation to the theatrical profession. The process occurs whenever actors look likely to attain respectability. Actors have always been admired, lusted after, even 'worshipped' in a peculiarly unhealthy way, but they have also long been the victims of an almost compulsive cutting down to size. Throughout history, hints and accusations of unspeakable vice and immorality have abounded. Until relatively recently the *Encyclopaedia Britannica* defined an actress as a type of prostitute, and theatres have always been closed at the drop of a hat by nervous governments. Actors are not immune to attack from their apparent allies, writers. Literature abounds with portraits of feather-brained gigglers, vicious grasping monsters or self-obsessed dolts, not least in plays. It is a precarious job and for years actors have accepted these stereotypes with forelock-tugging self-abasement. The treatment of black people as grinning ninnies and cowardly servants in decades-worth of Hollywood films is the most recognizable and offensive manifestation of this, but it is also firmly present in cosier, more heart-warming pieces such as *Stage Door*, *42nd Street* or *The Dresser*.

There have always been exceptions – serious artists taken seriously by society. In some ages there is a great deal more. In this country, in the 1960s and '70s there seemed to be a powerful move away from glamour

1

and trivia towards a new seriousness. Co-operatives were formed, new writing flourished, small companies thrived. A new breed of actor emerged, intellectually demanding, politically aware, witty and creative – an artist with muscle and opinion, not just a clever live toy. This growth was, perhaps, not entirely unconnected with subsidy. Society seemed to be honouring its artists, and respect breeds confidence.

There was a powerful backlash in the 1980s – the evolutionary process at work. In that decade of market forces and individual achievement, if you couldn't show a profit you went to the wall, and the profits of art have always been hard to quantify. Grants were cut, theatres closed, companies disbanded. Actors who were publically vocal were branded 'luvvies'. This irritating appellation was a highly efficient piece of spin-doctoring, guaranteed to rob actors of dignity and seriousness and shove them back onto their pedestals, where they could be admired and patronized, drooled over and disenfranchized.

Unfortunately, there's a great deal of self-inflicted foot-shooting. Nicholas Craig in *I, an Actor* has lampooned the ludicrous vanity of the compulsive self-exposer most brilliantly and embarassingly. This anthology is an attempt to redress the balance.

I have used the shape of a typical lifetime in the theatre, inasmuch as any life can be typical. Early games, school plays and visits to the theatre give way to amateur experiments, formal training, struggle, success (or sometimes failure) and eventual old age. The authors I have chosen are by no means all actors, or even playwrights. Tove Jansson, for instance, describes as well as anyone the nerves, agonies and rewards of a first night, yet she is a children's author with a cast of imaginary Scandinavian rodents.

I have tried where possible to avoid the Theatrical Anecdote. Like any in-joke they are fraught with peril. Those of us in the cast of *Bunty Pulls The Strings* at Torquay may roar to recall tumbling scenery, drunken colleagues or mishaps with the kippers but our tears of mirth are unlikely to be shared by anyone who wasn't actually *there*. On the contrary, a cold chill is likely to creep over the reader – the unmistakable sensation of having been buttonholed by a Bore. Accordingly there is more fiction than reminiscence, and when I have included actors talking about their work it is usually in a serious vein. An expert talking with passion and enthusiasm is always more entertaining than being beaten about the head with an old joke, however many famous names might be involved.

There is plenty of comedy, however, from the broad (Dickens' Mrs Porter exacting her revenge, Richmal Crompton's William mangling Hamlet) to the subtle (Dorothy Parker's agonizing 'Glory in The Daytime') as well as a theatrical cat in every way the equal of T. S. Eliot's more famous Gus.

Above all, I wanted to try and communicate the unique delight that the live theatre can give. It stretches imaginations and changes lives, not least the lives of everyone who works within it. When it *works*, it is the only art form that demands and receives collaborative creativity from its audience.

Acting is not as important as surgery or as physically gruelling and dangerous as mining, whatever some memoirs would have us believe – but it is important. We all need imaginative journeys to enrich and illuminate our lives. Actors make it their business to go on these journeys and to share the results with all of us. This book celebrates them.

PHILIP FRANKS, 1995

CHAPTER 1
CHILDHOOD

PANTOMIME POEM

'HE'S BEHIND YER!'
chorused the children
but the warning came too late.

The monster leaped forward
and fastening its teeth into his neck,
tore off the head.

The body fell to the floor
'MORE' cried the children

'MORE, MORE, MORE

MORE

MO

The bloodthirstiness of Roger McGough's children springs from their total involvement in what they have been watching. This is the first experience of theatre for many children – a glimpse into a parallel world, somehow more real than the day-to-day – and certainly more exciting. The wide-eyed wonder on a rapt child's face that a grown-up finds so touching and difficult to understand hides a multitude of complex feelings, beautifully expressed in this next poem.

CHILDREN LEAVING A PANTOMIME

Islands are places the sea would have eaten long ago
With its rolling and roaring for more like pantomime devils

Had not everything come right in the last scene
Before the walk-down and the wicked been sent empty away in
repentant surprise.

The matinee watchers of Sinbads, Whittingtons, Crusoes
Are those small ones who know islands are lonely places,
Are for the existers and the enduring people.

These tumble downstairs to the exits of theatres
After a pantomime, know navigations are not only

To islands, but to selves, that the Lost Wood
Is not the outside-night-dark-haunted-owl-cried-trees

But is the inside-Lost-Wood-under-the-Sea surging nightly
And formidable around the small bed clothes.

Help those who walk slowly, polite and still half-lost in the show
Down long stairs from circle to foyer,

Held still inside the dream inside the dream.

See in the unseeing eye another who sees
The sea knock endlessly at the privacy of islands.

Hears movements of stones and the call of seabirds
Help those who – blind with feeling and small –

Stumble with hand held helpfully out, back down to earth,
Who grow up later to know islands are hard personal places hardly
    won

Where the sea strikes always at each regular tide
And harsh things happen, needing a magic to survive stronger than
    pantomime.

Help those who live now on the mainland where the earth is flat,
The pavement smooth and traffic breaks in like an obscene noise

Upon the silence in which people say goodbye to love,
Where lovers and would-be kind family ask bright impossible
    questions about the magic

Like, 'Did you enjoy it, darling? Was it nice?'

STEPHEN SURREY

❧

From watching to doing. Joyce Grenfell perfected the character of the harassed primary-school teacher, vainly attempting to control her tiny charges, all with fierce wills of their own, and as alien to her as any Martian.

❧

Hello, Mrs Binton, I'm so glad you could get along to see a rehearsal of our Nativity Play! Can you squeeze in there? I'm afraid our chairs are a wee bitty wee, as they say north of the border!

Now then, children. We are going to start our rehearsal. Where are my Mary and Joseph?

That's right, Shirleen, take Denis by the hand and come sit nice and quietly on this bench in the middle.

Don't drag him. He'll come if you leave him alone!

Don't hit each other, Mary and Joseph were *friends.*

Now, who are my Wise Men?

You're a Wise Man, aren't you, Geoffrey?

Oh, aren't you? What are you then?

Oh, you're a cattle, are you? And you are going to low. Splendid! Go over to Miss Boulting, will you, please?

Miss Boulting ... You are organising the animals and the angels? He is one of yours.

7

Now, my Wise Men here, please!

Billy, Peter and George.

And George, Wise Men never do that ...

Now my Kings, please.

Of course, Mrs Binton, we know that by tradition the Wise Men and the Kings are one and the same, but we did want everyone in our Nursery School Nativity Play to have a chance, so we have taken a few liberties, and I don't think any one will mind.

Now Kings: Sidney, Neville, Cliff and Nikolas Anoniodes.

Four Kings, I'm afraid. We happen to have four lovely crowns, so it seemed a pity not to use them.

Sidney, put your crown on straight please, not over one eye. What have you got under your jersey?

That's not the place for a hamster, is it. Put him straight back in his little pen, please.

Sidney, which one have you got, General Amin or Harold Wilson?

Well, who's got General Amin?

Neville, put him back at once.

Poor General Amin and Harold Wilson, it isn't very Christmassy for them under your jersey.

Sidney, I think it serves you right if Harold Wilson bit you, and don't bite him back.

Because he's smaller than you are. Are you bleeding?

Then don't make such a fuss.

Cliff, put your crown on please.

It's too big? Let's see. Ah, yes it is ...

Where are you! Oh, there you are! Nice to see you again! Change with Nikolas.

Nikolas, you can manage a big crown, can't you? You've got just the ears for it.

I think if you pull your ears down a bit that will hold it up. And lean back a bit. That's it.

Stay like that, dear. Don't move.

Wise Men and Kings, don't muddle yourselves with each other.

Now then, Shepherds.

Jimmy, you are my First Shepherd and not a racing car.

Yes, Caroline, you're a shepherd.

No, dear you can't wear your Little Bo-Peep costume: because there aren't any little girl shepherdesses in our play. They're all boy shepherds, and you are a girl being a boy shepherd.

Yes, it is rotten. But we just have to settle for it. I think if you are very good perhaps you can wear a lovely grey beard; wouldn't that be fun?

George, what do Wise Men never do?

Yes ...

Jimmy, do you remember what you see up in the sky? Something lovely, isn't it?

No, not a baby. Try again.

It's a lovely silver star, and you are going to put your hand up and point to it. And what are you going to say when you do that?

No, Sidney, he isn't going to say, 'Please may I go to the bathroom?'

Children that isn't funny; it's a perfectly natural function, and we might as well get used to it.

Come on, Jimmy. You are going to say, 'Behold!' aren't you?

Yes, you are, dear. You said it yesterday.

You'd rather say it tomorrow?

Perhaps you are right.

We have broken the back of the play, so you may as well get ready to go home. Hand in your crowns gently, please. No, Sidney, you can't wear your crown home on the bus.

I think – I HOPE it will be all right on the night.

But you know, Mrs Binton, I think perhaps next year we might make do with a Christmas carol.

JOYCE GRENFELL, NATIVITY PLAY

Grenfell's children have not really caught the theatrical bug. Perhaps the inner fantasy life of a child doesn't need artificial expression until the child is older. Louisa M. Alcott's March girls are in their teens in this extract from *Little Women*. Marshalled by the imaginative, creative and uncontrollable Jo, they are about to perform a major verse tragedy, with music, in the safety and comfort of their own bedroom. They use theatre to cheer themselves up in an unsettled and frightening time: mid-nineteenth-century America during the Civil War. Their father is an army chaplain for the Yankees, away from home and facing death. Jo's play, though a fantasy, is full of violence and crisis. As is so often the case, theatre is giving expression to the inner life of the participants. Also, of course, it's *fun*.

On Christmas night, a dozen girls piled on to the bed, which was the dress-circle, and sat before the blue and yellow chintz curtains in a most flattering state of expectancy. There was a good deal of rustling and whispering behind the curtain, a trifle of lamp-smoke, and an occasional giggle from Amy, who was apt to get hysterical in the excitement of the moment. Presently a bell sounded, the curtains flew apart, and the Operatic Tragedy began.

'A gloomy wood', according to the one play-bill, was represented by a few shrubs in pots, green baize on the floor, and a cave in the distance. This cave was made with a clothes-horse for a roof, bureaus for walls; and in it was a small furnace in full blast, with a black spot on it, and an old witch bending over it. The stage was dark, and the glow of the furnace had a fine effect, especially as real steam issued from the kettle when the witch took off the cover. A moment was allowed for the first thrill to subside; then Hugo, the villain, stalked in with a clanking sword at his side, a slouched hat, black beard, mysterious cloak, and the boots. After pacing to and fro in much agitation, he struck his forehead, and burst out in a wild strain, singing of his hatred to Roderigo, his love for Zara, and his pleasing resolution to kill the one and win the other. The gruff tones of Hugo's voice, with an occasional shout when his feelings overcame him, were very impressive, and the audience applauded the moment he paused for breath. Bowing with the air of one accustomed to public praise, he stole to the cavern, and ordered Hagar to come forth with a commanding 'What ho, minion! I need thee!'

Out came Meg, with grey horse-hair hanging about her face, a red and black robe, a staff, and cabbalistic signs upon her cloak. Hugo demanded a potion to make Zara adore him, and one to destroy Roderigo. Hagar, in a fine dramatic melody, promised both, and proceeded to call up the spirit who would bring the love philtre:

> 'Hither, hither, from my home,
> Airy sprite, I bid thee come!
> Born of roses, fed on dew,
> Charms and potions canst thou brew?
>
> 'Bring me here, with elfin speed,
> The fragrant philtre which I need;
> Make it sweet and swift and strong,
> Spirit, answer now my song!'

A soft strain of music sounded, and then at the back of the cave appeared a little figure in cloudy white, with glittering wings, golden hair, and a garland of roses on its head. Waving a wand, it sang:

> 'Hither I come,
>   From my airy home,
> Afar in the silver moon.
>   Take this magic spell,
>   And use it well,
> Or its power will vanish soon!'

And, dropping a small, gilded bottle at the witch's feet, the spirit vanished. Another chant from Hagar produced another apparition – not a lovely one; for, with a bang, an ugly black imp appeared, and, having croaked a reply, tossed a dark bottle at Hugo, and disappeared with a mocking laugh. Having warbled his thanks and put the potions in his boots, Hugo departed; and Hagar informed the audience that, as he had killed a few of her friends in times past, she has cursed him, and intends to thwart his plans, and be revenged on him. Then the curtain fell, and the audience reposed and ate candy while discussing the merits of the play.

A good deal of hammering went on before the curtain rose again; but when it became evident what a masterpiece of stage-carpentering had been got up, no one murmured at the delay. It was truly superb! A tower rose to the ceiling; half-way up appeared a window, with a lamp burning at it, and behind the white curtain appeared Zara in a lovely blue and silver dress, waiting for Roderigo. He came in gorgeous array, with plumed cap, red cloak, chestnut love-locks, a guitar, and the boots, of course. Kneeling at the foot of the tower, he sang a serenade in melting tones. Zara replied, and, after a musical dialogue, consented to fly. Then came the grand effect of the play. Roderigo produced a rope ladder, with five steps to it, threw up one end, and invited Zara to descend. Timidly she crept from her lattice, put her hand on Roderigo's shoulder, and was about to leap gracefully down, when, 'Alas! alas for Zara!' she forgot her train – it caught in the window, the tower tottered, leant forward, fell with a crash, and buried the unhappy lovers in the ruins!

A universal shriek arose as the russet boots waved wildly from the wreck, and a golden head emerged, exclaiming, 'I told you so! I told you so!' With wonderful presence of mind, Don Pedro, the cruel sire, rushed in, dragged out his daughter, with a hasty aside:

'Don't laugh! Act as if it was all right!' – and, ordering Roderigo up, banished him from the kingdom with wrath and scorn. Though decidedly shaken by the fall of the tower upon him, Roderigo defied the old gentleman, and refused to stir. This dauntless example fired Zara: she also defied her sire, and he ordered them both to the deepest dungeons of the castle. A

11

stout little retainer came in with chains, and led them away, looking very much frightened, and evidently forgetting the speech he ought to have made.

Act third was the castle hall; and here Hagar appeared, having come to free the lovers and finish Hugo. She hears him coming, and hides; sees him put the potions into two cups of wine, and bid the timid little servant 'Bear them to the captives in their cells, and tell them I shall come anon.' The servant takes Hugo aside to tell him something, and Hagar changes the cups for two others which are harmless. Ferdinando, the 'minion', carries them away, and Hagar puts back the cup which holds the poison meant for Roderigo. Hugo, getting thirsty after a long warble, drinks it, loses his wits, and after a good deal of clutching and stamping, falls flat and dies; while Hagar informs him what she has done in a song of exquisite power and melody.

This was a truly thrilling scene, though some persons might have thought that the sudden tumbling down of a quantity of long hair rather marred the effect of the villain's death. He was called before the curtain, and with great propriety appeared, leading Hagar, whose singing was considered more wonderful than all the rest of the performance put together.

Act fourth displayed the despairing Roderigo on the point of stabbing himself, because he has been told that Zara has deserted him. Just as the dagger is at his heart a lovely song is sung under his window, informing him that Zara is true, but in danger, and he can save her, if he will. A key is thrown in, which unlocks the door, and in a spasm of rapture he tears off his chains, and rushes away to find and rescue his lady-love.

Act fifth opened with a stormy scene between Zara and Don Pedro. He wishes her to go into a convent, but she won't hear of it; and, after a touching appeal, is about to faint, when Roderigo dashes in and demands her hand. Don Pedro refuses, because he is not rich. They shout and gesticulate tremendously, but cannot agree, and Roderigo is about to bear away the exhausted Zara, when the timid servant enters with a letter and a bag from Hagar, who has mysteriously disappeared. The letter informs the party that she bequeaths untold wealth to the young pair, and an awful doom to Don Pedro, if he doesn't make them happy. The bag is opened, and several quarts of tin money shower down upon the stage, till it is quite glorified with the glitter. This entirely softens the 'stern sire': he consents without a murmur, all join in a joyful chorus, and the curtain falls upon the lovers kneeling to receive Don Pedro's blessing in attitudes of the most romantic grace.

Tumultuous applause followed, but received an unexpected check; for the cot-bed, on which the 'dress-circle' was built, suddenly shut up, and extinguished the enthusiastic audience. Roderigo and Don Pedro flew to the rescue, and all were taken out unhurt, though many were speechless with laughter. The excitement had hardly subsided, when Hannah appeared with 'Mrs March's compliments, and would the ladies walk down to supper'.

LOUISA M. ALCOTT, LITTLE WOMEN

Richmal Crompton's *Just William* books are among the funniest and least sentimental children's stories ever written. Her hero is a Napoleon in shorts – powerful, domineering, dangerous and destructive. In this extract from *William the Pirate* a lecture on *Hamlet*, unwisely given to William's form, has fired him with a passion to act, and nothing but the leading role will quite do.

Despite this contretemps, the preparations for the Shakespeare acting competition continued apace. Mr Welbecker had chosen Act III, Scene I, to be acted for the Shield. The parts of the Queen and Ophelia were to be played by boys, 'as was the custom in Shakespeare's time,' said Mr Welbecker, who seemed to cherish a pathetic delusion that no one had ever known anything about Shakespeare before his article appeared in the local press.

'I'm not going to be the woman that gets pushed into a pond,' said William firmly. 'I don't mind being the one that pushes her, and I don't mind being the one called Ham that poisons Shakespeare. I don't much mind which of them I am so long as I'm not the one that gets pushed into a pond, and as long as I've got a lot to say. When I'm in a play I like to have a lot to say.'

His interest in the play was increased by the fact that Dorinda Lane was once more staying at her aunt's in the village. Dorinda was a little girl with dark hair and dimples, who was the temporary possessor of William's heart, a hard-boiled organ that generally scorned thraldom to any woman. Dorinda, however, appeared on his horizon so seldom that, for the short duration of her visits, he could stoop from his heroic pinnacle of manliness to admire her without losing prestige in his own eyes.

'I'm goin' to be in a play at school,' he informed her the morning after Mr Welbecker's lecture.

She gave a little cry of excitement. Her admiration of William was absolute and unmixed.

'Oh, William!' she said, 'how lovely! What are you going to be?'

'I'm not quite sure,' said William, 'but anyway I'm goin' to be the most important person in it.'

'Oh, are you, William?'

'Yes, I'm going to be the one that poisons Bacon or that pushes Ham into a pond or something like that. Anyway, we had a lecture about it, and I was the only one that knew anything about it at the end, so they're going to give me the biggest part.'

'Oh, William, how lovely! Have they told you so?'

William hesitated.

'Well, they've as good as told me,' he said. 'I mean, I was the only one that knew anything about it when they'd finished giving this lecture, so they're sure to give me the biggest part. In fact' – finally surrendering to his imagination – 'in fact, they told me they were. They said: "You seem to be the only one that knows anything about this man Eggs what wrote the play so you choose what you'd like to be in it."'

'Oh, William,' said Dorinda, 'I think you're wonderful.'

After this William, convinced by his own eloquence, firmly believed that he was to be offered the best part in the scene, because of his masterly recapitulation of its plot. In order to be sure of making a good choice, he borrowed a Shakespeare from his father, turned to the scene (with much difficulty), and began to read it through. He found it as incomprehensible as if it had been written in a foreign language, but he was greatly struck by the speech beginning 'To be or not to be –' It was long, it was even more incomprehensible than the rest of the scene, it went with a weirdly impressive swing. William loved speeches that were long and incomprehensible and that went with a swing. He mouthed it with infinite gusto and many gesticulations, striding to and fro in his bedroom. He decided quite finally that he would be Hamlet.

His surprise and disgust, therefore, were unbounded when his form master told him that he was to be one of the attendants on the king, and that, as such, he would not be required to say anything at all.

'You just go in first of all and stand by the throne and then go out when the king goes out.'

'But I want to say something,' protested William.

'I've no doubt you do,' said his form master dryly. 'I've never known you yet when you didn't. But as it happens the attendant doesn't speak. By a strange oversight Shakespeare didn't write any lines for him.'

'Well, I don't mind writin' some myself. I'll write it and learn it.'

'If you learn it as well as you learnt your Latin verbs yesterday,' said the form master sarcastically, 'it'll be worth listening to.'

'Well, I don't *like* Latin verbs,' said William, 'and I *do* like acting.'

But it was in vain. His form master was adamant. He was to be one of the king's attendants and he was not to say anything. William's first plan was to feign illness on the day of the play and to tell Dorinda that a substitute had had to be hastily found for him but that he would have done the part much better. There were, however, obvious drawbacks to this course. For one thing he had never yet managed to feign illness with any success. His family doctor was a suspicious and, in William's eyes, inhuman being, who always drove William from his sickbed to whatever he was trying to avoid by draughts of nauseous medicine. ('It's better than bein' poisoned anyway,' William would say bitterly, as he finally abandoned his symptoms.) Moreover, even if he succeeded in outwitting the doctor (a thing he had never done yet) the whole proceeding would be rather tame. If there was anything going on William liked to be in it.

It was a chance remark of his father's that sent a ray of light into the gloom of the situation.

It happened that this same play was being acted at a London theatre, and that the actor who should have played Hamlet had been taken ill and the part played by another member of the cast at the last minute.

'This other fellow knew the part,' said his father, 'so he stepped into the breach.'

'Why did he do that?' said William.

'Do what?' asked his father.

'Step into that thing you said.'

'What thing?'

'You just said he stepped into something.'

'I said he played the part.'

'Well, you said he stepped into somethin', an' I thought perhaps he broke it like Robert did steppin' into one of the footlights when he was acting in that play the football club did.'

His father's only reply was a grunt that was obviously intended to close the conversation.

But William's way now lay clear before him. He would learn Hamlet's part, and on the night of the play, when Hamlet was taken ill, he would come forward to play the part for him. ('An' I won't go messin' about steppin' into things same as the one in London did,' he said sternly.)

In William's eyes the part of Hamlet consisted solely of the 'To be or not to be' speech. 'If I learn that I'll be all right,' he told himself. 'I can jus' make up the rest. Jus' say what comes into my head when they say things to me.'

Every night he repeated the speech before his looking-glass with eloquent and windmill-like gestures that swept everything off his dressing-table onto the floor in all directions.

As his head was the only part of his person that was visible in the look-ing-glass, he did not trouble to dress up more than his head for his part. Sometimes he clothed it Arab fashion in his towel, sometimes in his Red Indian head-dress, sometimes in his father's top hat, 'borrowed' for the occasion. On the whole he thought that the top hat gave the best effect.

'Are you *really* going to be the hero, William?' said Dorinda when next she met him.

'Yes, I have a speech that takes hours and hours to say. The longest there's every been in a play. I stand in the middle of the stage, and I go on talkin' an' talkin' sayin' the things in this speech with no one stoppin' me, or interruptin' me. For *hours.* 'Cause I'm the person the whole play's writ-ten about.'

'Oh, William, how lovely! What's the speech about?'

As William, though now able to repeat the speech almost perfectly, had not the faintest idea what it was about, he merely smiled mysteriously and said: 'Oh you'll have to wait and see.'

'Is it funny, William? Will it make me laugh? I *love* funny things.'

William considered. For all he knew the speech might be intended to be humorous. On the other hand, of course, it might not be. Having no key to its meaning, he could not tell.

'You'll have to wait and see,' he said with the air of one to whom weighty state secrets are entrusted, and who is bound on honour not to betray them.

He had now abandoned his looking-glass as an audience, and strode to and fro uttering his speech with its ample accompaniment of gestures to an audience of his wash-stand and a chair and a photograph of his mother's and father's wedding group that had slowly descended the ladder of impor-tance, working its way in the course of the years from the drawing-room to the dining-room, from the dining-room to the morning-room, from the morning-room to the hall, from the hall to the staircase, and then through his mother's, Robert's, and Ethel's bedrooms to the bottom rung of the ladder in William's. William, of course, did not see the wash-stand and the chair and the wedding group; he saw ranks upon serried ranks of intent faces, Dorinda's standing out from among them with startling clearness.

'To be or not to be,' he would declaim, 'that is the question, whether 'tis nobler in the slings to suffer.

The mind and arrows of opposing fortune

Or to die to sleep against a sea of troubles.

And by opposing end there.'

Even William did not pretend to get every word in its exact place. As he said to himself: 'It's as sens'ble as what's in the book, anyway, and it sounds all right.'

The subordinate part that he took in the rehearsals as the king's attendant did not trouble him in the least. He was not the king's attendant. He was Hamlet. He was the tall, dark boy called Dalrymple (he had adenoids and a slight lisp but excellent memory) who played Hamlet. It was he, William, not Dalrymple, who repeated that long and thrilling speech to an enthralled audience. So entirely did William trust in his star that he had not the slightest doubt that Dalrymple would develop some illness on the day of the play. William's mother had an enormous book with the title *Every-day Ailments*. William glanced through it idly and was much cheered by it. There were so many illnesses that it seemed impossible that Dalrymple – a mere mortal and susceptible to all the germs with which the air was apparently laden – should not be stricken down by one or another of them on the day of the play. Dorinda met him in the village the day before the performance.

'I'm *longing* for tomorrow, William,' she said.

And William, without the slightest qualm of doubt, replied:

'Oh, yes, it'll be jolly fine. You look out for my long speech.'

The day of the performance dawned. No news of any sudden illness of Dalrymple's reached William, yet he still felt no doubts. His star had marked him out for Hamlet, and Hamlet he would be. His mother, who was anxious for him not to be late, saw him off for the performance at what William considered an unduly early hour with many admonitions not to loiter on the way. She herself was coming later as part of the audience. William had a strong dislike of arriving too early at any objective. He considered that his mother had made him set off quite a quarter of an hour too soon, and therefore that he had a quarter of an hour to spend on the way. He still felt no doubts that he would play the part of Hamlet, but he was not narrow in his interests, and he realised even at that moment that there were other things in the world than Hamlet. There was the stream in Crown Woods (he had decided to go the longer way through Crown Woods in order to make up the quarter of an hour), there was a hedge sparrow's nest, there was a curious insect which William had never seen before and of which he thought that he must be the first discoverer, there was a path that William had not noticed on his previous visits to the wood and that had therefore to be explored, there was a tree whose challenge to climb it William could not possibly resist. Even William realised, on emerging from the wood, that he had spent in it more than the quarter of an hour that he considered his due.

He ran in the direction of the school. An excited group of people was standing at the gate, looking out for him. They received him with a stream of indignant reproaches, bundled him into his form room and began to pull off his clothes and hustle him into his attendant's uniform. ('It's time to *begin*. We've been waiting for you for *ages*. Why on *earth* couldn't you get here in time?') All the others had changed and were ready in their costumes. Hamlet looked picturesque in black velvet slashed with purple, wearing a silver chain. William tried to collect his forces, but his legs were being thrust into tights by one person, his hair was being mercilessly brushed by another, and his face was being made up by another. Whenever he opened his mouth to speak, it received a stick of make-up or an eyebrow pencil or a hare's foot.

'Now don't forget,' said the form master, who was also the producer, 'you go on first of all and stand by the throne. Stand quite stiffly, as I showed you, and in a few moments the king and the others will come on.'

And William, his faculties still in a whirl, was thrust unceremoniously upon the empty stage.

He stood there facing a sea of upturned, intent faces. Among them in the second row he discerned that of Dorinda, her eyes fixed expectantly upon him.

Instinctively and without a moment's hesitation, he stepped forward and with a sweeping gesture launched into his speech.

'To be or not to be that is the question

Whether 'tis nobler in the mind to suffer –'

'Come off, you young fool,' hissed the form master wildly from behind the scenes.

But William had got well into his stride and was not coming off for anyone.

'The stings and arrows of outrageous fortune.' (For a wonder he was getting the words in their right places.)

'Or to take arms against a sea of troubles.'

The best thing, of course, would have been to lower the curtain, but there was no curtain to lower.

Screens had been set along the edge of the stage and had been folded up when the performance was to begin.

'Come *off*, I tell you,' repeated the form master frantically.

'And by opposing end there. To sleep to die.'

William had forgotten everything in the world but himself, his words, and Dorinda. He was unaware of the crowd of distraught players hissing

18

and gesticulating off the stage; he was unaware of his form master's frenzied commands, of the frozen faces of the headmaster and Mr Welbecker, who sat holding his shield ready for presentation in the front row.

'No more and by a sleep to say an end.'

The form master decided to act. The boy had evidently gone mad. The only thing to do was to go boldly onto the stage and drag him off. This the form master attempted to do. He stalked onto the stage and put out his hand to seize William. William, vaguely aware that someone was trying to stop him saying his speech, reacted promptly, and dodged to the other side of the stage, still continuing his recital.

'The thousand natural shocks the flesh and hair is.'

The form master, whose blood was now up, plunged across the stage. Once more William dodged his outstretched hand, and, still breathlessly reciting, reached the other end of the stage again. Then followed the diverting spectacle of the form master chasing William round the stage – William dodging, doubling, and all the time continuing his speech. Someone had the timely idea of trying to set up the screens again, but it was a manoeuvre that defeated its own ends, for William (still reciting) merely dodged round and behind them and unfortunately one of them fell down on the top of the form master. A mighty roar ascended from the audience. Dorinda was rocking to and fro with mirth and clapping with all her might and main. The unseemly performance came to an end at last. The players joined the form master in the chase, and William, still reciting, was dragged ingloriously from the stage.

Mr Welbecker turned a purple face to the headmaster.

'This is an outrage,' he said; 'an insult. I should not dream of presenting my shield to a school in which I have seen this exhibition.'

'I agree that it's a most regrettable incident, Welbecker,' said the headmaster suavely, 'and I think that in the circumstances your decision is amply justified.'

Dorinda was wiping tears of laughter from her eyes. 'Wasn't William *wonderful*?' she said.

RICHMAL CROMPTON, *WILLIAM THE PIRATE*

๛

Sarah Bernhardt's first experience of acting is not that dissimilar to William's. Her convent school is alight with excitement at the forthcoming visit of the Archbishop of Paris. The nuns are planning an entertainment in the Archbishop's honour, the centrepiece of which is to be a short play entitled *Tobit Recovering His Eyesight*.

The little play was read to us by Mother St Thérèse, one Thursday, in the large assembly room. We were all in tears at the end, and Mother St Thérèse was obliged to make a great effort in order to avoid committing, if only for a second, the sin of pride.

I wondered anxiously what part I should take in this religious comedy, for, considering that I was now treated as a little personage, I had no doubt that some role would be given to me. The very thought of it made me tremble beforehand. I began to get quite nervous; my hands became quite cold, my heart beat furiously, and my temples throbbed. I did not approach, but remained sulkily seated on my stool when Mother St Thérèse said in her calm voice:

'Young ladies, please pay attention, and listen to your names and the different parts:

Tobit	EUGÉNIE CHARMEL
Tobias	AMÉLIE PLUCHE
Gabael	RENÉE D'ARVILLE
The Angel Raphael	LOUISE BUGUET
Tobias's mother	EULALIE LACROIX
Tobias's sister	VIRGINIE DEPAUL.'

I had been listening, although pretending not to, and I was stupefied, amazed, and furious. Mother St Thérèse then added. 'Here are your manuscripts, young ladies,' and a manuscript of the little play was handed to each pupil chosen to take part in it.

Louise Buguet was my favourite playmate, and I went up to her and asked her to let me see her manuscript, which I read over enthusiastically.

'You'll make me rehearse, when I know my part, won't you?' she asked, and I answered, 'Yes, certainly.'

'Oh, how frightened I shall be!' she said.

She had been chosen for the angel, I suppose, because she was as pale and sweet as a moonbeam. She had a soft, timid voice, and sometimes we used to make her cry, as she was so pretty then. The tears used to flow limpid and pearl-like from her grey, questioning eyes.

She began at once to learn her part, and I was like a shepherd's dog going from one to another among the chosen ones. It had really nothing to do with me, but I wanted to be 'in it.' The Mother Superior passed by, and as we all curtseyed to her she patted my cheek.

'We thought of you, little girl,' she said, 'but you are so timid when you are asked anything.'

'Oh, that's when it is history or arithmetic,' I said. 'This is not the same

20

thing, and I should not have been afraid.'

She smiled distrustfully and moved on. There were rehearsals during the next week. I asked to be allowed to take the part of the monster, as I wanted to have some role in the play at any cost. It was decided, though, that César, the convent dog, should be the fish monster.

A competition was opened for the fish costume. I went to an endless amount of trouble cutting out scales from cardboard that I had painted, and sewing them together afterwards. I made some enormous gills, which were to be glued on to César. My costume was not chosen; it was passed over for that of a stupid, big girl whose name I cannot remember. She had made a huge tail of kid and a mask with big eyes and gills, but there were no scales, and we should have to see César's shaggy coat. I nevertheless turned my attention to Louise Buguet's costume, and worked at it with two of the lay sisters, Sister St Cécile and Sister St Jeanne, who had charge of the linen room.

At the rehearsals not a word could be extorted from the Angel Raphael. She stood there stupefied on the little platform, tears dimming her beautiful eyes. She brought the whole play to a standstill, and kept appealing to me in a weeping voice. I prompted her, and getting up, rushed to her, kissed her, and whispered her whole speech to her. I was beginning to be 'in it' myself at last.

Finally, two days before the great solemnity, there was a dress rehearsal. The angel looked lovely, but, immediately on entering, she sank down on a bench, sobbing out in an imploring voice:

'Oh no; I shall never be able to do it, never!'

'Quite true, she never will be able to,' sighed Mother St Sophie.

Forgetting for the moment my little friend's grief, and wild with joy, pride, and assurance, I ran up to the platform and bounded on to the form on which the Angel Raphael had sunk down weeping.

'Oh, Mother, I know her part. Shall I take her place for the rehearsal?'

'Yes, yes!' exclaimed voices from all sides.

'Oh yes, you know it so well,' said Louise Buguet, and she wanted to put her band on my head.

'No, let me rehearse as I am, first,' I answered.

They began the second scene again, and I came in carrying a long branch of willow.

'Fear nothing, Tobias,' I commenced. 'I will be your guide. I will remove from your path all thorns and stones. You are overwhelmed with fatigue. Lie down and rest, for I will watch over you.' Whereupon Tobias, worn out, lay down by the side of a strip of blue muslin, about five yards of which, stretched out and winding about, represented the Tigris.

I then continued with a prayer to God whilst Tobias fell asleep. César next appeared as the Monster Fish, and the audience trembled with fear. César had been well taught by the gardener, Père Larcher, and he advanced slowly from under the blue muslin. He was wearing his mask, representing the head of a fish. Two enormous nut-shells for his eyes had been painted white, and a hole pierced through them, so that the dog could see. The mask was fastened with wire to his collar, which also supported two gills as large as palm leaves. César, sniffing the ground, snorted and growled, and then leaped wildly on to Tobias, who with his cudgel slew the monster at one blow. The dog fell on his back with his four paws in the air, and then rolled over on to his side, pretending to be dead.

There was wild delight in the house, and the audience clapped and stamped. The younger pupils stood up on their stools and shouted, 'Good, César! Clever César! Oh, good dog, good dog!' The sisters, touched by the efforts of the guardian of the convent, shook their heads with emotion. As for me, I quite forgot that I was the Angel Raphael, and I stooped down and stroked César affectionately. 'Ah, how well he has acted his part!' I said, kissing him and taking one paw and then the other in my hand, whilst the dog, motionless, continued to be dead.

The little bell was rung to call us to order. I stood up again, and, accompanied by the piano, we burst into a hymn of praise, a duet to the glory of God, who had just saved Tobias from the fearful monster.

After this the little green serge curtain was drawn, and I was surrounded, petted, and praised. Mother St Sophie came up on to the platform and kissed me affectionately. As to Louise Buguet, she was now joyful again and her angelic face beamed.

'Oh, well you knew the part!' she said. 'And then, too, every one can hear what you say. Oh, thank you so much!' She kissed me and I hugged her with all my might. At last I was in it!

SARAH BERNHARDT, *My Double Life*

❧

The next extract is from one of Tove Jansson's famous *Moomin* books, *Moominsummer Madness*. In it, the secure haven of Moomin valley is destroyed by a series of natural disasters – volcanoes, earthquakes, flooding. After this apocalypse, the Moomin family, adrift in a tiny boat, find a new home in a floating theatre, where of course they perform a play. This is the description of the dress rehearsal, and it is in every way accurate to the real experience. Particularly so is the character of Misabel. She is a fat, neurotic, self-indulgent depressive to whom theatre *happens*, and it transforms her life. I am sure many actors will experience a thrill of recognition.

ಟಿ

It was the day of the dress rehearsal of Moominpappa's play, and all the footlights were burning, although it was still only afternoon.

The beavers had been promised free tickets for the first night the following day if they would push the theatre back on an even keel, and now it was almost right, but the stage still slanted a little which made the acting slightly strained

The curtain was drawn, red and mysterious, and outside on the water a small flotilla of boats was curiously bobbing. They had waited since sunrise, and the people in them had brought their own dinners with them in paper bags, because dress rehearsals always take a lot of time.

'Mother, what's a dress rehearsal?' asked a poor hedgehog child in one of the boats.

'It's when they practise the play for the very last time to be quite sure that everything's in order,' explained the hedgehog mother. 'Tomorrow they'll act in real earnest, and then one has to pay to look at them. Today's free for poor hedgehogs like us.'

But the people behind the curtain were not at all sure that everything was in order. Moominpappa was rewriting his play. Misabel was crying.

'Didn't we *tell* you that we both wanted to die in the end!' exclaimed the Mymble's daughter. 'Why should only she be eaten by the lion? The Lion's Brides, we told you. Don't you remember?'

'All right, all right,' Moominpappa answered nervously. 'The lion shall devour, first you, and lastly Misabel. Don't disturb me, I'm trying to think in blank verse.'

'Have you got the family matters right now, dear?' Moominmamma asked worriedly. 'Yesterday the Mymble's daughter was married to your runaway son. Is it Misabel who's married to him now, and am I her mother? And is the Mymble's daughter unmarried?'

'I don't want to be unmarried,' the Mymble's daughter said at once.

'They can be sisters,' cried Moominpappa desperately. 'The Mymble's daughter is your daughter-in-law. I mean mine. Your aunt, that is.'

'I doubt it,' remarked Whomper. 'If Moominmamma's married to you, then it's *impossible* for your daughter-in-law to be our aunt.'

'It's all the same to me,' cried Moominpappa. 'There'll never be any play to perform, anyway!'

'Easy now, easy now,' said Emma with unexpected understanding.

'Everything's going to be all right. And anyway the audience won't understand a word.'

'Emma dear,' said Moominmamma. 'This dress is too narrow for me … it keeps slipping up in the back.'

'Now remember,' said Emma, her mouth full of pins, 'you mustn't look so happy when you come on the stage and tell him that your son has told him a pack of lies!'

'No, I promise,' said Moominmamma.

Misabel was reading her part. Suddenly she threw the paper away and cried: 'It's far too lighthearted! It doesn't suit me at all!'

'Hush, Misabel,' said Emma sternly. 'We start now. Are the spots ready?'

Whomper turned on the yellow spotlight.

'Red! Red!' the Mymble's daughter shouted. 'My entrance's red! Why must he always take the wrong light!'

'They all do,' said Emma calmly. 'Are you ready?'

'I can't remember my lines,' mumbled Moominpappa, panic-stricken. 'Not a word!'

Emma patted him on the shoulder. 'That's as it should be,' she said. 'Everything's exactly as it should be on a dress rehearsal.'

She thumped the floor three times with her broomstick, and silence fell over the boats outside. With a thrill of happiness in her old body she grasped the crank handle to raise the curtain.

Admiring whispers were heard among the sparse audience. Most of the hedgehogs had never been to the theatre before.

They saw a landscape of wild rocks, in red light.

To the right of the looking-glass cabinet (draped in black cloth), the Mymble's daughter was sitting, dressed in a tulle skirt, and a wreath of paper-flowers around her hairknot.

She studied the audience with great interest for some time and then spoke, rapidly and casually:

> If I must die tonight, in blooming youth,
> While all my innocence cries to high heav'n,
> Then into Blood may bloodily turn the sea
> And into dust the sprightliness of spring!
> A Rosebud, blushing still from childish sleep
> I'm slewn to earth by unrelenting Fate!

Behind the scenes rose a shrill chant. It was Emma:

> O Night, O Night, O Night, O Night of Fate!

Now Moominpappa entered from the left with a cloak carelessly draped over his shoulder, turned to the audience, and recited in a trembling voice:

> The bonds of Family and Friendship must
> Be broken at the sad command of Duty.
> Alas, shall then my crown be lifted off
> By th' sister of my daughter's nephew?

He felt that there was something wrong with the words, and resumed:

> Alas, shall then my crown be lifted off
> By the sister-in-law of my daughter's son?

Moominmamma put in her head from the wings and whispered: 'By the sister of my daughter's sister's son!'

'I know, I know,' said Moominpappa. 'I'll skip that part this time.'

He took a step towards the Mymble's daughter, who hid herself behind the cabinet, and continued:

> Then tremble, treacherous Mymble, tremble now
> And listen to the beastly lion's roar
> As hungrily he stamps about his cage
> Ululating at the moon!

A long silence followed.

'Ululating at the moon!' repeated Moominpappa, louder.

Nothing happened.

He turned to the left and asked: 'Why doesn't the lion ululate?'

'I wasn't to ululate until Whomper hoisted the moon,' replied Emma.

Whomper put out his head. 'Misabel promised to make a moon, and she hasn't,' he said.

'All right, all right' said Moominpappa hastily. 'We'll try Misabel's entrance now, because I'm not in the right mood anyway.'

Slowly Misabel glided on to the stage in her red velvet robe. For a long time she remained motionless with her paw over her eyes, feeling what it felt like to be a leading lady. It felt wonderful.

'O happiness,' prompted Moominmamma who thought she had forgotten her opening lines.

'I know, I'm just holding them spellbound!' Misabel hissed back. She staggered towards the footlights and reached out her arms to the audience. There was a click as Whomper started the wind machine behind the scenes.

'Is that a vacuum-cleaner?' asked the hedgehog child.

'Hush!' said the hedgehog mother.

Misabel started on her first great monologue:

> O happiness and joy when I behold
> Yourself beheaded at my own behest …

She took a rapid step, stumbled on the velvet trail and fell over the footlights straight down in the nearest hedgehog's boat.

The audience cheered and jointly lifted Misabel back up on the stage.

'Take my advice, miss,' said a middle-aged beaver, 'better cut off her head at once!'

'Whose head?' Misabel asked, wonderingly.

'Your son-in-law's niece's, of course,' replied the beaver encouragingly.

'They've misunderstood the whole thing,' whispered Moominpappa to Moominmamma. 'Come on at once, please.'

Moominmamma hastily gathered her skirts and appeared on the stage with a friendly and slightly shy smile.

> Now hide your face, I bring black tidings hither!
> Your son has told you but a pack of fibs!

she said happily.

Moominpappa stared nervously at her.

'Where is the lion,' she prompted helpfully.

'Where is the lion,' repeated Moominpappa. 'Where is the lion,' he said uncertainly once more. Finally, he shouted: 'Well, where is it?'

A great stamping could be heard behind the scenes. Then the lion entered. It consisted of a beaver in the fore-legs and another in the hind legs. The audience shouted with delight.

The lion hesitated. Then it walked up to the footlights and took a bow, and broke in the middle.

The audience clapped and began to row home.

'It isn't finished!' shouted Moominpappa.

'Dearest, they'll come back tomorrow,' said Moominmamma. 'And Emma says that the first night never succeeds if the dress rehearsal hasn't been a little so-so.'

'Does she really,' replied Moominpappa, reassured. 'Well, anyway they laughed several times!' he added happily.

But Misabel turned her back to the others for a while to quieten her thumping heart.

'They clapped!' she whispered to herself. 'Oh, how happy I am! I'll always, always feel happy after this!'

TOVE JANSSON, *MOOMINSUMMER MADNESS*

CHAPTER 2

BORN IN A
TRUNK

In George Cukor's version of the oft-remade film *A Star Is Born*, Judy Garland sings touchingly about her character's happy childhood as a professional vaudevillian. The song is the famous 'Born In A Trunk' and it is a perfect example of Hollywood's dishonesty, evasion and sentimentality, while contriving to be, at one and the same time, one of the great movie musical numbers. It is, of course, a sanitized biography of Garland's own appalling childhood. As a toddler, her pushy parents made her into one of the singing dancing Gumm sisters, all eyes, teeth and two shows a day. Then before she hit her teens she was hurled into the nightmare world of the studio system, force-fed with drugs to control her energy levels and putting out personality, charm and childhood on demand. Her story is a terrible warning to all would-be child actors and their parents. Noël Coward's recollections are less alarming, and while giving a vivid sense of the professional child's apartness from other children, he also shows us the compensations.

❧

THE BOY ACTOR
I can remember. I can remember,
The months of November and December

27

Were filled for me with peculiar joys
So different from those of other boys
For other boys would be counting the days
Until end of term and holiday times
But I was acting in Christmas plays
While they were taken to pantomimes.
I didn't envy their Eton suits,
Their children's dances and Christmas trees.
My life had wonderful substitutes
For such conventional treats as these.
I didn't envy their country larks,
Their organized games in panelled halls:
While they made snow-men in stately parks
I was counting the curtain calls.

I remember the auditions, the nerve-racking auditions:
Darkened auditorium and empty, dusty stage,
Little girls in ballet dresses practising 'positions',
Gentlemen with pince-nez asking you your age.
Hopefulness and nervousness struggling within you,
Dreading that familiar phrase, 'Thank you dear, no more'.
Straining every muscle, every tendon, every sinew
To do your dance much better than you'd ever done before.
Think of your performance. Never mind the others,
Never mind the pianist, talent must prevail.
Never mind the baleful eyes of other children's mothers
Glaring from the corners and willing you to fail.

I can remember. I can remember
The months of November and December
Were more significant to me
Than other months could ever be
For they were the months of high romance
When destiny waited on tip-toe,
When every boy actor stood a chance
Of getting into a Christmas show,
Not for me the dubious heaven
Of being some prefect's protégé!
Not for me the Second Eleven.
For me, two performances a day.

Ah those first rehearsals! Only very few lines:
Rushing home to mother, learning them by heart,
'Enter Left through window! – Dots to mark the cue lines:
'Exit with the others' – Still it was a part.
Opening performance; legs a bit unsteady,
Dedicated tension, shivers down my spine,
Powder, grease and eye-black, sticks of make-up ready
Leichner number three and number five and number nine.
World of strange enchantment, magic for a small boy
Dreaming of the future, reaching for the crown,
Rigid in the dressing-room, listening for the call-boy
'Overture, Beginners – Everybody Down!'

I can remember. I can remember.
The months of November and December,
Although climatically cold and damp,
Meant more to me than Aladdin's lamp.
I see myself, having got a job,
Walking on wings along the Strand,
Uncertain whether to laugh or sob
And clutching tightly my mother's hand,
I never cared who scored the goal
Or which side won the silver cup,
I never learned to bat or bowl
But I heard the curtain going up.

NOËL COWARD

&

'Never act with animals and children' is one of the hoariest of theatrical quotations. Like every cliché it is true. But why? Uta Hagan, the brilliant American actress and teacher, vividly describes being upstaged by a cat. She puts the animal's watchability down to a combination of lack of self-consciousness and absolute immediacy. An animal lives 'in the moment', without worrying about past or future, in exactly the way that an actor should and hardly ever can. Some child actors can achieve this same effect: Ricky Shroder in *The Champ*, Jenny Agutter in *The Railway Children* and the entire cast of Peter Brook's film of *The Lord of the Flies*, for instance. Occasionally a personality cult grows up around a child actor. It happened to Shirley Temple, possibly for murky reasons, which I can't go into here, not at least without risking the same legal troubles as beset

Graham Greene when he wrote about Miss Temple's charms for *Time and Tide*. As far as I know, Shirley Temple emerged unscathed from the furnace of popularity. Not so some others: Bobby Driscoll (the voice of Peter Pan) and River Phoenix are just two talented casualties. Even Macaulay Culkin would have been surprised at the cult that grew up around a young Irish boy at the beginning of the nineteenth century. William Betty was taken to see the great Sarah Siddons acting in Belfast. He became stage-struck and turned professional at twelve. He triumphed in Ireland, came to Birmingham and thence to Covent Garden, where he scored a huge hit in the tragedies *Barbarossa* and *Douglas*.

All London was now at his feet. His Life (not a very long one) was published, and sold like hot cakes. At their special request he was presented to the King and the Prince of Wales. The latter allowed him to roam all over Carlton House, and the former sent for him to Drury Lane, whither His Majesty had been to see the *School for Scandal*, more to his taste than *Lover's Vows*, in which Betty had been appearing 'over the way.' On Saturday, 9th December, he made his last appearance for the present at Covent Garden, and a rumour going round to the effect that it was his farewell of the stage, the crowd nearly wrecked the theatre in their endeavours to get in. The doors at the back of the circle were taken off their hinges and seats were erected beyond them, from which it was just possible the occupants might some time during the evening catch a glimpse of the 'Young Roscius.' Much of the same state of things occurred on Monday, 10th December, when he first appeared at Drury Lane as *Young Norval*. His playing of the part had improved, and his dying scene was averred to be a marvel of simplicity and unforced effect. His life seemed just to ebb away. There was not a dry eye in the audience as the last word 'mother' quivered on his dying lips. The scene had been played hundreds of times, on *East Lynne* lines, by maudlin, sentimental actors; but this gentle boy's passing, without a germ of self-consciousness or self-pity, was not sentiment, but tragedy, and tragedy of a very high order indeed. All his satellites followed him to Drury Lane, and he was feasted, fêted, and petted by the highest in the land, who waited for him outside the stage-door to take him to their houses in their carriages and chairs. It is scarcely surprising that towards the close of the season he fell ill of gastric trouble, which confined him to his room for some days.

At one time he was really very seriously ill, but he recovered and went to Bushey Park to recruit. During his illness public bulletins were issued, and he was treated generally as though he were a royal princeling. The bulletins caused some gibing and joking epigrams in the fashion of the time. Among the most popular was the following:

> A little Boy was sick with wine, punch, and full-eating,
> And the Public it was sick with a little Boy's Bulletin.

But he recovered, and the following season played twenty-four nights at each of the two great theatres, at an increased salary. London now saw his *Hamlet* for the first time, and the great Mr. Pitt adjourned the House of Commons that the members might be able to attend the performance! As a national attraction the Young Roscius vied with the Derby! He was presented to the Queen and Princesses by the King himself. In the interim between the two London seasons he had toured again in the north, making £2000 in little over a fortnight. London first saw his *Richard III* and *Macbeth* at the end of 1805, when he appeared on alternate nights. He does not seem to have quite succeeded in convincing in either of these characters, though the scene with the *Lady Anne* was said to be masterly! Of his *Macbeth* the less said the better – nothing much apparently *was* said! It was a mercy he never attempted *King Lear*! Towards the close of the season the enthusiasm began to abate, but it continued for some years longer in the provinces, and he added many more laurels to his crown, and many, many more guineas to the already ample fortune he had amassed.

His last appearance as an 'Infant Phenomenon' was made at Bath in March, 1808, when a dispute as to his abilities between two officers would have led to a duel, and possibly a death, but for the intervention of the authorities. Betty was then placed with a tutor until July, 1810, when he was entered as a fellow commoner of Christ's College, Cambridge. Whilst at Cambridge he could never bear any allusion to his days of glory. The conversation had only to turn on theatrical topics for him to lapse into silence. No one ever quite knew why, unless it was that he was an exceptionally sensible and sensitive boy, who perhaps felt that he had been made a public fool of. If his abilities had been exaggerated it was not his fault, and his private conduct had been beyond praise, thoroughly modest, manly, unassuming, and utterly unspoilt. He did not remain long at Cambridge or take his degree, as his father's death less than a year after his entrance into the University led to his withdrawal from it. He now determined to adopt the stage as a profession and made his re-entrée at Bath in February, 1812. The following November he appeared at Covent Garden in his old part of *Selim*. But though he was obviously an accomplished actor he seemed quite unable to establish any hold upon the hearts of his audience. He continued touring and acting at intervals in the provinces for twelve years. On one occasion he encountered the fiery Edmund Kean at Exeter, who sternly refused to play 'seconds' to him 'or any one else but John Kemble.' In Scotland, and at Newcastle and Birmingham, he appeared with Macready, who always affirmed that he had all the abilities but not the application necessary for a really great actor. In 1824 he finally retired from the stage after a farewell benefit at Southampton on 9th August, 1824. Exactly fifty years later, on 24th August, 1874, he died in London. The years of his retirement were passed in comfortable circumstances and tranquil enjoyment of the fruits of his early labours. At the age of thirty-three he had amassed a fortune very much larger than usually falls to the lot of the most successful actor after a full career. Betty realized this, appreciated his good fortune, and spent much of it doing good, and especially in assisting theatrical charities. He never gave himself any airs, but frankly admitted that his early abilities had been exaggerated, and that the enthusiastic worshippers of his genius had been deceived. One wonders how far they were so. Certainly it all seems too good to be true. But certain indisputable facts point to something very exceptional. His marvellously retentive memory and lightning grasp. He never had to be told a thing twice. The wonderful force that propelled him. He *had* to be an actor, or he would have died. The wonderful facility, simplicity and naturalness of such effects as were within his scope, all point to something very akin to genius. Was it really there and nipped in the early bud, or rather early bloom, by the unwise, forcing tactics of those responsible for him, or the exaggerated adulation which insisted upon the performance of characters utterly beyond his boyish mental grasp, wonderful though that was? Macready, who acted with him in after life, and many who saw him play, affirmed again and again that the powers were there, but an irresistible lethargy prevented his exerting them or exercising them on new material. After sifting all the evidence, it looks almost as though Master Betty was a real genius, whose powers were strangled at their birth by that most effective of all destroyers, premature success.

Of his amiable, modest character, it is impossible to speak too highly. In the height of his glory he was never known to 'put on side,' so to speak. There is only one instance, and that occurred in after life, and Macready is the authority, of anything approaching condescension on his part. What Macready had to say against any one was sometimes negligible. What he had to say for them was always dependable, and he had much to say for Master Betty.

CECIL ARMSTRONG, 'WILLIAM HENRY WEST BETTY'
IN *A CENTURY OF GREAT ACTORS*

Perhaps William Betty's prowess in tragedy is not so incomprehensible. After all, Shakespeare wrote Rosalind, Lady Macbeth and Cleopatra to be performed by a boy. In the next poem, Edwin Morgan imagines him giving last-minute notes to the boy playing Hermione in *The Winter's Tale*.

INSTRUCTIONS TO AN ACTOR

Now, boy, remember this is the great scene.
You'll stand on a pedestal behind a curtain,
the curtain will be drawn, and you don't move
for eighty lines; don't move, don't speak, don't breathe.
I'll stun them all out there, I'll scare them,
make them weep, but it depends on you.
I warn you eighty lines is a long time,
but you don't breathe, you're dead,
you're a dead queen, a statue,
you're dead as stone, new-carved,
new-painted and the paint not dry
– we'll get some red to keep your lip shining –
and you're a mature woman, you've got dignity,
some beauty still in middle-age, and
you're kind and true, but you're dead,
your husband thinks you're dead,
the audience thinks you're dead,
and you don't breathe, boy, I say
you don't even blink for eighty lines,
if you blink you're out!
Fix your eye on something and keep watching it.
Practise when you get home. It can be done.
And you move at last – music's the cue.
When you hear a mysterious solemn jangle
of instruments, make yourself ready.
Five lines more, you can lift a hand.
It may tingle a bit, but lift it –
slow, slow –
O this is where I hit them
right between the eyes, I've got them now –
I'm making the dead walk –
you move a foot, slow, steady, down,
you guard your balance in case you're stiff,

33

you move, you step down, down from the pedestal,
control your skirt with one hand, the other hand
you now hold out –
O this will melt their hearts if nothing does –
to your husband who wronged you long ago
and hesitates in amazement
to believe you are alive.
Finally he embraces you, and there's nothing
I can give you to say, boy,
but you must show that you have forgiven him.
Forgiveness, that's the thing. It's like a second life.
I know you can do it. – Right then, shall we try?

EDWIN MORGAN

My own favourite child actor appears in Charles Dickens's *Nicholas Nickleby*, a member of the glorious troupe led by Mr and Mrs Vincent Crummles and given unforgettable theatrical life by Trevor Nunn, John Caird, David Edgar and the Royal Shakespeare Company in the 1980s. Here is the entrance of the Infant Phenomenon.

As Mrs Vincent Crummles re-crossed back to the table, there bounded on to the stage from some mysterious inlet, a little girl in a dirty white frock with tucks up to the knees, short trousers, sandaled shoes, white spencer, pink gauze bonnet, green veil and curl-papers, who turned a pirouette, cut twice in the air, turned another pirouette, then looking off at the opposite wing shrieked, bounded forward to within six inches of the footlights, and fell into a beautiful attitude of terror, as a shabby gentleman in an old pair of buff slippers came in at one powerful slide, and chattering his teeth, fiercely brandishing a walking-stick.

'They are going through the Indian Savage and the Maiden,' said Mrs Crummles.

'Oh!' said the manager, 'the little ballet interlude. Very good, go on. A little this way, if you please, Mr Johnson. That'll do. Now!'

The manager clapped his hands as a signal to proceed, and the savage, becoming ferocious, made a slide towards the maiden, but the maiden avoided him in six twirls, and came down at the end of the last one upon the very points of her toes. This seemed to make some impression upon the savage, for, after a little more ferocity and chasing of the maiden into corners, he began to relent, and stroked his face several times with his right thumb and four fingers, thereby intimating that he was struck with admiration of the maiden's beauty. Acting upon the impulse of this passion, he (the savage) began to hit himself severe thumps in the chest, and to exhibit other indications of being desperately in love, which being rather a prosy proceeding, was very likely the cause of the maiden's falling asleep; whether it was or not, asleep she did fall, sound as a church, on a sloping bank, and the savage perceiving it, leant his left ear on his left hand, and nodded sideways, to intimate to all whom it might concern that she *was* asleep, and no shamming. Being left to himself, the savage had a dance, all alone, and just as he left off the maiden woke up, rubbed her eyes, got off the bank, and had a dance all alone too – such a dance that the savage looked on in ecstasy all the while, and when it was done, plucked from a neighbouring tree some botanical curiosity, resembling a small pickled cabbage, and offered it to the maiden, who at first wouldn't have it, but on the savage shedding tears relented. Then the savage jumped for joy; then the maiden jumped for rapture at the sweet smell of the pickled cabbage. Then the savage and the maiden danced violently together, and, finally, the savage dropped down on one knee, and the maiden stood on one leg upon his other knee; thus concluding the ballet, and leaving the spectators in a state of pleasing uncertainty, whether she would ultimately marry the savage, or return to her friends.

'Very well indeed,' said Mr Crummles; 'bravo!'

'Bravo!' cried Nicholas, resolved to make the best of everything. 'Beautiful!'

'This, sir,' said Mr Vincent Crummles, bringing the maiden forward, 'this is the infant phenomenon – Miss Ninetta Crummles.'

'Your daughter?' inquired Nicholas.

'My daughter – my daughter,' replied Mr Vincent Crummles; 'the idol of every place we go into, sir. We have had complimentary letters about this girl, sir, from the nobility and gentry of almost every town in England.'

'I am not surprised at that,' said Nicholas; 'she must be quite a natural genius.'

'Quite a – !' Mr Crummles stopped; language was not powerful enough to describe the infant phenomenon. 'I'll tell you what, sir,' he said; 'the talent of this child is not to be imagined. She must be seen, sir – seen – to be ever so faintly appreciated. There; go to your mother, my dear.'

'May I ask how old she is?' inquired Nicholas.

'You may, sir,' replied Mr Crummles, looking steadily in his questioner's face as some men do when they have doubts about being implicitly believed in what they are going to say. 'She is ten years of age, sir.'

'Not more!'

'Not a day.'

'Dear me!' said Nicholas, 'it's extraordinary.'

It was; for the infant phenomenon, though of short stature, had a comparatively aged countenance, and had moreover been precisely the same age – not perhaps to the full extent of the memory of the oldest inhabitant, but certainly for five good years. But she had been kept up late every night, and put upon an unlimited allowance of gin-and-water from infancy, to prevent her growing tall, and perhaps this system of training had produced in the infant phenomenon these additional phenomena.

CHARLES DICKENS, *NICHOLAS NICKLEBY*

CHAPTER 3

AM DRAM

For many people interested in acting, the logical next step after the school play is some form of amateur dramatics. Shakespeare introduces his amateur troupe, The Mechanicals, in *A Midsummer Night's Dream*, at the moment of the casting session. Peter Quince, the long-suffering director, is handing out the roles in the tragedy of *Pyramus and Thisbe*.

❧

[*ACT I, sc. ii*]
Enter Quince the Carpenter, and Snug the Joiner, and Bottom the Weaver, and Flute the Bellows Mender, and Snout the Tinker, and Starveling the Tailor.

QUINCE. Is all our company here?
BOTTOM. You were best to call them generally, man by man, according to the scrip.
QUINCE. Here is the scroll of every man's name, which is thought fit, through all Athens, to play in our interlude before the Duke and the Duchess, on his wedding day at night.
BOTTOM. First, good Peter Quince, say what the play treats on; then read the names of the actors; and so grow to a point.
QUINCE. Marry, our play is, 'The most lamentable comedy, and most cruel

death of Pyramus and Thisby.'

BOTTOM. A very good piece of work, I assure you, and a merry. Now, good Peter Quince, call forth your actors by the scroll. Masters, spread yourselves.

QUINCE. Answer as I call you. Nick Bottom, the weaver.

BOTTOM. Ready. Name what part I am for, and proceed.

QUINCE. You, Nick Bottom, are set down for Pyramus.

BOTTOM. What is Pyramus? A lover, or a tyrant?

QUINCE. A lover that kills himself, most gallant, for love.

BOTTOM. That will ask some tears in the true performing of it: if I do it, let the audience look to their eyes. I will move storms. I will condole in some measure. To the rest: yet my chief humour is for a tyrant. I could play Ercles rarely, or a part to tear a cat in, to make all split.

> The raging rocks
> And shivering shocks
> Shall break the locks
>   Of prison gates;
> And Phibbus' car
> Shall shine from far,
> And make and mar
>   The foolish Fates.

This was lofty! Now name the rest of the players. This is Ercles' vein, a tyrant's vein. A lover is more condoling.

QUINCE. Francis Flute, the bellows mender.

FLUTE. Here, Peter Quince.

QUINCE. Flute, you must take Thisby on you.

FLUTE. What is Thisby? A wand'ring knight?

QUINCE. It is the lady that Pyramus must love.

FLUTE. Nay, faith, let not me play a woman. I have a beard coming.

QUINCE. That's all one. You shall play it in a mask, and you may speak as small as you will.

BOTTOM. An I may hide my face, let me play Thisby too, I'll speak in a monstrous little voice, 'Thisne, Thisne!' 'Ah Pyramus, my lover dear! Thy Thisby dear, and lady dear!'

QUINCE. No, no; you must play Pyramus; and, Flute, you Thisby.

BOTTOM. Well, proceed.

QUINCE. Robin Starveling, the tailor.

STARVELING. Here, Peter Quince.

QUINCE. Robin Starveling, you must play Thisby's mother. Tom Snout,

38

the tinker.

SNOUT. Here, Peter Quince.

QUINCE. You, Pyramus' father: myself, Thisby's father: Snug, the joiner; you, the lion's part. And I hope here is a play fitted.

SNUG. Have you the lion's part written? Pray you, if it be, give it me, for I am slow of study.

QUINCE. You may do it extempore, for it is nothing but roaring.

BOTTOM. Let me play the lion too. I will roar that I will do any man's heart good to hear me. I will roar, that I will make the Duke say, 'Let him roar again, let him roar again.'

QUINCE. An you should do it too terribly, you would fright the Duchess and the ladies, that they would shriek; and that were enough to hang us all.

ALL. That would hang us, every mother's son.

BOTTOM. I grant you, friends, if you should fright the ladies out of their wits, they would have no more discretion but to hang us: but I will aggravate my voice so that I will roar you as gently as any sucking dove; I will roar you an 'twere any nightingale.

QUINCE. You can play no part but Pyramus; for Pyramus is a sweet-faced man; a proper man as one shall see in a summer's day; a most lovely, gentlemanlike man: therefore you must needs play Pyramus.

BOTTOM. Well, I will undertake it. What beard were I best to play it in?

QUINCE. Why, what you will.

BOTTOM. I will discharge it in either your straw-colour beard, your orange-tawny beard, your purple-in-grain beard, or your French-crown-colour beard, your perfect yellow.

QUINCE. Some of your French crowns have no hair at all, and then you will play barefaced. But masters, here are your parts; and I am to entreat you, request you, and desire you, to con them by tomorrow night; and meet me in the palace wood, a mile without the town, by moonlight. There will we rehearse, for if we meet in the city, we shall be dogged with company, and our devices known. In the meantime I will draw a bill of properties, such as our play wants. I pray you, fail me not.

BOTTOM. We will meet; and there we may rehearse most obscenely and courageously. Take pains; be perfect; adieu.

QUINCE. At the Duke's Oak we meet.

BOTTOM. Enough; hold or cut bowstrings. (*Exeunt.*)

WILLIAM SHAKESPEARE, *A MIDSUMMER NIGHT'S DREAM*

à

In *Mansfield Park*, Jane Austen has a group of her characters indulge in amateur theatricals, masterminded by the charismatic but untrustworthy brother and sister combo Henry and Mary Crawford. Austen seems to disapprove of the whole venture and makes the morally upright and 'sympathetic' Fanny and Edmund disapprove of it too. However, despite a certain po-facedness which a modern sensibility finds hard to stomach (or do I just feel she's getting at me?) she handles her casting session with characteristic insight and malice exposing vanity, greed and selfishness with great delicacy.

ᑐ

Fanny seemed nearer being right than Edmund had supposed. The business of finding a play that would suit every body, proved to be no trifle; and the carpenter had received his orders and taken his measurements, had suggested and removed at least two sets of difficulties, and having made the necessity of an enlargement of plan and expense fully evident, was already at work, while a play was still to seek. Other preparations were also in hand. An enormous roll of green baize had arrived from Northampton, and been cut out by Mrs Norris (with a saving, by her good management, of full three quarters of a yard), and was actually forming into a curtain by the housemaids, and still the play was wanting; and as two or three days passed away in this manner, Edmund began almost to hope that none might ever be found.

There were, in fact, so many things to be attended to, so many people to be pleased, so many best characters required, and above all, such a need that the play should be at once both tragedy and comedy, that there did seem as little chance of a decision, as any thing pursued by youth and zeal could hold out.

On the tragic side were the Miss Bertrams, Henry Crawford, and Mr Yates; on the comic, Tom Bertram, not *quite* alone, because it was evident that Mary Crawford's wishes, though politely kept back, inclined the same way; but his determinateness and his power, seemed to make allies unnecessary; and independent of this great irreconcileable difference, they wanted a piece containing very few characters in the whole, but every character first-rate, and three principal women. All the best plays were run over in vain. Neither Hamlet, nor Macbeth, nor Othello, nor Douglas, nor the Gamester, presented any thing that could satisfy even the tragedians; and the Rivals, the School for Scandal, Wheel of Fortune, Heir at Law, and a long etcetera, were successively dismissed with yet warmer objections. No piece could be proposed that did not supply somebody with a difficulty, and on one side or the other it was a continual repetition of, 'Oh! no, *that* will never do. Let us have no ranting tragedies. Too many characters – Not a tolerable woman's part in the play – Any thing but *that,* my dear Tom. It would be impossible to fill it up – One could not expect anybody to take such a part – Nothing but buffoonery from beginning to end. *That* might do, perhaps, but for the low parts – If I *must* give my opinion, I have always thought it the most insipid play in the English language – I do not wish to make objections, I shall be happy to be of any use, but I think we could not choose worse.'

Fanny looked on and listened, not unamused to observe the selfishness which, more or less disguised, seemed to govern them all, and wondering how it would end. For her own gratification she could have wished that something might be acted, for she had never seen even half a play, but every thing of higher consequence was against it.

'This will never do,' said Tom Bertram at last. 'We are wasting time most abominably. Something must be fixed on. No matter what, so that something is chosen. We must not be so nice. A few characters too many, must not frighten us. We must *double* them. We must descend a little. If a part is insignificant, the greater our credit in making any thing of it. From this moment *I* make no difficulties. I take any part you choose to give me so as it be comic. Let it but be comic, I condition for nothing more.'

For about the fifth time he then proposed the Heir at Law, doubting only whether to prefer Lord Duberley or Dr Pangloss for himself, and very earnestly, but very unsuccessfully, trying to persuade the others that there were some fine tragic parts in the rest of the Dramatis Personae.

The pause which followed this fruitless effort was ended by the same speaker, who taking up one of the many volumes of plays that lay on the table, and turning it over, suddenly exclaimed, 'Lovers' Vows! And why should not Lovers' Vows do for *us* as well as for the Ravenshaws? How came it never to be thought of before? It strikes me as if it would do exactly. What say you all? – Here are two capital tragic parts for Yates and Crawford, and here is the rhyming butler for me – if nobody else wants it – a trifling part, but the sort of thing I should not dislike, and as I said before, I am determined to take any thing and do my best. And as for the rest, they may be filled up by any body. It is only Count Cassel and Anhalt.'

The suggestion was generally welcome. Every body was growing weary of indecision, and the first idea with every body was, that nothing had been proposed before so likely to suit them all. Mr Yates was particularly pleased; he had been sighing and longing to do the Baron at Ecclesford, had grudged every rant of Lord Ravenshaw's, and been forced to re-rant it all in his own room. To storm through Baron Wildenhaim was the height of his theatrical ambition, and with the advantage of knowing half the scenes by heart already, he did now with the greatest alacrity offer his services for the part. To do him justice, however, he did not resolve to appropriate it – for remembering that there was some very good ranting ground in Frederick, he professed an equal willingness for that. Henry Crawford was ready to take either. Whichever Mr Yates did not choose, would perfectly satisfy him, and a short parley of compliment ensued. Miss Bertram feeling all the interest of an Agatha in the question, took on her to decide it, by observing to Mr Yates, that this was a point in which height and figure out to be considered, and that *his* being the tallest, seemed to fit him peculiarly for the Baron. She was acknowledged to be quite right, and the two parts being accepted accordingly, she was certain of the proper Frederick. Three of the characters were now cast, besides Mr Rushworth, who was always answered for by Maria as willing to do any thing; when Julia, meaning like her sister to be Agatha, began to be scrupulous on Miss Crawford's account.

'This is not behaving well by the absent,' said she. 'Here are not women enough. Amelia and Agatha may do for Maria and me, but here is nothing for your sister, Mr Crawford.'

Mr Crawford desired *that* might not be thought of; he was very sure his sister had no wish of acting, but as she might be useful, and that she would not allow herself to be considered in the present case. But this was immediately opposed by Tom Bertram, who asserted the part of Amelia to be in every respect the property of Miss Crawford if she would accept it. 'If falls as naturally, as necessarily to her,' said he, 'as Agatha does to one or other of my sisters. It can be no sacrifice on their side, for it is highly comic.'

A short silence followed. Each sister looked anxious; for each felt the best claim to Agatha, and was hoping to have it pressed on her by the rest. Henry Crawford, who meanwhile had taken up the play, and with seeming carelessness was turning over the first act, soon settled the business. 'I must entreat Miss *Julia* Bertram,' said he, 'not to engage in the part of Agatha, or it will be the ruin of all my solemnity. You must not, indeed you must not – (turning to her.) I could not stand your countenance dressed up in woe and paleness. The many laughs we have had together would infallibly come across me, and Frederick and his knapsack would be obliged to run away.'

Pleasantly, courteously it was spoken; but the manner was lost in the matter to Julia's feelings. She saw a glance at Maria, which confirmed the injury to herself; it was a scheme – a trick; she was slighted, Maria was preferred; the smile of triumph which Maria was trying to suppress shewed how well it was understood, and before Julia could command herself enough to speak, her brother gave his weight against her too, by saying, 'Oh! yes, Maria must be Agatha. Maria will be the best Agatha. Though Julia fancies she prefers tragedy, I would not trust her in it. There is nothing of tragedy about her. She has not the look of it. Her features are not tragic features, and she walks too quick, and speaks too quick, and would not keep her countenance. She had better do the old countrywoman; the Cottager's wife; you had, indeed, Julia. Cottager's wife is a very pretty part I assure you. The old lady relieves the high-flown benevolence of her husband with a good deal of spirit. You shall be Cottager's wife.'

'Cottager's wife!' cried Mr Yates. 'What are you talking of? The most trivial, paltry, insignificant part; the merest common-place – not a tolerable speech in the whole. Your sister do that! It is an insult to propose it. At Ecclesford the governess was to have done it. We all agreed that it could not be offered to any body else. A little more justice, Mr Manager, if you please. You do not deserve the office, if you cannot appreciate the talents of your company a little better.'

'Why as to *that,* my good friend, till I and my company have really acted there must be some guess-work; but I mean no disparagement to Julia. We cannot have two Agathas, and we must have one Cottager's wife; and I am sure I set her the example of moderation myself in being satisfied with the old Butler. If the part is trifling she will have more credit in making something of it; and if she is so desperately bent against every thing humorous, let her take Cottager's speeches instead of Cottager's wife's, and so change the parts all through; he is solemn and pathetic enough I am sure. It could make no difference in the play; and as for Cottager himself, when he has got his wife's speeches, *I* would undertake him with all my heart.'

'With all your partiality for Cottager's wife,' said Henry Crawford, 'it will be impossible to make any thing of it fit for your sister, and we must not suffer her good nature to be imposed on. We must not *allow* her to accept the part. She must not be left to her own complaisance. Her talents will be wanted in Amelia. Amelia is a character more difficult to be well represented than even Agatha. I consider Amelia as the most difficult character in the whole piece. It requires great powers, great nicety, to give her playfulness and simplicity without extravagance. I have seen good actresses fail in the part. Simplicity, indeed, is beyond the reach of almost every actress by profession. It requires a delicacy of feeling which they have not. It requires a gentlewoman – a Julia Bertram. You *will* undertake it I hope?' turning to her with a look of anxious entreaty, which softened her a little; but while she hesitated what to say, her brother again interposed with Miss Crawford's better claim.

'No, no, Julia must not be Amelia. It is not at all the part for her. She

43

would not like it. She would not do well. She is too tall and robust. Amelia should be a small, light, girlish, skipping figure. It is fit for Miss Crawford and Miss Crawford only. She looks the part, and I am persuaded will do it admirably.'

Without attending to this, Henry Crawford continued his supplication. 'You must oblige us,' said he, 'indeed you must. When you have studied the character, I am sure you will feel it suit you. Tragedy may be your choice, but it will certainly appear that comedy chooses *you*. You will be to visit me in prison with a basket of provisions; you will not refuse to visit me in prison? I think I see you coming in with your basket.'

The influence of his voice was felt. Julia wavered: but was he only trying to soothe and pacify her, and make her overlook the previous affront? She distrusted him. The slight had been most determined. He was, perhaps, but at treacherous play with her. She looked suspiciously at her sister; Maria's countenance was to decide it; if she were vexed and alarmed – but Maria looked all serenity and satisfaction, and Julia well knew that on this ground Maria could not be happy but at her expense. With hasty indignation therefore, and a tremulous voice, she said to him, 'You do not seem afraid of not keeping your countenance when I come in with a basket of provisions – though one might have supposed – but it is only as Agatha that I was to be so overpowering!' – She stopped – Henry Crawford looked rather foolish, and as if he did not know what to say. Tom Bertram began again.

'Miss Crawford must be Amelia – She will be an excellent Amelia.'

'Do not be afraid of *my* wanting the character,' cried Julia with angry quickness; – 'I am *not* to be Agatha, and I am sure I will do nothing else; and as to Amelia, it is of all parts in the world the most disgusting to me. I quite detest her. An odious, little, pert, unnatural, impudent girl. I have always protested against comedy, and this is comedy in its worst form.' And so saying, she walked hastily out of the room, leaving awkward feelings to more than one, but exciting small compassion in any except Fanny, who had been a quiet auditor of the whole, and who could not think of her as under the agitations of *jealousy*, without great pity.

A short silence succeeded her leaving them; but her brother soon returned to business and Lovers' Vows, and was eagerly looking over the play, with Mr Yates's help, to ascertain what scenery would be necessary – while Maria and Henry Crawford conversed together in an under voice, and the declaration with which she began of, 'I am sure I would give up the part to Julia most willingly, but that though I shall probably do it very ill, I feel persuaded *she* would do it worse,' was doubtless receiving all the compliments it called for.

When this had lasted some time, the division of the party was completed by Tom Bertram and Mr Yates walking off together to consult farther in the room now beginning to be called *the Theatre,* and Miss Bertram's resolving to go down to the Parsonage herself with the offer of Amelia to Miss Crawford; and Fanny remained alone.

The first use she made of her solitude was to take up the volume which had been left on the table, and begin to acquaint herself with the play of which she had heard so much. Her curiosity was all awake, and she ran through it with an eagerness which was suspended only by intervals of astonishment, that it could be chosen in the present instance – that it could be proposed and accepted in a private Theatre! Agatha and Amelia appeared to her in their different ways so totally improper for home representation – the situation of one, and the language of the other, so unfit to be expressed by any woman of modesty, that she could hardly suppose her cousins could be aware of what they were engaging in; and longed to have them roused as soon as possible by the remonstrance which Edmund would certainly make.

JANE AUSTEN, *MANSFIELD PARK*

ða

The play having been cast, rehearsals commence. We return to Shakespeare's Mechanicals, rehearsing at night in an enchanted wood. They encounter all the usual challenges of the eager inexperienced: how not to offend the audience, how to put a lion on stage, or moonlight, or a brick wall. They find imaginative solutions to all their problems, leading instinctively towards real theatrical magic. As ever, execution falls short of intention – a very familiar scenario.

ða

[ACT III, sc. i]
Enter the clowns: [Quince, Snug, Bottom, Flute, Snout, and Starveling].

BOTTOM. Are we all met?

QUINCE. Pat, pat; and here's a marvellous convenient place for our rehearsal. This green plot shall be our stage, this hawthorn brake our tiring house, and we will do it in action as we will do it before the Duke.

BOTTOM. Peter Quince?

QUINCE. What sayest thou, bully Bottom?

BOTTOM. There are things in this comedy of Pyramus and Thisby that will never please. First, Pyramus must draw a sword to kill himself; which the ladies cannot abide. How answer you that?

SNOUT. By'r lakin, a parlous fear.

STARVELING. I believe we must leave the killing out, when all is done.

BOTTOM. Not a whit. I have a device to make all well. Write me a prologue, and let the prologue seem to say, we will do no harm with our swords, and that Pyramus is not killed indeed; and, for the more better assurance, tell them that I Pyramus am not Pyramus, but Bottom the weaver. This will put them out of fear.

QUINCE. Well, we will have such a prologue, and it shall be written in eight and six.

BOTTOM. No, make it two more; let it be written in eight and eight.

SNOUT. Will not the ladies be afeared of the lion?

STARVELING. I fear it, I promise you.

BOTTOM. Masters, you ought to consider with yourselves. To bring in – God shield us! – a lion among ladies, is a most dreadful thing. For there is not a more fearful wild fowl than your lion living; and we ought to look to't.

SNOUT. Therefore another prologue must tell he is not a lion.

BOTTOM. Nay, you must name his name, and half his face must be seen through the lion's neck, and he himself must speak through, saying thus, or to the same defect – 'Ladies' – or,'Fair ladies – I would wish you' – or, 'I would request you' – or, 'I would entreat you – not to fear, not to tremble: my life for yours. If you think I come hither as a lion, it were pity of my life. No, I am no such thing. I am a man as other men are.' And there indeed let him name his name, and tell them plainly, he is Snug the joiner.

QUINCE. Well, it shall be so. But there is two hard things; that is, to bring the moonlight into a chamber; for, you know, Pyramus and Thisby meet by moonlight.

SNOUT. Doth the moon shine that night we play our play?

BOTTOM. A calendar, a calendar! Look in the almanac; find out moonshine, find out moonshine.

QUINCE. Yes, it doth shine that night.

BOTTOM. Why, then may you leave a casement of the great chamber window, where we play, open, and the moon may shine in at the casement.

QUINCE. Ay; or else one must come in with a bush of thorns and a lantern, and say he comes to disfigure, or to present, the person of Moonshine. Then, there is another thing: we must have a wall in the great chamber; for Pyramus and Thisby, says the story, did talk through the chink of a wall.

SNOUT. You can never bring in a wall. What say you, Bottom?

BOTTOM. Some man or other must present Wall; and let him have some plaster, or some loam, or some roughcast about him, to signify Wall; and let him hold his fingers thus, and through that cranny shall Pyramus and Thisby whisper.

QUINCE. If that may be, then all is well. Come, sit down, every mother's son, and rehearse your parts. Pyramus, you begin. When you have spoken your speech, enter into that brake; and so everyone according to his cue.

Enter Robin [Puck]

PUCK. What hempen homespuns have we swagg'ring here,
So near the cradle of the Fairy Queen?
What, a play toward! I'll be an auditor;
An actor too perhaps, if I see cause.

QUINCE. Speak, Pyramus. Thisby, stand forth.

PYRAMUS [BOTTOM]. Thisby, the flowers of odious savours sweet –

QUINCE. Odours, odours.

PYRAMUS. –odours savours sweet:
So hath thy breath, my dearest Thisby dear.
But hark, a voice! Stay thou but here awhile,
And by and by I will to thee appear.   *Exit*

PUCK. A stranger Pyramus than e'er played here!   *[Exit.]*

THISBY [FLUTE]. Must I speak now?

QUINCE. Ay, marry, must you. For you must understand he goes but to see a noise that he heard, and is to come again.

THISBY. Most radiant Pyramus, most lily-white of hue,
Of colour like the red rose on triumphant brier,
Most brisky Juvenal, and eke most lovely Jew,
As true as truest horse, that yet would never tire,
I'll meet thee, Pyramus, at Ninny's tomb.

QUINCE. 'Ninus' tomb,' man. Why, you must not speak that yet. That you answer to Pyramus. You speak all your part at once, cues and all. Pyramus enter. Your cue is past; it is 'never tire.'

THISBY. O – as true as truest horse, that yet would never tire.

[Re-enter Puck, and Bottom with an ass's head.]

PYRAMUS. If I were fair, Thisby, I were only thine.

QUINCE. O monstrous! O strange! We are haunted. Pray, masters! Fly, masters! Help!

[Exeunt all the clowns but Bottom.]

PUCK. I'll follow you, I'll lead you about a round,

Through bog, through bush, through brake, through brier
Sometime a horse I'll be, sometime a hound,
    A hog, a headless bear, sometime a fire;
And neigh, and bark, and grunt, and roar, and burn,
    Like horse, hound, hog, bear, fire, at every turn.   *[Exit]*
BOTTOM. Why do they run away? This is a knavery of them to make me
    afeard.

Enter Snout.

SNOUT. O Bottom, thou art changed! What do I see on thee?
BOTTOM. What do you see? You see an ass head of your own, do you?
                                                          [Exit Snout.]

Enter Quince.

QUINCE. Bless thee, Bottom! Bless thee! Thou art translated.   *Exit.*
BOTTOM. I see their knavery. This is to make an ass of me; to fright me, if
    they could. But I will not stir from this place, do what they can. I will
    walk up and down here, and I will sing, that they shall hear I am not
    afraid.   *[Sings.]*
            WILLIAM SHAKESPEARE, *A MIDSUMMER NIGHT'S DREAM*

In Timberlake Wertembaker's play *Our Country's Good,* based on Thomas
Keneally's novel *The Playmaker,* amateur dramatics are powerfully thera-
peutic. A group of transported convicts, under the direction of an idealistic
young lieutenant, are to perform Farquhar's *The Recruiting Officer.*
Gradually, the experience of creating the play lifts them out of their
lethargy and fear, frees their voices and their spirits and gives them, and us,
a sense that life can be better. When I saw the play at the Royal Court in
1988, I found it a tremendously moving and optimistic picture of the
transforming power of art, and Lesley Sharp's final tremor of excitement,
just before the curtain rises on Mary's simple line 'I love this', is an unforgettable theatrical memory.

ACT TWO:SCENE TEN
BACKSTAGE

NIGHT. *The Aborigine.*
THE ABORIGINE: Look: oozing pustules on my skin, heat on my forehead.
    Perhaps we have been wrong all this time and this is not a dream at all.

48

The Actors come on.

MARY: Are the savages coming to see the play as well?

KETCH: They come around the camp because they're dying: smallpox.

MARY: Oh.

SIDEWAY: I hope they won't upset the audience.

MARY: Everyone is here. All the officers too.

LIZ *(to Duckling)*: Dabby could take your part.

DUCKLING: No. I will do it. I will remember the lines.

MARY: I've brought you some bread. They've thrown her out of Harry
    Brewer's tent.

WISEHAMMER: Why? He wouldn't have wanted that.

DUCKLING: Major Ross said a whore was a whore and I was to go into the
    women's camp. They've taken all of Harry's things.

She bursts into tears.

MARY: I'll talk to the Lieutenant.

LIZ: Let's go over your lines. And if you forget them, touch my foot and I'll
    whisper them to you.

SIDEWAY: *(who has been practising on his own)*: We haven't rehearsed the bow.
    Garrick used to take his this way: you look up to the circle, to the sides,
    down, make sure everyone thinks you're looking at them. Get in a line.

They do so.

ARSCOTT: I'll be in the middle, I'm the tallest.

SIDEWAY: Dabby, you should be next to Mary.

DABBY: I won't take the bow.

SIDEWAY: It's not the biggest part, Dabby, but you'll be noticed.

DABBY: I don't want to be noticed.

SIDEWAY: Let's get this right. If we don't all do the same thing, it will look
    a mess.

They try.

DABBY: Hurray, hurray, hurray.

SIDEWAY: No, they will be shouting bravo, but we're not in a line yet.

DABBY: I wasn't looking at the bow, I saw the whole play, and we all knew
    our lines, and Mary, you looked so beautiful, and after that, I saw Devon
    and they were shouting bravo, bravo Dabby, hurray, you've escaped,
    you've sailed thousands and thousands of miles on the open sea and
    you've come back to your Devon, bravo Dabby, bravo.

MARY: When are you doing this, Dabby?

DABBY: Tonight.

MARY: You can't.

DABBY: I'll be in the play till the end, then in the confusion, when it's over, and all the convicts are going back to the camp and the officers aren't paying attention, we can slip away. The tide is up, the night will be dark, everything's ready.

MARY: The Lieutenant will be blamed, I won't let you.

DABBY: If you say anything to the Lieutenant, I'll refuse to act in the play.

ARSCOTT: When I say my lines, I think of nothing else. Why can't you do the same?

DABBY: Because it's only for one night. I want to grow old in Devon.

MARY: They'll never let us do another play, I'm telling the Lieutenant.

ALL: No, you're not.

DABBY: Please, I want to go back to Devon.

WISEHAMMER: I don't want to go back to England now. It's too small and they don't like Jews. Here, no one has more of a right than anyone else to call you a foreigner. I want to become the first famous writer.

MARY: You can't become a famous writer until you're dead.

WISEHAMMER: You can if you're the only one.

SIDEWAY: I'm going to start a theatre company. Who wants to be in it?

WISEHAMMER: I will write you a play about justice.

SIDEWAY: Only comedies, my boy, only comedies.

WISEHAMMER: What about a comedy about unrequited love?

LIZ: I'll be in your company, Mr Sideway.

KETCH: And so will I. I'll play all the parts that have dignity and gravity.

SIDEWAY: I'll hold auditions tomorrow.

DABBY: Tomorrow.

DUCKLING: Tomorrow.

MARY: Tomorrow.

LIZ: Tomorrow

A long silence. (Un ange passe.)

MARY: Where are my shoes?

RALPH comes in.

RALPH: Arscott, remember to address the soldiers when you talk of recruiting. Look at them: you are speaking to them. And don't forget, all of you, to leave a space for people to laugh.

ARSCOTT: I'll kill anyone who laughs at me.

RALPH: They're not laughing at you, they're laughing at Farquhar's lines. You must expect them to laugh.

ARSCOTT: That's all right, but if I see Major Ross or any other officer laughing at me, I'll kill them.

MARY: No more violence. By the way, Arscott, when you carry me off the stage as Jack Wilful, could you be a little more gentle? I don't think he'd be so rough with a young gentleman.

RALPH: Where's Caesar?

KETCH: I saw him walking towards the beach earlier. I thought he was practising his lines.

ARSCOTT: Caesar!

He goes out.

WISEHAMMER: When I say 'Do you love fishing, madam?', do you say something then? −

RALPH: *(goes over to Duckling):* I am so sorry, Duckling. Harry was my friend.

DUCKLING: I loved him. But now he'll never know that. I thought that if he knew he would become cruel.

RALPH: Are you certain you don't want Dabby to take your part?

DUCKLING: No! I will do it. I want to do it.

Pause

He liked to hear me say my lines.

RALPH *(to Mary):* How beautiful you look.

MARY: I dreamt I had a necklace of pearls and three children.

RALPH: If we have a boy we will call him Harry.

MARY: And if we have a girl?

RALPH: She will be called Betsey Alicia.

Arscott comes in with Caesar drunk and dishevelled.

ARSCOTT: Lying on the beach, dead drunk.

CAESAR: I can't. All those people. My ancestors are angry, they do not want me to be laughed at by all those people.

RALPH: You wanted to be in this play and you will be in this play −

KETCH: I'm nervous too, but I have overcome it. You have to be brave to be an actor.

CAESAR: My ancestors will kill me.

He swoons. Arscott hits him.

ARSCOTT: You're going to ruin my first scene.

CAESAR: Please, Lieutenant, save me.

RALPH: Caesar, if I were back home, I wouldn't be in this play either. My ancestors wouldn't be very pleased to see me – here with people not of my sort. But our ancestors are thousands of miles away.

CAESAR: I cannot be a disgrace to Madagascar.

ARSCOTT: You will be more of a disgrace if you don't come out with me on that stage.

MARY: Think of us as your family.

SIDEWAY: What do you think of this bow?

RALPH: Caesar, I am your Lieutenant and I command you to go on that stage. If you don't you will be tried and hanged for treason.

KETCH: I'll tie the rope in such a way you'll dangle there for hours full of piss and shit.

RALPH: What will your ancestors think of that, Caesar?

Caesar cries but pulls himself together.

KETCH *(to Liz):* I couldn't have hanged you.

LIZ: –

RALPH: Dabby, have you got your chickens?

DABBY: My chickens? Yes. Here.

RALPH: Are you all right?

DABBY: Yes. *(Pause.)* I was dreaming.

RALPH: Of your future success?

DABBY: Yes. Of my future success.

RALPH: And so is everyone here, I hope. Now. Arscott.

ARSCOTT: Yes, Sir!

RALPH: Calm.

ARSCOTT: I have been used to danger, Sir.

SIDEWAY: Here.

LIZ: What's that?

SIDEWAY: Salt. For good luck.

RALPH: Where did you get that from?

SIDEWAY: I have been saving it from my rations. I have saved enough for each of us to have some.

WISEHAMMER: Lieutenant?

RALPH: Yes, Wisehammer.

WISEHAMMER: There's – there's –

MARY: There's his prologue.

RALPH: The prologue. I forgot.

Pause.

Let me hear it again.

WISEHAMMER: From distant climes o'er wide-spread seas we come.
 Though not with much éclat or beat of drum,
 True patriots all; for be it understood,
 We left our country for our country's good;
 No private views disgraced our generous zeal,
 What urg'd our travels was our country's weal,
 And none will doubt but that our emigration
 Has prov'd most useful to the British nation.

Silence.

RALPH: When Major Ross hears that, he'll have an apopleptic fit.

MARY: I think it's very good.

DABBY: So do I. And true.

SIDEWAY: But not theatrical.

RALPH: It is very good, Wisehammer, it's very well written, but it's too-too political. It will be considered provocative.

WISEHAMMER: You don't want me to say it.

RALPH: Not tonight. We have many people against us.

WISEHAMMER: I could tone it down. I could omit 'We left our country for our country's good.'

DABBY: That's the best line.

RALPH: It would be wrong to cut it.

WISEHAMMER: I worked so hard on it.

LIZ: It rhymes.

SIDEWAY: We'll use it in the Sideway Theatre.

RALPH: You will get much praise as Brazen, Wisehammer.

Wisehammer: It isn't the same as writing.

RALPH: The theatre is like a small republic, it requires private sacrifices for the good of the whole. That is something you should agree with, Wisehammer.

Pause.

And now, my actors. I want to say what a pleasure it has been to work with you. You are on your own tonight and you must do your utmost to provide the large audience out there with a pleasureable, intelligent and memorable evening.

LIZ: We will do our best, Mr Clark.

MARY: I love this.

RALPH: Arscott.

ARSCOTT *(to Caesar):* You walk three steps ahead of me. If you stumble once, you know what will happen to you later? Move.

RALPH: You're on.

ARSCOTT: 'If any gentlemen soldiers, or others, have a mind to serve Her Majesty, and pull down the French King; if any prentices have severe masters, any children have undutiful parents; if any servants have too little wages, or any husband too much wife; let them repair to the noble Sergeant Kite, at the Sign of the Raven, in this good town of Shrewsbury, and they shall receive present relief and entertainment …

TIMBERLAKE WERTEMBAKER, OUR COUNTRY'S GOOD

We never see the convicts' play, and in a way of course it doesn't matter if it's good or bad – the process is the important thing. Virginia Woolf, in her last novel, *Between the Acts*, deals with the anguish of performance. An amateur pageant play on an historical theme provides the opportunity for some very funny parody. The pageant also allows her to provide insights into the desperate yearning of the author, director and performers for the piece to 'work', to have the desired effect, to create that fragile and elusive relationship between performer and audience that is the unique property of theatre out of all the arts. Miss La Trobe, whose project it is, is gnawing her knuckles behind a bush, waiting for the audience to assemble and the pageant to begin.

Rows of chairs, deck chairs, gilt chairs, hired cane chairs, and indigenous garden seats had been drawn up on the terrace. There were plenty of seats for everybody. But some preferred to sit on the ground. Certainly Miss La Trobe had spoken the truth when she said: 'The very place for a pageant!' The lawn was as flat as the floor of a theatre. The terrace, rising, made a natural stage. The trees barred the stage like pillars. And the human figure was seen to great advantage against a background of sky. As for the weather, it was turning out, against all expectation, a very fine day. A perfect summer afternoon.

'What luck!' Mrs Carter was saying. 'Last year … ' Then the play began. Was it, or was it not, the play? Chuff, chuff, chuff sounded from the bushes. It was the noise a machine makes when something has gone wrong. Some sat down hastily; others stopped talking guiltily. All looked at the bushes. For the stage was empty. Chuff, chuff, chuff the machine buzzed in the bushes. While they looked apprehensively and some finished their sentences, a small girl, like a rosebud in pink, advanced; took her stand on a mat, behind a conch, hung with leaves and piped:

> *Gentles and simples, I address you all ...*

So it was the play then. Or was it the prologue?

> *Come hither for our festival* (she continued)
> *This is a pageant, all may see*
> *Drawn from our island history.*
> *England am I ...*

'She's England,' they whispered. 'It's begun.' 'The prologue,' they added, looking down at the programme.

'*England am I*', she piped again; and stopped.

She had forgotten her lines.

'Hear! Hear!' said an old man in a white waistcoat briskly. 'Bravo! Bravo!'

'Blast 'em!' cursed Miss La Trobe, hidden behind the tree. She looked along the front row. They glared as if they were exposed to a frost that nipped them and fixed them all at the same level. Only Bond the cowman looked fluid and natural.

'Music!' she signalled. 'Music!' But the machine continued: Chuff, chuff, chuff.

'*A child new born ...* ' she prompted.

'*A child new born*,' Phyllis Jones continued,

> *Sprung from the sea*
> *Whose billows blown by mighty storm*
> *Cut off from France and Germany*
> *This isle.*

She glanced back over her shoulder. Chuff, chuff, chuff, the machine buzzed. A long line of villagers in shirts made of sacking began passing in and out in single file behind her between the trees. They were singing, but not a word reached the audience.

England am I, Phyllis Jones continued, facing the audience,

> *Now weak and small*
> *A child, as all may see ...*

Her words peppered the audience as with a shower of hard little stones.

Mrs Manresa in the very centre smiled; but she felt as if her skin cracked when she smiled. There was a vast vacancy between her, the singing villagers and the piping child.

Chuff, chuff, chuff, went the machine like a corn-cutter on a hot day. The villagers were singing, but half their words were blown away.

Cutting the roads ... up to the hill top ... we climbed. Down in the valley ...
sow, wild boar, hog, rhinoceros, reindeer ... Dug ourselves in to the hill top ...
Ground roots between stones ... Ground corn ... till we too ... lay under
g–r–o–u–n–d ...

The words petered away. Chuff, chuff, chuff, the machine ticked. Then at last the machine ground out a tune!

> *Armed against fate*
> *The valiant Rhoderick*
> *Armed and valiant*
> *Bold and blatant*
> *Firm elatant*
> *See the warriors – here they come ...*

The pompous popular tune brayed and blared. Miss La Trobe watched from behind the tree. Muscles loosened; ice cracked. The stout lady in the middle began to beat time with her hand on her chair. Mrs Manresa was humming:

My home is at Windsor, close to the Inn.

Royal George is the name of the pub.

And boys you'll believe me,

I don't want no asking ...

She was afloat on the stream of the melody. Radiating royalty, complacency, good humour, the wild child was Queen of the festival. The play had begun.

But there was an interruption. 'O,' Miss La Trobe growled behind her tree, 'the torture of these interruptions!'

'Sorry I'm so late,' said Mrs Swithin. She pushed her way through the chairs to a seat beside her brother.

'What's it all about? I've missed the prologue. England? That little girl? Now she's gone ... '

Phyllis had slipped off the mat.

'And who's this?' asked Mrs Swithin.

It was Hilda, the carpenter's daughter. She now stood where England had stood.

'*O, England's grown* … ' Miss La Trobe prompted her.
'*O, England's grown a girl now,*' Hilda sang out.
('What a lovely voice!' someone exclaimed.)

> *With roses in her hair,*
> *Wild roses, red roses,*
> *She roams the lanes and chooses*
> *A garland for her hair.*

'A cushion? Thank you so much,' said Mrs Swithin, stuffing the cushion behind her back. Then she leant forward.

'That's England in the time of Chaucer, I take it. She's been maying, nutting. She has flowers in her hair … But those passing behind her –' she pointed. 'The Canterbury pilgrims? Look!'

All the time the villagers were passing in and out between the trees. They were singing; but only a word or two was audible ' … *wore ruts in the grass … built the house in the lane* … ' The wind blew away the connecting words of their chant, and then, as they reached the tree at the end they sang:

'*To the shrine of the Saint … to the tomb … lovers … believers … we come* … '

They grouped themselves together.

Then there was a rustle and an interruption. Chairs were drawn back. Isa looked behind her. Mr and Mrs Rupert Haines, detained by a breakdown on the road, had arrived. He was sitting to the right, several rows back, the man in grey.

Meanwhile the pilgrims, having done their homage to the tomb, were, it appeared, tossing hay on their rakes.

> *I kissed a girl and let her go,*
> *Another did I tumble,*
> *In the straw and in the hay* …

– that was what they were singing, as they scooped and tossed the invisible hay, when she looked round again.

'Scenes from English history,' Mrs Manresa explained to Mrs Swithin. She spoke in a loud cheerful voice, as if the old lady were deaf. 'Merry England.'

She clapped energetically.

The singers scampered away into the bushes. The tune stopped. Chuff, chuff, chuff, the machine ticked. Mrs Manresa looked at her programme. It would take till midnight unless they skipped. Early Briton; Plantagenets; Tudors; Stuarts – she ticked them off, but probably she had forgotten a reign or two.

'Ambitious, ain't it?' she said to Bartholomew, while they waited. Chuff, chuff, chuff went the machine. Could they talk? Could they move? No, for the play was going on. Yet the stage was empty; only the cows moved in the meadows; only the tick of the gramophone needle was heard. The tick, tick, tick seemed to hold them together, tranced. Nothing whatsoever appeared on the stage.

'I'd no notion we looked so nice,' Mrs Swithin whispered to William. Hadn't she? The children; the pilgrims; behind the pilgrims the trees, and behind them the fields – the beauty of the visible world took his breath away. Tick, tick, tick the machine continued.

'Marking time,' said old Oliver beneath his breath.

'Which don't exist for us,' Lucy murmured. 'We've only the present.'

'Isn't that enough?' William asked himself. Beauty – isn't that enough? But here Isa fidgeted. Her bare brown arms went nervously to her head. She half turned in her seat. 'No, not for us, who've the future,' she seemed to say. The future disturbing our present. Who was she looking for? William, turning, following her eyes, saw only a man in grey.

The ticking stopped. A dance tune was put on the machine. In time to it, Isa hummed: 'What do I ask? To fly away, from night and day, and issue where – no partings are – but eye meets eye – and ... O', she cried aloud: 'Look at her!'

Everyone was clapping and laughing. From behind the bushes issued Queen Elizabeth – Eliza Clark, licensed to sell tobacco. Could she be Mrs Clark of the village shop? She was splendidly made up. Her head, pearl-hung, rose from a vast ruff. Shiny satins draped her. Sixpenny brooches glared like cats' eyes and tigers' eyes; pearls looked down; her cape was made of cloth of silver – in fact swabs used to scour saucepans. She looked the age in person. And when she mounted the soap box in the centre, representing perhaps a rock in the ocean, her size made her appear gigantic. She could reach a flitch of bacon or haul a tub of oil with one sweep of her arm in the shop. For a moment she stood there, eminent, dominant, on the soap box with the blue and sailing clouds behind her. The breeze had risen.

The Queen of this great land ...

– those were the first words that could be heard above the roar of laughter and applause.

Mistress of ships and bearded men (she bawled)
Hawkins, Frobisher, Drake,

Tumbling their oranges, ingots of silver,
Cargoes of diamonds, ducats of gold,
Down on the jetty, there in the west land, –
(she pointed her fist at the blazing blue sky)
Mistress of pinnacles, spires and palaces –
(her arm swept towards the house)
For me Shakespeare sang –
(a cow mooed. A bird twittered)
The throstle, the mavis (she continued)
In the green wood, the wild wood,
Carolled and sang, praising England, the Queen,
Then there was heard too
On granite and cobble
From Windsor to Oxford
Loud laughter, low laughter
Of warrior and lover,
The fighter, the singer.
The ashen haired babe
(she stretched out her swarthy, muscular arm)
Stretched his arm in contentment
As home from the Isles came
The sea faring men ...

Here the wind gave a tug at her head dress. Loops of pearls made it top-heavy. She had to steady the ruffle which threatened to blow away.

'Laughter, loud laughter,' Giles muttered. The tune on the gramophone reeled from side to side as if drunk with merriment. Mrs Manresa began beating her foot and humming in time to it.

'Bravo! Bravo!' she cried. 'There's life in the old dog yet!' And she trolloped out the words of the song with an abandonment which, if vulgar, was a great help to the Elizabethan age. For the ruff had become unpinned and great Eliza had forgotten her lines. But the audience laughed so loud that it did not matter.

The gramophone blared. Dukes, priests, shepherds, pilgrims, and serving men took hands and danced. The idiot scampered in and out. Hands joined, heads knocking, they danced round the majestic figure of the Elizabethan age personified by Mrs Clark, licensed to sell tobacco, on her soap box.

It was a mellay; a medley; an entrancing spectacle (to William) of dappled light and shade on half clothed, fantastically coloured, leaping, jerking, swinging legs and arms. He clapped till his palms stung.

Mrs Manresa applauded loudly. Somehow she was the Queen; and he (Giles) was the surly hero.

'Bravo! Bravo!' she cried, and her enthusiasm made the surly hero squirm on his seat. Then the great lady in the bath chair, the lady whose marriage with the local peer had obliterated in his trashy title a name that had been a name when there were brambles and briars where the Church now stood – so indigenous was she that even her body, crippled by arthritis, resembled an uncouth, nocturnal animal, now nearly extinct – clapped and laughed loud – the sudden laughter of a startled jay.

'Ha, ha, ha!' she laughed and clutched the arms of her chair with ungloved twisted hands.

'A-maying, a-maying,' they bawled. 'In and out and round about, a-maying, a-maying … '

It didn't matter what the words were; or who sang what. Round and round they whirled, intoxicated by the music. Then, at a sign from Miss La Trobe behind the tree, the dance stopped. A procession formed. Great Eliza descended from her soap box. Taking her skirts in her hand, striding with long strides, surrounded by Dukes and Princes, followed by the lovers arm in arm, with Albert the idiot playing in and out, and the corpse on its bier concluding the procession, the Elizabethan age passed from the scene.

'Curse! Blast! Damn 'em!' Miss La Trobe in her rage stubbed her toe against a root. Here was her downfall; here was the Interval. Writing this skimble-skamble stuff in her cottage, she had agreed to cut the play here; a slave to her audience, – to Mrs Sands' grumble – about tea; about dinner; – she had gashed the scene here. Just as she had brewed emotion, she spilt it. So she signalled: Phyllis! And, summoned, Phyllis popped up on the mat again in the middle.

> *Gentles and simples, I address you all* (she piped.)
> *Our act is done, our scene is over.*
> *Past is the day of crone and lover.*
> *The bud has flowered; the flower has fallen.*
> *But soon will rise another dawning,*
> *For time whose children shall we be*
> *Hath in his keeping, you shall see,*
> *You shall see …*

Her voice petered out. No one was listening. Heads bent, they read 'Interval' on the programme. And, cutting short her words, the megaphone announced in plain English: 'An interval.' Half an hour's interval, for tea. Then the gramophone blared out:

> *Armed against fate,*
> *The valiant Rhoderick,*
> *Bold and blatant*
> *Firm, elatant, etc., etc.*

At that, the audience stirred. Some rose briskly; others stooped, retrieving walking-sticks, hats, bags. And then, as they raised themselves and turned about, the music modulated. The music chanted: *Dispersed are we.* It moaned: *Dispersed are we.* It lamented: *Dispersed are we*, as they streamed, spotting the grass with colour, across the lawns, and down the paths: *Dispersed are we.*

VIRGINIA WOOLF, BETWEEN THE ACTS

𝕫𝕒

Sometimes, vary rarely it is true, but sometimes a play will have an effect it was supposed to have. Probably all actors go through their lives hoping to change somebody the way they themselves were once changed. In Chekhov's *The Seagull*, Konstantin Gavrilovitch Trepliov's amateur play has collapsed in chaos, ruined by his mother's selfishness. Konstantin is devastated, but the performance has had a profound effect on the ageing lady's man Dr Dorn. Unfortunately, as so often in Chekhov's plays, the characters are incapable of communicating properly – Konstantin is too preoccupied to take in the very thing that he most wants to hear.

𝕫𝕒

[All go out except DORN.]

DORN [*alone*]. I don't know, maybe I don't understand anything, maybe I've gone off my head, but I did like that play. There is something in it. When that child was holding forth about loneliness, and later when the devil's red eyes appeared, I was so moved that my hands were shaking. It was fresh, unaffected … Ah! I think he's coming along now. I feel like telling him a lot of nice things about it.

TREPLIOV [*enters*]. They've all gone already!

DORN. I'm here.

TREPLIOV. Mashenka has been looking for me all over the park. Insufferable creature!

DORN. Konstantin Gavrilovich, I liked your play exceedingly. It's a bit strange and, of course, I didn't hear the end, and yet it made a deep

61

impression on me. You've got talent and you must carry on.

[*Trepliov shakes his hand warmly and embraces him impulsively.*]

Tut-tut! How strung up you are! Tears in your eyes! ... What I mean to say is this. You took your subject from the realm of abstract ideas. That was as it should be, because a work of art must without fail convey some great idea. Only things conceived in high seriousness can be beautiful. How pale you are!

TREPLIOV. So you're telling me to carry on?

DORN. Yes. But you must depict only what is significant and permanent. You know, I've lived a varied life, I've chosen my pleasures with discrimination. I'm satisfied. But if it had ever been my lot to experience the exaltation an artist feels at the moment of creative achievement, I believe I should have come to despise this material body of mine and all that goes with it, and my soul would have taken wings and soared into the heights.

TREPLIOV. Forgive me, where's Zaryechnaia?

DORN. There's one more thing. A work of art must express a clear, definite idea. You must know what you are aiming at when you write, for if you follow the enchanted path of literature without a definite goal in mind, you'll lose your way and your talent will ruin you.

TREPLIOV. [*impatiently*]. Where is Zaryechnaia?

DORN. She's gone home.

TREPLIOV [*in despair*]. What shall I do? I want to see her ... I've got to see her ... I'm going ... [*enter Masha.*]

DORN [*to Trepliov*]. Do be a little calmer, my friend.

TREPLIOV. But I'm going all the same. I must go.

MASHA. Please, Konstantin Gavrilovich, come indoors. Your Mamma is waiting for you. She's worried.

TREPLIOV. Tell her I've gone away. And I beg you – all of you – leave me alone! Leave me alone! Don't follow me about.

DORN. But ... but, my dear boy ... you shouldn't ... That's not right.

TREPLIOV [*tearfully*]. Good-bye, Doctor. Thank you. ... [*Goes out.*]

DORN [*with a sigh*]. Youth will have its own way! Youth! ...

MASHA. When people can't think of anything else to say, they say: youth! youth! ... [*Takes snuff.*]

Dorn [*takes the snuff box from her and flings it into the bushes*]. Disgusting!

[*A pause*]

I think I can hear music in the house. We ought to go in.

MASHA. Wait a moment.

DORN. What is it?

Masha. There's something I want to tell you again. ... I feel like talking ...
[*Agitated.*] I'm not really fond of my father, but I've a soft spot in my
heart for you. For some reason I feel a sort of deep affinity with you ...
You must help me. Help me, or I'll do something stupid, something
that'll make a mockery of my life and mess it up ... I can't go on like
this ...

DORN But what is it? How am I to help you?

MASHA. I'm so unhappy. Nobody, nobody knows how unhappy I am!
[*Leaning her head against his breast, softly.*] I love Konstantin.

DORN. How distraught they all are! How distraught! And what a quantity
of love about! ... It's the magic lake! [*Tenderly.*] But what can I do, my
child? Tell me, what can I do? What?

ANTON CHEKHOV, *THE SEAGULL*

๛

After the yearning and anguish of Chekhov, some robust comedy from
the young Charles Dickens. 'Mrs Joseph Porter' is one of the *Sketches
by Boz*, and as well as being very funny gives some indication of the high
seriousness with which the Victorians went about their 'private theatricals'. *Plus ça change* – the earnest amateur today will lose no opportunity to
tell you that his production of *The Winter's Tale* you have just suffered
through has been judged by Many Who Know as infinitely superior to
anything the National or the RSC could come up with.

๛

Most extensive were the preparations at Rose Villa, Clapham Rise, in the
occupation of Mr Gattleton (a stockbroker in especially comfortable circumstances), and great was the anxiety of Mr Gattleton's interesting family,
as the day fixed for the representation of the Private Play which had been
'many months in preparation', approached. The whole family was infected
with the mania for Private Theatricals; the house, usually so clean and tidy,
was, to use Mr Gattleton's expressive description, 'regularly turned out o'
windows'; the large dining-room, dismantled of its furniture and orna-
ments, presented a strange jumble of flats, flies, wings, lamps, bridges,
clouds, thunder and lightning, festoons and flowers, daggers and foil, and
various other messes in theatrical slang included under the comprehensive
name of 'properties'. The bedrooms were crowded with scenery, the
kitchen was occupied by carpenters. Rehearsals took place every other

night in the drawing-room, and every sofa in the house was more or less damaged by the perseverance and spirit with which Mr Sempronius Gattleton, and Miss Lucina, rehearsed the smothering scene in *Othello* – it having been determined that the tragedy should form the first portion of the evening's entertainments.

'When we're a *leetle* more perfect, I think it will go admirably,' said Mr Sempronius, addressing his *corps dramatique*, at the conclusion of the hundred and fiftieth rehearsal. In consideration of his sustaining the trifling inconvenience of bearing all the expenses of the play, Mr Sempronius had been, in the most handsome manner, unanimously elected stage-manager. 'Evans,' continued Mr Gattleton, the younger, addressing a tall, thin, pale young gentleman, with extensive whiskers – 'Evans, you play *Roderigo* beautifully.'

'Beautifully,' echoed the three Miss Gattletons; for Mr Evans was pronounced by all his lady friends to be 'quite a dear'. He looked so interesting, and had such lovely whiskers: to say nothing of his talent for writing verses in albums and playing the flute! *Roderigo* simpered and bowed.

'But I think,' added the manager, 'you are hardly perfect in the – fall – in the fencing-scene, where you are – you understand?'

'It's very difficult,' said Mr Evans, thoughtfully; 'I've fallen about, a good deal, in our counting-house lately, for practice, only I find it hurts one so. Being obliged to fall backward you see, it bruises one's head a good deal.'

'But you must take care you don't knock a wing down,' said Mr Gattleton, the elder, who had been appointed prompter, and who took as much interest in the play as the youngest of the company. 'The stage is very narrow, you know.'

'Oh! Don't be afraid,' said Mr Evans, with a very self-satisfied air; 'I shall fall with my head "off", and then I can't do any harm.'

'But, egad,' said the manager, rubbing his hands, 'we shall make a decided hit in *Masaniello*. Harleigh sings that music admirably.'

Everybody echoed the sentiment. Mr Harleigh smiled, and looked foolish – not an unusual thing with him – hummed 'Behold how brightly breaks the morning', and blushed as red as the fisherman's nightcap he was trying on.

'Let's see,' resumed the manager, telling the number on his fingers, 'we shall have three dancing female peasants, besides *Fenella,* and four fishermen. Then, there's our man Tom; he can have a pair of ducks of mine, and a check shirt of Bob's, and a red nightcap, and he'll do for another – that's five. In the choruses, of course, we can sing at the sides; and in the market-scene we can walk about in cloaks and things. When the revolt takes place, Tom must keep rushing in on one side and out on the other, with a pick-axe, as fast as he can. The effect will be electrical; it will look exactly as if there were an immense number of 'em. And in the eruption-scene we must burn the red fire, and upset the tea-trays, and make all sorts of noises – and it's sure to do.'

'Sure! sure!' cried all the performers *una voce* – and away hurried Mr Sempronius Gattleton to wash the burnt cork off his face, and superintend the 'setting up' of some of the amateur-painted, but never-sufficiently-to-be-admired, scenery.

Mrs Gattleton was a kind, good-tempered, vulgar soul, exceedingly fond of her husband and children, and entertaining only three dislikes. In the first place, she had a natural antipathy to anybody else's unmarried daughters; in the second, she was in bodily fear of anything in the shape of ridicule; lastly – almost a necessary consequence of this feeling – she regarded, with feelings of the utmost horror, one Mrs Joseph Porter over the way. However, the good folks of Clapham and its vicinity stood very much in awe of scandal and sarcasm; and thus Mrs Joseph Porter was courted, and flattered, and caressed, and invited, for much the same reason that induces a poor author, without a farthing in his pocket, to behave with extraordinary civility to a two-penny postman.

'Never mind, ma,' said Miss Emma Porter, in colloquy with her respected relative, and trying to look unconcerned; 'if they had invited me, you know that neither you nor pa would have allowed me to take part in such an exhibition.'

'Just what I should have thought from your high sense of propriety,' returned the mother. 'I am glad to see, Emma, you know how to designate the proceeding.' Miss P., by-the-bye, had only the week before made 'an exhibition' of herself for four days, behind a counter at a fancy fair, to all and every of her Majesty's liege subjects who were disposed to pay a shilling each for the privilege of seeing some four dozen girls flirting with strangers, and playing at shop.

'There!' said Mrs Porter, looking out of window; 'there are two rounds of beef and a ham going in – clearly for sandwiches; and Thomas, the pastry-cook, says, there have been twelve dozen tarts ordered, besides blanc-mange and jellies. Upon my word! think of Miss Gattletons in fancy dresses, too!'

'Oh, it's too ridiculous!' said Miss Porter, hysterically.

'I'll manage to put them a little out of conceit with the business, however,' said Mrs Porter; and out she went on her charitable errand.

'Well, my dear Mrs Gattleton,' said Mrs Joseph Porter, after they had been closeted for some time, and when, by dint of indefatigable pumping, she had managed to extract all the news about the play, 'Well, my dear, people may say what they please; indeed we know they will, for some folks are so ill-natured. Ah, my dear Miss Lucina, how d'ye do? I was just telling your mamma that I have heard it said, that –'

'What?'

'Mrs Porter is alluding to the play, my dear,' said Mrs Gattleton; 'she was, I am sorry to say, just informing me that –'

'Oh, now pray don't mention it,' interrupted Mrs Porter; 'it's most absurd – quite as absurd as young What's-his-name saying he wondered how Miss Caroline, with such a foot and ankle, could have the vanity to play *Fenella.*'

'Highly impertinent, whoever said it,' said Mrs Gattleton, bridling up.

'Certainly, my dear,' chimed in the delighted Mrs Porter; 'most undoubtedly! Because, as I said, if Miss Caroline *does* play *Fenella,* it doesn't follow, as a matter of course, that she should think she has a pretty foot – and then – such puppies as these young men are – he had the impudence to say that –'

How far the amiable Mrs Porter might have succeeded in her pleasant purpose, it is impossible to say, had not the entrance of Mr Thomas Balderstone, Mrs Gattleton's brother, familiarly called in the family 'Uncle Tom', changed the course of conversation, and suggested to her mind an excellent plan of operation on the evening of the play.

Uncle Tom was very rich, and exceedingly fond of his nephews and nieces: as a matter of course, therefore, he was an object of great importance in his own family. He was one of the best-hearted men in existence: always in a good temper, and always talking. It was his boast that he wore top-boots on all occasions, and had never worn a black silk neckerchief; and it was his pride that he remembered all the principal plays of Shakespeare from beginning to end – and so he did. The result of this parrot-like accomplishment was, that he was not only perpetually quoting himself, but that he could never sit by, and hear a misquotation from the *Swan of Avon* without setting the unfortunate delinquent right. He was also something of a wag; never missed an opportunity of saying what he considered a good thing, and invariably laughed until he cried at anything that appeared to him mirth-moving or ridiculous.

'Well, girls!' said Uncle Tom, after the preparatory ceremony of kissing and how-d'ye-do-ing had been gone through, 'how d'ye get on? Know your parts, eh? – Lucina, my dear, act ii., scene I – place, left – cue – "Unknown fate," – What's next, eh? – Go on – "The Heavens – "'

'Oh, yes,' said Miss Lucina, 'I recollect –

"The heavens forbid
But that our loves and comforts should increase
Even as our days do grow!" '

'Make a pause here and there,' said the old gentleman, who was a great critic. "But that our loves and comforts should increase" – emphasis on the last syllable "crease," loud "even", – one, two, three, four; then loud again, "as our days do grow"; emphasis on *days*. That's the way, my dear; trust to your uncle for emphasis. Ah! Sem, my boy, how are you?'

'Very well, thankee, uncle,' returned Mr Sempronius, who had just appeared, looking something like a ringdove, with a small circle round each eye: the result of his constant corking. 'Of course we see you on Thursday.'

'Of course, of course, my dear boy.'

'What a pity it is your nephew didn't think of making you prompter, Mr Balderstone!' whispered Mrs Joseph Porter; 'you would have been invaluable.'

'Well, I flatter myself, I *should* have been tolerably up to the thing,' responded Uncle Tom.

'I must bespeak sitting next you on the night,' resumed Mrs Porter; 'and then, if our dear young friends here, should be at all wrong, you will be able to enlighten me. I shall be so interested.'

'I am sure I shall be most happy to give you any assistance in my power.'

'Mind, it's a bargain.'

'Certainly.'

'I don't know how it is,' said Mrs Gattleton to her daughters, as they were sitting round the fire in the evening, looking over their parts, 'but I really very much wish Mrs Joseph Porter wasn't coming on Thursday, I am sure she's schemeing something.'

'She can't make *us* ridiculous, however,' observed Mr Sempronius Gattleton, haughtily.

The long-looked-for Thursday arrived in due course, and brought with it, as Mr Gattleton senior, philosophically observed, 'no disappointments, to speak of'. True, it was yet a matter of doubt whether *Cassio* would be enabled to get into the dress which had been sent for him from the masquerade warehouse. It was equally uncertain whether the principal female singer would be sufficiently recovered from the influenza to make her appearance; Mr Harleigh, the *Masaniello* of the night, was hoarse, and rather unwell, in consequence of the great quantity of lemon and sugar-candy he had eaten to improve his voice; and two flutes and a violoncello had pleaded severe colds. What of that? the audience were all coming.

Everybody knew his part: the dresses were covered with tinsel and span-gles; the white plumes looked beautiful; Mr Evans had practised falling until he was bruised from head to foot and quite perfect; *Iago* was sure that, in the stabbing-scene, he should make 'a decided hit'. A self-taught deaf gentleman, who had kindly offered to bring his flute, would be a most valuable addition to the orchestra; Miss Jenkins's talent for the piano was too well known to be doubted for an instant; Mr Cape had practised the violin accompaniment with her frequently; and Mr Brown, who had kindly undertaken, at a few hours' notice, to bring his violoncello, would, no doubt, manage extremely well.

Seven o'clock came, and so did the audience; all the rank and fashion of Clapham and its vicinity was fast filling the theatre. There were the Smiths, the Gubbinses, the Nixons, the Dixons, the Hicksons, people with all sorts of names, two aldermen, a sheriff in perspective, Sir Thomas Glumper (who had been knighted in the last reign for carrying up an address on somebody's escaping from nothing); and last, not least, there were Mrs Joseph Porter and Uncle Tom, seated in the centre of the third row from the stage; Mrs P. amusing Uncle Tom with all sorts of stories, and Uncle Tom amusing every one else by laughing most immoderately.

Ting, ting, ting! went the prompter's bell at eight o'clock precisely, and dash went the orchestra into the overture to 'The Men of Prometheus'. The pianoforte player hammered away with laudable perseverance; and the violoncello, which struck in at intervals, 'sounded very well, considering'. The unfortunate individual, however, who had undertaken to play the flute accompaniment 'at sight', found, from fatal experience, the perfect truth of the old adage, 'ought of sight, out of mind'; for being very near-sighted, and being placed at a considerable distance from his music-book, all he had an opportunity of doing was to play a bar now and then in the wrong place, and put the other performers out. It is, however, but justice to Mr Brown to say that he did this to admiration. The overture, in fact, was not unlike a race between the different instruments; the piano came in first by several bars, and the violoncello next, quite distancing the poor flute; for the deaf gentleman *too-too*'d away, quite unconscious that he was at all wrong, until apprised, by the applause of the audience, that the over-ture was concluded. A considerable bustle and shuffling of feet was then heard upon the stage, accompanied by whispers of 'Here's a pretty go! – what's to be done?' &c. The audience applauded again, by way of raising the spirits of the performers; and then Mr Sempronius desired the prompter, in a very audible voice, to 'clear the stage, and ring up'.

Ting, ting, ting! went the bell again. Everybody sat down; the curtain shook; rose sufficiently high to display several pair of yellow boots paddling about; and there remained.

Ting, ting, ting! went the bell again. The curtain was violently convulsed, but rose no higher; the audience tittered; Mrs Porter looked at Uncle Tom; Uncle Tom looked at everybody, rubbing his hands, and laughing with perfect rapture. After as much ringing with the little bell as a muffin-boy would make in going down a tolerably long street, and a vast deal of whispering, hammering, and calling for nails and cord, the curtain at length rose, and discovered Mr Sempronius Gattleton *solus,* and decked for *Othello.* After three distinct rounds of applause, during which Mr Sempronius applied his right hand to his left breast, and bowed in the most approved manner, the manager advanced and said:

'Ladies and Gentlemen – I assure you it is with sincere regret, that I regret to be compelled to inform you, that *Iago* who was to have played Mr Wilson – I beg your pardon, Ladies and Gentlemen, but I am naturally somewhat agitated (applause) – I mean, Mr Wilson, who was to have played *Iago,* is – that is, has been – or, in other words, Ladies and Gentlemen, the fact is, that I have just received a note, in which I am informed that *Iago* is unavoidably detained at the Post-office this evening. Under these circumstances, I trust – a-a-amateur performance – a-nother gentleman undertaken to read the part request indulgence for a short time courtesy and kindness of a British audience.' Over-whelming applause. Exit Mr Sempronius Gattleton, and curtain falls.

The audience were, of course, exceedingly good-humoured; the whole business was a joke; and accordingly they waited for an hour with the utmost patience, being enlivened by an interlude of rout-cakes and lemonade. It appeared by Mr Sempronius's subsequent explanation, that the delay would not have been so great, had it not so happened that when the substitute *Iago* had finished dressing, and just as the play was on the point of commencing, the original *Iago* unexpectedly arrived. The former was therefore compelled to undress, and the latter to dress for his part; which, as he found some difficulty in getting into his clothes, occupied no inconsiderable time. At last, the tragedy began in real earnest. It went off well enough, until the third scene of the first act, in which *Othello* addresses the Senate: the only remarkable circumstance being, that as *Iago* could not get on any of the stage boots, in consequence of his feet being violently swelled with the heat and excitement, he was under the necessity of playing the part in a pair of Wellingtons, which contrasted rather oddly with his richly embroidered pantaloons. When *Othello* started with his address to the Senate (whose dignity was represented by, the *Duke,* a carpenter, two men engaged on the recommendation of the gardener, and a boy), Mrs Porter found the opportunity she so anxiously sought.

Mr Sempronius proceeded:

> 'Most potent, grave, and reverend signiors,
> My very noble and approv'd good masters,
> That I have ta'en away this old man's daughter,
> It is most true; – rude am I in my speech –'

'Is that right?' whispered Mrs Porter to Uncle Tom.

'No.'

'Tell him so, then.'

'I will. Sem!' called out Uncle Tom, 'that's wrong, my boy.'

'What's wrong, uncle?' demanded *Othello,* quite forgetting the dignity of his situation.

'You've left out something. "True, I have married – " '

'Oh, ah!' said Mr Sempronius, endeavouring to hide his confusion as much and as ineffectually as the audience attempted to conceal their half-suppressed tittering, by coughing with extraordinary violence –

> " ' – true I have married her: –
> The very head and front of my offending
> Hath this extent; no more"

(Aside) Why don't you prompt, father?'

'Because I've mislaid my spectacles,' said poor Mr Gattleton, almost dead with the heat and bustle.

'There, now it's "rude am I", 'said Uncle Tom.

'Yes, I know it is,' returned the unfortunate manager, proceeding with his part.

It would be useless and tiresome to quote the number of instances in which Uncle Tom, now completely in his element, and instigated by the mischievous Mrs Porter, corrected the mistakes of the performers; suffice it to say, that having mounted his hobby, nothing could induce him to dismount; so, during the whole remainder of the play, he performed a kind of running accompaniment, by muttering everybody's part as it was being delivered, in an undertone. The audience were highly amused, Mrs Porter delighted, the performers embarrassed; Uncle Tom never was better pleased in all his life; and Uncle Tom's nephews and nieces had never, although the declared heirs to his large property, so heartily wished him gathered to his fathers as on that memorable occasion.

Several other minor causes, too, united to damp the ardour of the *drama-*

tis personae. None of the performers could walk in their tights, or move their arms in their jackets; the pantaloons were too small, the boots too large, and the swords of all shapes and sizes. Mr Evans, naturally too tall for the scenery, wore a black velvet hat with immense white plumes, the glory of which was lost in 'the flies'; and the only other inconvenience of which was, that when it was off his head he could not put it on, and when it was on he could not take it off. Notwithstanding all his practice, too, he fell with his head and shoulders as neatly through one of the side scenes, as a harlequin would jump through a panel in a Christmas pantomime. The pianoforte player, overpowered by the extreme heat of the room, fainted away at the commencement of the entertainments, leaving the music of 'Masaniello' to the flute and violoncello. The orchestra complained that Mr Harleigh put them out, and Mr Harleigh declared that the orchestra prevented his singing a note. The fishermen, who were hired for the occasion, revolted to the very life, positively refusing to play without an increased allowance of spirits; and, their demand being complied with, getting drunk in the eruption-scene as naturally as possible. The red fire, which was burnt at the conclusion of the second act, not only nearly suffocated the audience, but nearly set the house on fire into the bargain; and, as it was, the remainder of the piece was acted in a thick fog.

In short, the whole affair was, as Mrs Joseph Porter triumphantly told everybody, 'a complete failure'. The audience went home at four o'clock in the morning, exhausted with laughter, suffering from severe headaches, and smelling terribly of brimstone and gunpowder. The Messrs Gattleton, senior and junior, retired to rest, with the vague idea of emigrating to Swan River early in the ensuing week.

Rose Villa has once again resumed its wonted appearance; the dining-room furniture has been replaced; the tables are as nicely polished as formerly; the horsehair chairs are ranged against the wall, as regularly as ever; Venetian blinds have been fitted to every window in the house to intercept the prying gaze of Mrs Joseph Porter. The subject of theatricals is never mentioned in the Gattleton family, unless, indeed, by Uncle Tom, who cannot refrain from sometimes expressing his surprise and regret at finding that his nephews and nieces appear to have lost the relish they once possessed for the beauties of Shakespeare, and quotations from the works of that immortal bard.

CHARLES DICKENS, *SKETCHES BY BOZ*

CHAPTER 4
TRAINING
AND THEORY

This chapter is about the theory of acting and the training required to become one. It also touches on the importance of acting, both to its practitioners and as an art form. I'm well aware that I'm on very dodgy ground here – much of the literature on this subject is wide open to parody. Self-importance and vanity lurk around every corner in a broad-brimmed hat and clutching a book of press-cuttings. John Dexter managed it succinctly in his posthumous autobiography *The Honourable Beast*: 'The solution (if you're ever going to find it) to what, why, how one spends one's time doing something as seemingly meaningless as theatre is a question of faith, belief in that object itself, in theatre as religion.'

Of course, no-one becomes a fully-fledged actor by divine intervention, or not in my experience. To produce the necessary controlled passion, with the actor in command technically yet emotionally free, takes time, effort and training. Theories on how to achieve this are legion, but Hamlet's advice to the Players is still the best starting point.

≈

SCENE ii
Enter HAMLET *and three of the* PLAYERS.

HAMLET. Speak the speech, I pray you, as I pronounced it to you, trippingly on the tongue; but if you mouth it as many of your players do, I had as lief the town-crier spoke my lines. Nor do not saw the air too much with your hand, thus, but use all gently; for in the very torrent, tempest, and, as I may say, whirlwind of your passion, you must acquire and beget a temperance that may give it smoothness. O, it offends me to the soul to hear a robustious periwig-pated fellow tear a passion to tatters, to very rags, to split the ears of the groundlings, who for the most part are capable of nothing but inexplicable dumb-shows and noise. I would have such a fellow whipped for o'erdoing Termagant. It out-Herods Herod. Pray you avoid it.

1ST PLAYER. I warrant your honour.

HAMLET. Be not too tame neither, but let your own discretion be your tutor. Suit the action to the word, the word to the action, with this special observance, that you o'erstep not the modesty of nature. For anything so o'erdone is from the purpose of playing, whose end, both at the first and now, was and is to hold as 'twere the mirror up to nature; to show virtue her feature, scorn her own image, and the very age and body of the time his form and pressure. Now this overdone or come tardy off, though it makes the unskilful laugh, cannot but make the judicious grieve, the censure of the which one must in your allowance o'erweigh a whole theatre of others. O, there be players that I have seen play – and heard others praise, and that highly – not to speak it profanely, that neither having th'accent of Christians, nor the gait of Christian, pagan, nor man, have so strutted and bellowed that I have thought some of Nature's journeymen had made men, and not made them well, they imitated humanity so abominably.

1ST PLAYER. I hope we have reformed that indifferently with us.

HAMLET. O reform it altogether. And let those that play your clowns speak no more than is set down for them – for there be of them that will themselves laugh, to set on some quantity of barren spectators to laugh too, though in the meantime some necessary question of the play be then to be considered. That's villainous, and shows a most pitiful ambition in the fool that uses it. Go make you ready.   *[Exeunt Players.]*

WILLIAM SHAKESPEARE, *HAMLET*

The next three extracts are from the writings of four of the most influential theatre practitioners of the twentieth century. Konstantin Stanislavsky, as artistic director of the Moscow Arts Theatre, staged premieres of plays by Chekhov and Gorky among others. As an actor, he created Astrov, Gayev and Vershinin, and as a theorist he wrote eight volumes of work on acting and theatre that are still required reading.

Lee Strasberg, creator of 'The Method', transformed Stanislavsky's teachings into a highly personal and psychoanalytical way of working.

Julian Beck and Judith Malina founded The Living Theatre in 1947, though the decade with which their work is most associated is the 1960s. Passionate, political, committed, adventurous, Living Theatre pioneered the explosion in experimental work on both sides of the Atlantic.

ᵂ

The actor must first of all believe in everything that takes place on the stage, and most of all he must believe in what he himself is doing. And one can believe only in the truth. Therefore it is necessary to feel this truth at all times, to know how to find it, and for this it is inescapable to develop one's artistic sensitivity to truth. It will be said, 'But what kind of truth can this be, when all on the stage is a lie, an imitation, scenery, cardboard, paint, make-up, properties, wooden goblets, swords and spears. Is all this truth?' But it is not of this truth I speak. I speak of the truth of emotions, of the truth of inner creative urges which strain forward to find expression, of the truth of the memories of bodily and physical perceptions. I am not interested in a truth that is without myself; I am interested in the truth that is within myself, the truth of my relation to this or that event on the stage, to the properties, the scenery, the other actors who play parts in the drama with me, to their thoughts and emotions.

The actor says to himself:

'All these properties, make-ups, costumes, the scenery, the publicness of the performance, are lies. I know they are lies, I know I do not need any of them. But *if* they were true, then I would do this and this, and I would behave in this manner and this way towards this and this event.'

I came to understand that creativeness begins from that moment when in the soul and imagination of the actor there appears the magical, creative *if*. While only actual reality exists, only practical truth which a man naturally cannot but believe, creativeness has not yet begun. Then the creative *if* appears, that is, the imagined truth which the actor can believe as sincerely and with greater enthusiasm than he believes practical truth, just as the child believes in the existence of its doll and of all life in it and around it.

From the moment of the appearance of *if* the actor passes from the plane of actual reality into the plane of another life, created and imagined by himself. Believing in this life, the actor can begin to create.

Scenic truth is not like truth in life; it is peculiar to itself. I understood that on the stage truth is that in which the actor sincerely believes. I understood that even a palpable lie must become a truth in the theatre so that it may become art. For this it is necessary for the actor to develop to the highest degree his imagination, a childlike naïvety and trustfulness, an artistic sensitivity to truth and to the truthful in his soul and body. All these qualities help him to transform a coarse scenic lie into the most delicate truth of his relation to the life imagined. All these qualities, taken together, I shall call the *feeling of truth*. In it there is the play of the imagination and the creation of creative faith; in it there is a barrier against scenic lies; in it is the feeling of true measure; in it is the tree of childlike naïvety and the sincerity of artistic emotion. The feeling of truth, as one of the important elements of the creative mood, can be both developed and practised. But this is neither the time nor the place to speak of the methods and means of such work. I will only say now that this ability to feel the truth must be developed to such an extent that absolutely nothing would take place on the stage, that nothing would be said and nothing listened to, without a preparatory cleansing through the filter of the artistic feeling of truth.

If this were true, then all my scenic exercises in loosening the muscles as well as in concentration had been performed incorrectly. I had not cleansed them through the filter of spiritual and physical truth. I took a certain pose on the stage. I did not believe in it physically. Here and there I weakened the strain. It was better. Now I changed the pose somewhat. Ah! I understood. When one stretches himself in order to reach something, this pose is the result of such stretching. And my whole body and after it my soul, began to believe that I was stretching towards an object which I needed very much.

It was only with the help of the feeling of truth, and the inner justification of the pose, that I was able more or less to reach the loosening of the muscles in actual life and on the stage during performances.

From that time on all my scenic exercises in the loosening of muscles and in concentration passed under the strict control of my feeling of truth.

KONSTANTIN STANISLAVSKY, *MY LIFE IN ART*

The extraordinary thing about acting is that life itself is actually used to create artistic results. In every other art the means only pretend to deal with reality. Music can often capture something more deeply than any other way, but it only tells you something about reality. Painting tells something *about* the painter, *about* the thing painted, and *about* the combination of the two. But since the actor is also a human being, he does not pretend to use reality. He can literally use everything that exists. The actor uses thought – not thought transcribed into colour and line as the painter does, but actual, real thought. The actor uses real sensation and real behaviour. That actual reality is the material of our craft.

The things that fed the great actors of the past as human beings were of such strength and sensitivity that when these things were added to conscious effort, they unconsciously and subconsciously led to the results in all great acting, the great performances accomplished by people who would say if asked, 'I don't know how I do it.' In themselves as human beings were certain sensitivities and capacities which made it possible for them to create these great performances even though they were unaware of the process.

The actor's human nature not only makes possible his greatness, but also is the source of his problems. Here in the Studio we have become aware that the opposite is also true, that an individual can possess the technical ability to do certain things and yet may have difficulty in expressing them because of his emotional life, because of the problems of his human existence. The approach to this actor's problem must therefore deal first with relieving whatever difficulties are inherent in himself that negate his freedom of expression and block the capacities he possesses.

All actors who have worked at their craft have found it hard to describe what they have done. Stanislavsky had difficulty because he didn't think abstractly. But this was wonderful because it kept him from arriving at the abstract conclusions with which most people had previously satisfied their minds. Most people suppose they have really solved something when in fact they have only made an impressive formula. It means something to them but is not cogent enough to mean anything to anybody else.

The clearest and most precise statement about acting to be found is a fifteen-page essay written by the great French actor Talma – one of the greatest actors of all time. In it he states everything you need to know about acting. For example, sensibility without control or intelligence is wrong; there must be a unification of inner and outer resources; intelligence and intellectual control must be involved to ensure a proper use of all elements. Talma's essay is the best ever written about acting, but nobody can understand it who has not already found out what it means. It has made no impression on the theatre because it is abstract.

One of the most brilliant descriptions of the actor's problem comes from

Jacques Copeau. He describes the difficulties the actor has with his 'blood,' as he calls it. The actor tells his arm, 'Come on now, arm, go out and make the gesture,' but the arm remains wooden. The 'blood' doesn't flow; the muscles don't move; the body fights within itself; it's a terrifying thing. To someone on the outside this sounds like verbalization or poetry. But we know, because we have often felt what it means to stand on the stage and know that what you are doing is not what you mean to do, that you meant to move your arm differently and you meant to come over to the audience with ease and warmth, and instead you're standing there like a stick. Copeau calls it 'the battle with the blood of the actor.'

Copeau was also the first to bring to my attention the marvellous phrase Shakespeare used about acting. Remember where Hamlet says, 'Is it not monstrous that this player here, but in a fiction, in a dream of passion, could force his soul so to his own conceit … ?' Isn't it monstrous that someone should have this capacity? The profession of acting, the basic art of acting, is a monstrous thing because it is done with the same flesh-and-blood muscles with which you perform ordinary deeds, real deeds. The body with which you make real love is the same body with which you make fictitious love with someone whom you don't like, whom you fight with, whom you hate, by whom you hate to be touched. And yet you throw yourself into his arms with the same kind of aliveness and zest and passion as with your real lover – not only with your real lover, with your realest lover. In no other art do you have this monstrous thing.

The basic thing in acting is what William Gillette calls 'the illusion of the first time.' It must seem that this has never taken place before, that no one has seen it before, that this actress has never done this before, and that in fact she's not an actress. Even in stylized forms of theatre, unless you feel that what you are seeing is somehow at that moment being creatively inspired, you say, 'Well, he's repeating,' or, 'It's very good, but seems mechanical; it seems imitative,' or 'It seems as if he's getting tired of it.' The conditions of acting demand that you know in advance what you are going to do while the art of acting demands that you should seem not to know. This would appear to make acting impossible, but that is not so in practice. It is just that there is a slight confusion about the problem.

A piano is a precise instrument. It exists outside of yourself. When we say that the pianist is doing something real, we mean that he knows the music, that with a definite finger of a particular hand he will hit a certain note, and that he knows he means to hit it with a certain amount of energy and a certain amount of feeling, and therefore not only of physical pressure but also of rhythmic and mood pressure. However – and this is what preserves the illusion of the first time – when his hand comes down on the piano, because it is a real instrument and cannot be misled by the pianist's intention, the sound that comes out is the precise result of the amount of energy that he employed. But the actor has no piano. In the actor pianist and piano are the same. When the actor attempts to hit on some key of himself, on some mood, thought, feeling, or sensation, what comes out is not necessarily what he thinks he should have hit, but what he actually hits. He may consciously follow the same procedure which he employed on a previous occasion to evoke the desired response, but instead some unconscious pattern may well trigger an entirely different and unwanted response. There is no such situation in any other art ...

Edwin Booth was an intelligent actor though never an actor of passion. One day he was playing Hamlet. His daughter was sitting in a box, and as he started to speak about Ophelia, thoughts of his daughter's being trapped in Ophelia's situation came to his mind, and he was very moved. He became emotional. Tears flowed. And he was shocked and surprised when people at the end told him, 'It was a very bad performance you gave today. What happened?' He assumed that it should have been a good performance.

The human being who acts is the human being who lives. That is a terrifying circumstance. Essentially the actor acts a fiction, a dream; in life the stimuli to which we respond are always real. The actor must constantly respond to stimuli that are imaginary. And yet this must happen not only just as it happens in life, but actually more fully and more expressively. Although the actor can do things in life quite easily, when he has to do the same things on the stage under fictitious conditions he has difficulty because he is not equipped as a human being merely to playact at imitating life. He must somehow believe. He must somehow be able to convince himself of the rightness of what he is doing in order to do things fully on the stage.

When the actor comes off the stage, he often knows that something went wrong, but because of the ego that is involved in acting he is usually ashamed and afraid to ask what people are referring to when they say, 'What the hell happened today?' It is not merely that the actor fears he was bad. He is much more afraid that he will find out he was fooling himself by thinking that what was bad was really good. That would mean that he literally doesn't know what is happening on the stage, that he goes on without knowing what is going to happen. He is then in a desperate situation. To go on then, he must have either an absence of ego – which is impossible – or a degree of faith that is equally impossible.

LEE STRASBERG, *STRASBERG AT THE STUDIO*

79

MESSAGES
The Theatre of Changes
Change the world. Marx. Change life. Rimbaud.
How to be what we are and not what we seem to be.

Toilet Paper
Rufus Collins, an actor of physical and psychological intensity, ended an impassioned improvisation by throwing a wad of toilet paper at the audience.

Bill Shari, who is quite a scrupulous pacifist, said that he couldn't play the breathing scene that precedes this improvisation if Rufus persisted in that kind of insult to the spectator. Rufus said: 'I'm not only playing Rufus Collins, I'm playing the Black Man crying out, rising up, anguished and angry.'

Bill Shari shook his head.

That night after the breathing, Rufus gave an incredible outcry and afterwards swiftly threw the toilet paper on the stage floor.

The Theatre of Pain
The child feels pain, the child cries, the elders find ways to suppress the crying. What does this mean to the actor?

The crying that represents the pain is hard for the elders to take. It reminds them of their own. And so we suppress it, but we do not eliminate it, and we go on to our eternal ruin with music and fatal pomp of flowers, with toys, distractions and coffee breaks to ease, for instance, the pain and boredom of hated labour. But the pain remains.

When the spectator begins to feel the pain, then the actor begins to accomplish a vivid purpose: to heighten awareness.

Acting Lesson
Acting Lesson: Open your ears. Do you hear the screaming? You don't? Why? Are they too far away, the ones dying because we haven't saved them? The hungry, because we haven't found a way to feed them? Don't you hear the people ripped apart by wars we haven't found a way to stop? The choking miners? The slaves to hated toil? Listen to them. Then, when you hear them, open your mouth. And let their needs speak through it. Move. Towards them, toward yourself in them.

Now, anytime you don't hear them, stop and listen. If you don't hear them you've shut your inner ear to the sound of your brother's blood crying out from the earth. Don't act when you don't hear them. Stop and listen till you do. Then act.

Now be joyous.

Awareness

Intellectual Awareness is not enough. We have been intellectually aware for thousands of years. We have to be physically aware. If we could feel the pain, we could not tolerate it and would find the means to eliminate it. Artaud.

Passion, Anger, Sadness, Weeping

When the actors cry out against the pain, our detractors say: 'They are filled with hate.' Imagine! They can't tell the difference between passion and anger.

It is better to rage against the preventable suffering

/because it leads to the

suggestion of gorgeous alternatives/

than to express our sadness. We could do a whole evening (maybe a lifetime) of just weeping, and say (as we always do anyway): 'This is a play about the human condition.'

Why do we go to the theatre?

To crack your head open and let in the oxygen. To revivify the brain, inform the senses, awaken the body, consciousness physical and mental, to what's happening to you, to you, the person watching. To go beyond watching into action. To find the keys to salvation (a ceremony in which the actor serves as a guide). To find out how to enter The Theatre of Life. To enter The Theatre of Daily Life.

How the Acting Exercise leads to the playing of the scene.

Acting exercises: We develop an exercise to create a scene that needs such an exercise. Sometimes we do some breathing work. A Yogin from the circus in Perugia teaches some of the actors his breathing. Allen Ginsberg does Mantras with us in Brooklyn. Things like that.

But our major exercise is in practising an increasing, an uncanny, an extraordinary sensitivity to one another. And this we do in our everyday lives which include rehearsal and performance, but no less our packing the cars, or our meals, or our teaching of our children:

Gene Gordon says he feels vibrations in his heart when Jenny coughs. Luke Theodore knows when to console me with jokes and when to be silent. Rufus is always visibly shaken when any of the children are sick. We sense each others' details like lovers. We know when Mary Mary wears pale colours ... And onstage we are beginning to deal with each other in a language we can only call magic because it has no other category.

That's the exercise.

To include the audience in this sensitivity and this language and to let the audi-

81

ence include the world in this sensitivity and this language is playing the scene for which this exercise is created.

The Theatre of Fiction

At this stage of our development the portrayal of character is not sufficient work for a man. An actor is a man, he has to do more than span experience by being a fictitious character. For 2,500 years we have had this great form of acting to illustrate how man can extend his consciousness to include consciousness of characters other than his own. We have reached that stage in our development at which The Theatre of Fictional Character thus becomes reactionary by confining man to the limits of character. Can we go beyond that to the next theatre, permanent change, permanent revolution: to Theatre of Joy (Nearness to God)? May we be alive to live it. And to do it.

Giving Notes

In giving notes during rehearsals, Living Theatre actors often preface their notes with: 'Look, we are all musicians … '

The Trouble with Rational Theatre

The Rational Theatre of intellectual discussion in which we all remain cool, unparticipating, cut off from real feeling and real experience, reinforces our own lifelessness, our feelinglessness, our state of cutoff.

We must fly. Eric Gutkind.

Fear of Chaos and Revolutionary Trust

The traditionalists accuse the revolutionary theatre of being no-form no-content antitheatre. At the same time they accuse it of a hodgepodge of ancient ritual, barbaric traditions, age-old festival and ceremonies.

Isn't that what it's about: to accept nothing and everything.

To assault the total culture totally is to be free to use all the fruits of mankind's wisdom and experience without the rotten structure in which these glories are encased and encrusted.

In breaking open this dead shell all the real works of man will emerge, useful, excellent, and if at first crude and haphazard, eventually finding their fundamental harmony, their subtlety and their real relationships.

The 'disorder' is a wave of purity breaking down the painted scenery of the mind in the way that radical theatre of the 1920s broke down the painted scenery of the stage.

But the mind offers greater resistances to keep its neatly painted flats and papier-mâché gardens in order.

The new actors say, 'Don't be afraid of chaos.' The surface orderliness, like the pseudocleanliness of the existing culture is a lie protected by the partially hidden violence of the law enforcers, armies, jails, and psychiatric hospitals.

The natural order will emerge only if we let go of the fear of the disorder. If we trust each other.

During the Rite of Study in Paradise Now, Bill Shari invented the mantra: 'Trust is a Revolutionary Change.'

How can we fly?

How can we fly? Not by watching and observing. It will not happen to us. We have to do it.

Sure, by making the proper preparations, by figuring it out, by observing and then by taking the route that will bring on the MUTATION, by trying.

Why should we fly?

Because we have dreamed of it for so long that we have to. Because it is useful. Because once we are able to fly it will mean that we are capable of so much else. And because, when we dream it, it is because we dream of being free. Since this yearning to be free is a fundamental component of the truth of everyman, the actor has always to be expressing this yearning, this yearning to fly, to be free. .

The Actor's Reality

Steven Ben Israel, playing the Creature in Frankenstein, fell from the top of the three-tier set during a rehearsal and broke his back. Michele Mareck was playing a scene from Ibsen's When We Dead Awaken on the bottom tier. As he fell she heard him say: 'I don't believe this.'

Things to play:

The mutilation of cell structure by the diseases of life.

The recoiling of muscles at the onslaught of capitalism.

The causes of violence.

The crippling of character within the authoritarian class structure. (This is particularly important for the playing of all the roles in Shakespeare.)

The remembrance of Eden. Of the ocean.

The Impatience.

The Creative.

The Lusts of the Flesh which win every battle.

The joy of still being alive.

The changes.

The Other.

The interior conflict between the Superior-Man-Within and Things As
They Are.

The electrochemical transmissions.

The automatic responses to any impetus.

The voice attached to the nerves, the muscles, the organs, as opposed to
the voice as slave of the brain.

The Natural Man.

Et Cetera.

How do you play these things?

What exercises do you do?

This is the work that the actor is engaged in.

Working on the Brink of Breakthrough

We work as if every moment we are about to make the Great Discovery.

How to suffuse everything with joyous utility.

How to speak so that we are believed.

How to dissolve the barrier between art and life.

(The Wall: it must be torn down).

How to destroy the false imprisoning structure so that it shall fall without injur-
ing anyone or burying any human heart in the rubble.

Beauty and the Beast

There is no reason why the consciously aware actor should continue to
exemplify the criteria of beauty created by the Ruling Clawss. That is, the
esthetics of, for instance, the Troubadour poets, or of the Ancient World,
which still dominate our cultural perceptions, might simply be false defini-
tions of what is beautiful. The beauty created for the critical approbation, and
admiration, of the Masters (certainly not the Slaves) might be just as corrupt
as the beauty created by Modern Advertisers. Both keep the People in thrall.

The new definition of beauty cannot be found In The Theatre of
Fiction, in which established esthetics and ethics are portrayed, but in a
theatre in which acting is the process of entering into a state of being, the
very process of which would be a state of discovery. In which even the per-
ception of the actor changes.

Are you a Messenger or a Beauty Queen?

To stand up on the stage is to say to many people: 'Look at me.' How can you
do that without speaking the only truth you know? There is no such thing as an
uncommitted actor.

84

Mottoes

Don't enact. Act.
Don't re-create. Create.
Don't imitate life. Live.
Don't make graven images. Be.

Motto:

The best motto is: If you don't like it, change it.

JULIAN BECK AND JUDITH MALINA, *ACTORS ON ACTING*

≈

An example now of theory in practice. Peter Brook's *US* for the Royal Shakespeare Company in 1966 was experimental theatre in a large public space. A devised piece on the Vietnam war and the British response, it was made possible by the faith and courage of a subsidized company. There was no script at the start of the rehearsal period, no design, no music, no single playwright, just a group of people willing to investigate. I find it almost inconceivable that a large company would take a comparable risk now, though I very much hope I'm wrong. This is a glimpse of the rehearsal process.

≈

TUESDAY, AUGUST 30

In the tiny back room at the Donmar Rehearsal Theatre were: Brook, Hunt, Reeves, Mitchell, Kustow, Cannan and Mark Jones. A very delicate exercise was about to take place, based on the situation of Cannan's proposed final scene. 'You are in Grosvenor Square,' said Brook to Mark Jones, 'with your petrol-can and your matches. You have come to burn yourself.' Mark started to make preparations. Along came Cannan, working off a clipboard of questions. He stopped Mark in midstream, and probed the reasons for his action, the effect he hoped it would have, what he thought of other people and their capacity for change.

It was a sustained, John-Whiting-like assault on man's (and Mark's) presumption, using harsh anecdotes and Socratic dialectic to try to undermine Mark's resolution. But it didn't connect with the pitch of utter decision which Mark had achieved, the dogged, almost animal-like honesty with which he held to his choice. Against this impervious sincerity, even the sharpest flints of Cannan's arguments could not pierce.

Mitchell then tried to sway Mark. 'Can't you see that it's self-sacrifice? Have you really tried every other possible route?'

Hunt read Mark a list of the many people who had committed suicide by fire in Britain over the past two years, for reasons that were pathetic, foolish, mad, or just plain inexplicable. Mark's reaction was that however others cared to interpret it, he knew his motives, and in that sense at least was untroubled.

Brook sat down on the floor with Mark. Very close to him. 'Look me in the eyes. What is cruelty? Unlimited exercise of power over others. Do you have power over other people? Do you have power over yourself? Aren't you being cruel to your own flesh by setting it on fire? Aren't you alive? What is you? There is something called life and it's there in you. Have you the right to destroy it? What you want to do to yourself is what the world is doing to itself. You want life for the world, why don't you allow yourself to live? If you stop now, one less act of cruelty has taken place. It takes more courage to face the situation than to burn yourself. It takes the same kind of courage for the super-powers involved in this war to back down from their prepared positions.'

Mark put his head in his hands. There was silence for five minutes. The exercise had lasted nearly two hours. We all sat still. I was very aware of the different kind of contact Brook had made with the actor compared with the others. Brook's questioning had been much more physical, much closer to a confessional.

We tried to discuss the results of this exercise afterwards. Hunt feared the sense of a soothing catharsis which such an intense trial-by-fire-and-argument would generate. Brook said the silence at the end must be 'an open mouth, not a shut eye.' 'Commitment is a changing relationship, like a love affair; not a deal, like a bad marriage. And let's not overestimate the potential effect of the show. An analyst has one person on the couch for maybe twelve years: we have 1000 people on the equivalent of Waterloo Station for three hours. We must work like acupuncture: find the precise spot on the tensed muscle that will cause it to relax. If we succeed, we won't end the war or anything drastic like that, but one person out of our thousand might act differently because of what they experienced in the theatre that night.'

MICHAEL KUSTOW, THE BOOK OF US

The production that changed my life, as it did so many others, was also directed by Peter Brook. It was the RSC's *A Midsummer Night's Dream* from the 1970s. I have always remembered the following programme note, by the Russian symbolist director Meyerhold: 'There is a fourth *creator* in addition to the author, the director and the actor – namely the spectator ... from the friction between the actors' creativity and the spectators' imagination, a clear flame is kindled.'

The next stage in an actor's life is encountering an audience. In Howard Barker's first prologue to his play *The Bite of the Night*, he sets out lucidly and touchingly the relationship which most actors would wish to achieve with that audience.

❧

THE FIRST PROLOGUE TO *THE BITE OF THE NIGHT*
They brought a woman from the street
And made her sit in the stalls
By threats
By bribes
By flattery
Obliging her to share a little of her life with actors

But I don't understand art

Sit still, they said

But I don't want to see sad things

Sit still, they said.

And she listened to everything
Understanding some things
But not others
Laughing rarely, and always without knowing why
Sometimes suffering disgust
Sometimes thoroughly amazed
And in the light again said

If that's art I think it is hard work
It was beyond me
So much of it beyond my actual life

But something troubled her
Something gnawed her peace
And she came a second time, armoured with friends

Sit still, she said

And again, she listened to everything
This time understanding different things
This time untroubled that some things could not be understood
Laughing rarely but now without shame
Sometimes suffering disgust
Sometimes thoroughly amazed
And in the light again said

That is art, it is hard work

And one friend said, too hard for me
And the other said if you will
I will come again

Because I found it hard I felt honoured

HOWARD BARKER, *THE BITE OF THE NIGHT*

CHAPTER 5

STARTING OUT

*'MRS WORTHINGTON, DON'T PUT YOUR DAUGHTER ON
THE STAGE'*

A Song

Regarding yours, dear Mrs Worthington,
Of Wednesday the 23rd,
Although your baby,
May be,
Keen on a stage career,
How can I make it clear,
That this is not a good idea.
For her to hope,
Dear Mrs Worthington,
Is on the face of it absurd.
Her personality
Is not in reality
Inviting enough,
Exciting enough
For this particular sphere.

Don't put your daughter on the stage, Mrs Worthington,
Don't put your daughter on the stage,
The profession is overcrowded
And the struggle's pretty tough
And admitting the fact
She's burning to act,
That isn't quite enough.
She has nice hands, to give the wretched girl her due,
But don't you think her bust is too
Developed for her age.
I repeat
Mrs Worthington,
Sweet
Mrs Worthington,
Don't put your daughter on the stage.

Don't put your daughter on the stage,
Mrs Worthington,
Don't put your daughter on the stage,
Though they said at the school of acting
She was lovely as Peer Gynt,
I'm afraid on the whole
An ingénue role
Would emphasize her squint.

She's a big girl, and though her teeth are fairly good
She's not the type I ever would
Be eager to engage,
No more buts,
Mrs Worthington,
NUTS,
Mrs Worthington,
Don't put your daughter on the stage.

Don't put your daughter on the stage, Mrs Worthington,
Don't put your daughter on the stage,
She's a bit of an ugly duckling
You must honestly confess,
And the width of her seat
Would surely defeat

Her chances of success,
It's a loud voice, and though it's not exactly flat,
She'll need a little more than that
To earn a living wage.
On my knees
Mrs Worthington,
Please! Mrs Worthington,
Don't put your daughter on the stage.

Don't put your daughter on the stage, Mrs Worthington,
Don't put your daughter on the stage,
One look at her bandy legs should prove
She hasn't got a chance,
In addition to which
The son of a bitch
Can neither sing nor dance,
She's a vile girl and uglier than mortal sin,
One look at her has put me in
A tearing bloody rage,
That sufficed,
Mrs Worthington,
Christ!
Mrs Worthington,
Don't put your daughter on the stage.

NÖEL COWARD

è.

Despite Noël Coward's awful warning, Worthingtons of both sexes hurl themselves on to the stage in droves and often get a nasty shock. In January 1984 John Osborne joined a number two tour of West End success called *No Room at the Inn*, as an acting ASM. The first date of the tour was the Theatre Royal, Cardiff.

è.

Apart from the leading lady, Diana King, I was the only new member of the company. The young Irishman who played a sailor client joined us the following day. There were four second-class carriages reserved for the company. I was claimed on arrival by Bert, the stage carpenter, and his wife, the wardrobe mistress, and bustled into one of the two carriages that appeared to be reserved for the staff and stage management – wardrobe mistress; stage carpenter; two ASMs, including myself; stage director; Mrs Garnsey, mother of the leading child actress; the three older girls and a small boy. The actors had their own carriages and it was soon clear that there was an accepted system of Officers and Other Ranks in the operation of company train calls. Bert made it obvious that my place was among the Ranks, with the *News of the World, Sunday Pictorial* and Mrs Garnsey's charges, who reminded me of the most deprived and appalling inmates of the convalescent home. Apart from the star, Rita, they too looked as if they were plagued with lice, bed-wetting and malnutrition, like the inmates at Deathaboys Hall.

The actors' carriages were littered with folded copies of the *Observer* and *Sunday Times*. The young juvenile, Sheila, a twenty-two-year-old who played the leading evacuee with elfin Elstree winsomeness, swooped in during the journey. With her Joan Buffen accent, unteased schoolgirl's hair, above all her enthusiasm, goshing rather than gushing, she was almost a shock after the memory of Renee, hair carefully rolled, her corsage – for that is what it was – flattened on what was already a bosom. It was a shape I had found exciting as well as comforting, but it would soon burgeon into what was then known as a roll-top desk; not something to be despised, but Renee was still barely eighteen. Sheila was twenty-two and her own roll-top seemed some more careless years away. Childhood still beckoned to her from behind at a time when the word 'gamin' was popular with film publicists.

Bert was quite agreeable, although his wife, Lily, was a very bad-tempered crone. He was a dedicated Tory voter (*'You* put them in, *you* get them out,' he would intone every time he read something about the Labour Government in the papers). He sucked up to the actors shamelessly. The stage staff were itinerant forelock-pullers, and lucky to be so. Bert would rush out on to the platform on our frequent stops offering one of the more haughty actors a choice of sandwiches or tea. 'Can I get you something more, Miss Atkins?' he would wheedle. 'No thank you, Bert. That's very kind of you.' Miss Atkins turned out to be a particularly churlish actress given to waspish tea-shop outbursts, which she may have intended to be Mrs Patrick Campbell gestures to style.

One of my jobs as ASM was to act as call boy, not only calling the half-hour, quarter, five and Beginners, but giving individual calls throughout the play. It was undemanding enough, simply requiring the actor's acknowledgement. This established, he had no excuse for missing his cue. An ASM, I was told, should always wait for the acknowledging 'Thank You' or accept responsibility for a missed entrance. However, actors rarely blamed dozy lads for their own unpreparedness. Calling the artists seemed a gratuitiously servile and unnecessary tradition to me but I soon found it was a friendly, bantering business. Not so with Miss Atkins. She had a trick of occasionally ignoring the most insistent knock, deliberately missing her cue, hurling insults like stale scones at the Prompt Corner and demanding abject apologies in her dressing-room, when her artistic sensibilities had recovered. She was extremely cunning about when and how often she chose not to answer the call. Someone should have warned me against her for I soon discovered that a couple of ill reports to the company manager could, in theory, cost me my job. The only remedy was to knock relentlessly until she was forced to snap back a reply. I won this war of attrition at the Hippodrome Theatre, Bristol, by knocking on the door and entering immediately as she was inserting a Tampax. She never tried the trick again. I once found myself needing to provide an actor with a prop fountain pen. Asking him at the dress rehearsal if he could do this for me, he replied, 'I have eight fountain pens. But it is your job to provide me with one.' It was this sort of actor's kitchen *hubris* that nowadays would bring subsidized companies to a standstill.

JOHN OSBORNE, *A BETTER CLASS OF PERSON*

ॐ

Osborne's beady view of a grimy and selfish world is light years away from the rarefied atmosphere of Peter Brook's rehearsals. However, they are both aspects of an actor's life and we've all got to start somewhere. Even Isadora Duncan, a byword for rigorous standards and a worshipper at the sacred flame of Art if ever there was one, started out in pantomime, graduating to a fairy in *A Midsummer Night's Dream*. Having been spotted by impresario Augustin Daly dancing in Chicago, she came to New York in 1899 and reported to him at his theatre.

ॐ

My first impression of New York was that it had far more beauty and art in it than Chicago. Again, I was glad to be by the sea once more. I have always felt stifled in inland cities.

We stopped at a boarding-house in one of the side-streets off Sixth Avenue. There was a strange collection of people in this boarding-house. They, like the Bohemians, seemed to have but one thing in common: none were able to pay their bills, and they lived in a constant proximity to ejection.

One morning I reported at the stage door of Daly's theatre. Again I was admitted into the presence of a great man. I wanted to explain to him anew my ideas, but he seemed very busy and worried.

'We have brought over the great pantomime star, Jane May,' he said, 'from Paris. And there is a part for you if you can act in pantomime.'

Now pantomime to me has never seemed an art. Movement is lyrical and emotional expression, which can have nothing to do with words, and in pantomime people substitute gestures for words, so that it is neither the art of the dancer nor that of the actor, but falls between the two in hopeless sterility. However, there was nothing to do but take the part. I took it home to study, but the whole thing seemed to me very stupid and quite unworthy of my ambitions and ideals.

The first rehearsal was a horrible disillusion. Jane May was a little lady with an extremely violent temper who took every occasion for bursting into a rage. When I was told that I must point to her to say YOU, press my heart to say LOVE, and then violently hit myself on the chest to say ME, it all seemed to be too ridiculous. And, having no heart in it, I did it so badly that Jane May was quite disgusted. She turned to Mr Daly and explained that I had no talent whatever and could not possibly carry the part. When I heard this, I realized it would mean all of us being stranded in a terrible boarding-house at the mercy of a relentless landlady. I had in my mind's eye the vision of a little chorus girl who had been turned out into the streets the day before without her trunk, and I recalled all that my poor mother had gone through in Chicago. When I thought of all this, the tears came into my eyes and rolled down my cheeks. I suppose I looked very tragic and miserable, for Mr Daly assumed a more kindly expression. He patted me on the shoulder and said to Jane May:

'You see, she is very expressive when she cries. She'll learn.'

But these rehearsals were martyrdom to me. I was told to make movements which I considered very vulgar and silly and which had no real connection with the music to which they were made. However, youth is adaptable, and I finally managed to fall into the humour of the part.

Jane May acted the part of Pierrot, and there was a scene where I was to make love to Pierrot. To three different bars in the music I must approach and kiss Pierrot three times on the cheek. At the dress rehearsal I did this with such energy that I left my red lips on Pierrot's white cheek. At which Pierrot turned into Jane May, perfectly furious, and boxed my ears. A charming entrance into theatrical life!

And yet, as the rehearsals advanced, I could not help but admire the extraordinary and vibrant expression of this pantomime actress. If she had not been imprisoned in the false and vapid form of pantomime, she might have been a great dancer. But the form was too limited. I always felt I wanted to say of pantomime:

'If you want to speak, why don't you speak? Why all this effort to make gestures as in a deaf and dumb asylum?'

The first night came. I wore a Directoire costume of blue silk, a blonde wig, and a big straw hat. Alas for the revolution of art which I had come to give the world! I was completely disguised and not myself. My dear mother sat in the first row, and she was rather bewildered. Even then she did not suggest that we should go back to San Francisco, but I could see that she was terribly disappointed. For so much striving to arrive at such a poor result!

During the rehearsals for that pantomime we had no money. We were put out of the boarding-house and took two bare rooms with nothing in them at all in 180th Street. There was no money for car-fare, and often I had to go on foot down to Augustin Daly's in 29th Street. I used to run on dirt, skip on pavement, and walk on wood to make the way seem shorter. I had all sorts of systems for that. I didn't eat lunch because I had no money, so I used to hide in the stage box during the lunch hour and sleep from exhaustion, then start rehearsing again in the afternoon without any food. I rehearsed for six weeks in this way before the pantomime opened, and then performed for a week before any payment was made.

After three weeks in New York the company went on the road on one-night stands. I received fifteen dollars a week to pay all my expenses, and sent half home to my mother that she might live. When we descended at a station, I did not go to a hotel, but carried my valise and went on foot looking for a boarding-house which would be cheap enough. My limit was fifty cents a day, everything included, and sometimes I had to trudge weary miles before I found this. And sometimes the quest landed me in very strange neighbourhoods. I remember one place where they gave me a room without a key and where the men of the house – mostly drunk – kept making continual attempts to get into my room. I was terrified and, dragging the heavy wardrobe across the room, barricaded the door with it. Even then I did not dare to go to sleep, but sat up on guard all night. I can't imagine any more God-forsaken existence than what they call 'on the road' with a theatrical troupe.

Jane May was indefatigable. She called a rehearsal every day, and nothing ever suited her.

I had a few books with me, and I read incessantly. Every day I wrote a long letter to Ivan Miroski; I do not think I told him quite how miserable I was.

After two months of this touring, the pantomime returned to New York. The whole venture had been a distressing financial failure for Mr Daly, and Jane May returned to Paris.

What was to become of me? Again I saw Mr Daly and tried to interest him in my Art. But he seemed quite deaf and indifferent to anything I could offer him.

'I am sending out a company with *Midsummer Night's Dream*,' he said. 'If you like, you might dance in the fairy scene.'

My ideas on the dance were to express the feelings and emotions of humanity. I was not at all interested in fairies. But I consented, and proposed that I should dance to the Scherzo of Mendelssohn in the wood scene before the entrance of Titania and Oberon.

When *Midsummer Night's Dream* opened, I was dressed in a long straight tunic of white and gold gauze with two tinsel wings, I objected very much to the wings. It seemed to me that they were ridiculous. I tried to tell Mr Daly that I could express wings without putting on papier-mâché ones, but he was obdurate. The first night I came on the stage alone to dance. I was delighted. Here, at last, I was alone on a great stage with a great public before me, and I could dance. And I did dance – so well that the public broke into spontaneous applause. I had made what they call a hit. When I came out in the wings, I expected to find Mr Daly delighted and receive his congratulations. Instead of this, he was in a towering rage. 'This isn't a music-hall!' he thundered. Unheard of that the public should applaud this dance! Next night, when I came on to dance, I found all the lights were turned out. And each time I danced in *Midsummer Night's Dream* I danced in the dark. Nobody could see anything on the stage but a white fluttering thing.

After two weeks in New York, *Midsummer Night's Dream* also went on the road, and again I had the dreary journeys and the hunting for boarding-houses. Only, my salary was raised to twenty-five dollars a week.

A year passed by in this way.

I was extremely unhappy. My dreams, my ideals, my ambition: all seemed futile. I made very few friends in the company. The regarded me as queer. I used to go about behind the scenes with a book of Marcus Aurelius. I tried to adopt a stoic philosophy to alleviate the constant misery which I felt. However, I made one friend on that trip – a young girl called Maud Winter who played Queen Titania. She was very sweet and sympathetic. But she had a strange mania of living on oranges and refusing other food. I suppose she was not made for this earth, for some years afterwards I read of her death from pernicious anaemia.

The star in Augustin Daly's company was Ada Rehan – a great actress, though a most unsympathetic person to her subordinates – and the only joy I had in the company was when I could watch her act. She was seldom with the road company with which I went, but when I returned to New

York I often used to watch her performances of Rosalind, Beatrice, and Portia. She was one of the supremely great actresses of the world. But this great artist in ordinary life did not take any care to make herself loved by the people in the company. She was very proud and reserved and seemed to feel that it was an effort even to say good day to us, for one day the following notice was posted in the wings:

'The Company are informed that they need not say good day to Miss Rehan!'

Indeed, in all the two years that I was with the Augustin Daly company I never had the pleasure of speaking with Miss Rehan. She evidently considered all the minor people of the company as quite beneath her notice. I remember one day, when she was kept waiting by some grouping of Daly's, she swept her hand over the heads of us all and exclaimed: 'Oh, Guv'nor, how can you keep me waiting for these nonentities!' (I being one of the nonentities, did not appreciate the allusion!) I cannot understand how so great an artist and fascinating a woman as Ada Rehan could have made this mistake, and I can only account for it by the theory that at that time she was nearly fifty years old. She had long been the adoration of Augustin Daly, and perhaps she resented his subsequently picking out of the company some pretty girl who would be for two or three weeks – or two or three months – suddenly lifted into leading parts for no apparent reason whatever, but possibly for some reason to which Miss Rehan objected. As an artist I had the greatest admiration for Ada Rehan, and at that time it would have meant very much in my life to have had a little kindly encouragement from her. But in all those two years she never looked at me. Indeed, once I remember at the end of *The Tempest*, where I danced for the pleasure of Miranda and Ferdinand at their nuptials, she distinctly turned away her head during the whole dance, which embarrassed me so much that I could hardly continue.

In the course of our tournée with *Midsummer Night's Dream* we finally arrived one day at Chicago. I was overjoyed to find my supposed fiancé. It was again summer, and every day that there was no rehearsal we went out into the woods and had long walks, and I learned more and more to appreciate the intelligence of Ivan Miroski. When, a few weeks later, I left for New York, it was with the understanding that he was to follow me there and that we would be married. My brother, hearing of this, fortunately made enquiries and found out that he had already a wife in London. My mother, aghast, insisted on our separation.

ISADORA DUNCAN, *MY LIFE*

I t is rather comforting to find oneself in the same company as Osborne and Isadora Duncan when it comes to remembering one's first job. My own involved arriving in Edinburgh on New Year's Day. No one had told me that on the day after Hogmanay no Scot gets out of bed. It was like landing on the moon. My university dreams of experimenting on Jacobean texts to an understanding and appreciative audience were sharply rapped on the head as we piled into a minibus in a blizzard to take an hour-long *Billy Budd* to a class of grim-faced school children in Musselburgh.

Every so often, however, something extraordinary happens at the beginning of a career. Micheál MacLiammóir and Hilton Edwards were running the Dublin Gate Theatre Studio in 1931 when a young actor arrived for an audition.

ॐ

For some time people had been begging us to do Ashley Duke's adaptation of *Jew Süss*. With Hilton Edwards as Süss and Betty Chancellor as Naomi we were safe enough, but we ransacked our lists for nights for a new actor to play the Duke and could find no one. Then one day Hilton walked into the scene dock and said 'Somebody strange has arrived from America. Come and see what you think of it'.

'What,' I asked, 'is it?'

'Tall, young, fat: says he's been with the Guild Theatre in New York. Don't believe a word of it, but he's interesting. I want him to give me an audition. Says he's been in Connemara with a donkey, and I don't see what that's got to do with me. Come and have a look at him.'

We found, as he had hinted, a very tall young man with a chubby face, full powerful lips, and disconcerting Chinese eyes. His hands were enormous and very beautifully shaped, like so many American hands; they were coloured like champagne and moved with a sort of controlled abandon never seen in a European. The voice, with its brazen transatlantic sonority, was already that of a preacher, a leader, a man of power; it bloomed and boomed its way through the dusty air of the scene dock as though it would crush down the little Georgian walls and rip up the floor; he moved in a leisurely manner from foot to foot and surveyed us with magnificent patience as though here was our chance to do something beautiful at last – yes, sir – and were we going to take it? Well, well, just too bad for us if we let the moment slip. And all this did not come from mere youth, though the chubby tea-rose cheeks were as satin-like as though the razor had never known them – that was the big moment waiting for the razor – but from some ageless and superb inner confidence that no one could blow out. It was unquenchable. That was his secret. He knew that he was precisely what he himself would have chosen to be had God consulted him on the subject at his birth; he fully appreciated and approved what had been bestowed, and realized that he couldn't have done the job better himself, in fact he would not have changed a single item. Whether we and the world felt the same – well, that was for us to decide.

'I've just told Mr Edwards some of the things I've done, Mr MacL'móir,' he said, 'but I haven't told him everything; there wouldn't be time. I've acted with the Guild. I've written a couple of plays, I've toured the States as a sword-swallowing female impersonator. I've flared through Hollywood like a firecracker. I've lived in a little tomato-coloured house on the Great Wall of China on two dollars a week. I've wafted my way with a jackass through Connemara. I've eaten dates all over the burning desert and crooned Delaware squaws asleep with Serbian rhapsodies. But I haven't told you everything. No; there wouldn't be time.'

And he threw back his head and laughed, a frenzy of laughter that involved a display of small white teeth, a buckling up of the eyes into two oblique slits, a perplexed knitting of the sparse darkly coloured brows, and a totally unexpected darting forth of a big pale tongue. The tongue vanished almost at once and he frowned.

'Don't you want to see what I can do?' he asked.

I emerged from the jungle whence he had dragged me and said, 'Why not?'

'I'd rather see it than hear about it,' said Hilton.

'Well, gimme a book then. Anything you want, I don't mind: James Joyce or Florence Barclay, what the hell, I want to act for you. I can't keep things in my head. They'd go bad there.'

Hilton performed a conjuring trick. He pulled from his pocket a copy of *Jew Süss*.

'Read the Duke,' he said, 'look, this speech here. And this one,' and he marked the book in two places.

'Oh, I don't want to read the Duke, I want to read the Jew. Lemme read the Jew! Lemme read little Naomi. I don't want to read the Duke!'

'Read the Duke,' said Hilton with unforeseen calm; to see him deal with this American prodigy reminded me of those drunken men who can only be sobered by the sudden spectacle of another man in the throes of D.T.s, at which moment they become steadfast as Florence Nightingale: 'Read the Duke. Come on.'

And he led him to the stage.

There followed one of the strangest sights I have witnessed in my life.

The young man, looking larger, taller, softer and broader in the face than ever, bounded on to the stage with our poor little book in his hand. He confronted us with glaring eyes and seemed, as far as we could judge from our seats at the back of the two-and-fourpennies, in a towering rage. A chair was hurled through the air, and he struck an attitude suggestive of sated repose. Then he thought better of that and a small table followed the chair. A violent cloud of dust, like a miniature sand-storm, and an accompanying desiccated rustle of paper and twigs informed me that some branches of plum blossom were sharing the same fate. A few books and a harmless necessary cushion or two concluded the holocaust, and after a brief prayer of gratitude that the valuable clock used in Act Three was in the prop room and that I myself was out of reach for the moment – my partner I was sure could take care of himself – I began to wonder what was to be left of our theatre before it was ready for this young man to play in it.

'I hope to God the act drop's safe,' I whispered to Hilton, but he was shaking with silent guffaws and throwing out his hands with broad Italianate gestures as if to encourage our new friend to further frenzies. At last the storm died down and the stranger advanced to the front of the stage, a lurid silhouette against the wreckage.

'Is this all the light you can give me?' he said in a voice like a regretful oboe.

We hadn't given him any at all yet, so that was settled, and he began. It was an astonishing performance, wrong from beginning to end but with all the qualities of fine acting tearing their way through a chaos of inexperience. His diction was practically perfect, his personality, in spite of his fantastic circus antics, was real and varied; his sense of passion, of evil, of drunkenness, of tyranny, of a sort of demoniac authority was arresting; a preposterous energy pulsated through everything he did. One wanted to bellow with laughter, yet the laughter died on one's lips. One wanted to say, 'Now, now, *really* you know,' but something stopped the words from coming. And that was because he was real to himself, because it was something more to him than a show, more than the mere inflated exhibitionism one might have suspected from his previous talk, something much more.

'Thanks, that's all right,' Hilton shouted; 'come down and talk.'

And the young man unfolded himself from the floor and came to meet us with a grin that showed suddenly how very young he was.

'Terrible, wasn't it?' he said.

'Yes, bloody awful,' Hilton answered. 'But you can play the part.'

A short pause followed, during which the stranger's face softened, but he made no other sign.

'That is,' the other went on, 'if you'll make me a promise. Don't obey me blindly, but listen to me. More important still, listen to yourself. I can help you how to play this part, but you must see and hear what's good about yourself and what's lousy.'

'But I know that already.'

'Then act on it. How old are you?'

'I'm eighteen,' he said so defiantly that we knew there was something wrong. A mystic voice, like Joan of Arc's, had probably whispered to him that an actor, like a lady, should never be quite accurate about his age, and it struck me incredibly that he could not have been older than eighteen and must therefore be younger.

'Do you want any money?'

'I only want what'll buy me a seat on a trolley-car. Gimme –' and he named a sum so absurdly low that we thought he must be joking. But he wasn't. Like many born romantics he had a mind fundamentally honest and clear-sighted: he knew that with all his talent he had had no experience, he would for a while be learning, not performing: why should he be paid for being taught the first letters of an alphabet whose entire meaning he grasped with such brilliant chaos?

'You're an extraordinary young man,' Hilton said.

'I know. So's Ireland an extraordinary country. I won't want more than that here if I can play the Duke.'

He laughed once more, and once more the jungle gloomed and yawned about us. When that was over Hilton said, 'What's your name?'

'Oh, didn't I tell you? Orson Welles.'

MICHEÁL MacLIAMMÓIR, *ALL FOR HECUBA*

Emlyn Williams wrote two volumes of autobiography, *George* and *Emlyn,* which are full of enthusiasm and wisdom – a world away from the 'then I played X with darling Y in the cast and we were *marvellous'* school of theatrical memoir. This is from the very end of the first volume and describes the young Williams's first job in the theatre. He had already turned his life upside-down by leaving the Welsh Valleys for Oxford University and is about to do it again.

Saturday morning, walking through Bloomsbury to my newly acquired furnished room, I held a committee meeting with myself. Though I had written that I would be unable to save, I was determined to. Plate and spoon from Woolworth's so I can keep cornflakes in a cupboard for breakfast, all other meals in A.B.Cs or Lyons or at coffee-stalls, no fares, walk to the theatre and back – if I stick to this, I can put by a pound a week, by Schools I'll have saved eight pounds ... The room was in Mecklenburg Street, a dingy top-floor back single with three clothes-hooks and one chair with a burst seat, but it was ten-and-six a week and within walking distance of the Strand. I cut the theatre-list out of a newspaper I had picked up in the train and stuck it on a nail beside my bed; an hour later the slatternly landlady entered to find me washing the window and the woodwork, and looked so taken aback I thought she was going to fetch a policeman. I walked to Leicester Square, to Frizell's the chemist to buy my make-up, 'a stick of five and a stick of nine', then down to the Savoy to rehearse with Mr Storie the stage-manager, ready for Monday. In the rack, a letter, Miss Cooke's writing, 'Emlyn Williams Esq., Stage Door, Savoy Theatre, London W.C.2.' Had she written that with sorrow in her heart? 'Hmmm, I was afraid of this. But I have faith, and three cheers for Mr Fagan of Trinity.'

I was happy to find that I had six lines in my part, now dictated to me by Mr Storie; under the dim working light, I stood scribbling them on the back of Miss Cooke's envelope. My bit opened the play: curtain up on street scene, enter Pelling's Prentice carrying hare, knock at Pepys's front door, opened by Blackamoor. 'Is Mistress Pepys within ... '

Sunday I spent at Campbell's. Walking I wondered – for the first time, realistically – what sort of an actor I would have to be, to make the success which I assumed I would achieve say by ten years' time. Ten, I would be thirty-one – no, say nine ... I reminded myself that the stars of today, Nares, du Maurier, Ainley, as well as the actors on the brink of success, Ion Swinley, Francis Lister, Ian Hunter, Frank Vosper, were all cast in the heroic gentlemanly mould; my face clouded. To appeal to an audience was it not enough to be interesting? A wild creature like Heathcliff? Keats? A criminal like that pantry-boy Jacoby who murdered his old benefactress? Do they *all* have to be six foot six, and can't young character actors be romantic or tragic, instead of just comic relief? There must be plays ... But I felt my first part burning a hole in my pocket, on the back of an envelope, and the cloud was gone.

Easter Monday, 18 April 1927, I was to join the cast at the matinée. On my way I called at the British Museum, a gesture of propitiation to my academic gods, and arranged a card to the Reading Room. Then I walked, in the spring sun, down Southampton Row; walking I fore-dreamed, but this time practical. I would work in the Museum daily, even matinée afternoons, for after my bit I could be out by ten to three, and after my Schools in June before America (America!) I would get down to writing a play, a thriller which had been hovering over my mind for weeks. Miss Cooke had decreed that a play respecting the Unities of Time and Place was the most difficult: well, this one, a ghost story, would carry the Unities to the utmost lengths, for the Time would be the time of the performance, and the Place the stage of the theatre in which the piece would be played. I had the title, *A Murder Has Been Arranged*. Once I had made enough money to be out of work for a year, I would get my parents out of 314a and build a bungalow for them, say on the genteel slopes around Hawarden, a bathroom ...

By this time I was in the Strand, thronged with holiday-makers celebrating my début in the spring sun. A red bus flashed round from Waterloo Bridge, with across it 'AND SO TO BED'; the next said 'EMLYN WILLIAMS' twice the size. I looked again. 'EVAN WILLIAMS Shampoo', near enough; I walked along the pavement from which Drake-Brockman had pointed out Nelson's Column. For *George, His Story*, what would be today's illustration? 'A deathly hush as he stood in the wings, then ... the curtain was up ... ' Outside the Savoy, a new poster, 250th Performance SPECIAL MATINEE TODAY. At the stage-door Bill Bragg the rosy old man handed me four envelopes. Not bad, nearly one for every line in my part.

I raced up to the stifling hot chorus-room where I was to dress with six other people, and there found the amiable boy who was being moved to the Irish play, George More O'Ferrall, come to wish me luck. He introduced the new boy to the rest of the form, and sitting down I hoped it would not be too clear from the way I handled my five-and-nine that I was not used to them. I got into ballet shirt, brown knee-breeches and short jacket – must buy a cheap dressing-gown – and examined my mail: a telegram from Campbell and his family, another from the Fagans and two notes, from Miss Cooke and our Tom, 'All send love, I was clearing the shed yesterday and found your poultices in hundreds, we had a good laugh ... ' Then I got nervous and went down to the stage, holding More O'Ferrall's late matted wig. I muttered my part, heard the audience coming in, my audience, and felt suddenly cold. Mr Storie took me in to Yvonne Arnaud in the star dressing-room, a radiant bubble in a wrapper, gurgling – in between brushing her teeth – her own brand of English. We spoke French, she asked me had I done Rostand at Oxford; I made a note to mention to Miss Cooke that actresses know about Rostand, went down to the stage again, stood in front of the long mirror in the half-dark wings, and felt my hands tremble as I pulled on the wig.

A click, and the dark was stabbed by great fingers of light from the street scene within: the fire into which I must walk ... At the same moment there struck up the gay music of Lully, harpsichord and viola da gamba, wrapping us round in our Restoration world. They may have played it two hundred and forty-nine times before, but this Easter afternoon they were playing it for me. The Blackamoor was already at her post inside the Pepys house, a coloured lady named Emma Williams. 'You two,' whispered Mr Storie, 'ought to go on the halls together.'

Beyond the theatre walls, the faint rumble of the sunlit Strand; in the sacred daylight-dark at the pulsating core of the great city, here I stood at last, admitted. All over London the curtains were rising, on *The Letter, The Constant Nymph, The Gold Diggers, On Approval, The Marquise, The Dybbuk, Interference, The Fanatics, The Ringer, Marigold, The Transit of Venus, The Constant Wife, Yellow Sands, The Greatest Love, The Beaux' Stratagem,* and I was a part of it, together with all the people on my bedside list; and now, as I stood waiting, they streamed in breathless procession across my excited mind, Marie Tempest Ronald Squire Gladys Cooper Ernest Milton Ellis Jeffreys Gerald du Maurier Valerie Taylor Herbert Marshall Angela Baddeley John Gielgud Jean Forbes-Robertson Nicholas Hannen Cathleen Nesbitt Cedric Hardwicke Dorothy Dickson Robert Harris Ursula Jeans Leslie Faber Alison Leggatt Keneth Kent Mary Clare Leslie Banks Athlene Seyler Lewis Casson Edna Best Raymond Massey Tallulah Bankhead Allan Aynesworth Fay Compton Frank Vosper Sybil Thorndike Ralph Richardson Edith Evans ...

The music came to a spirited close, applause, silence; above me a voice muttered 'House out'. Under a distant light I could see Miss Grey, drinking water and whispering to a footpad and a fop; she blew me a kiss. I was suddenly gripped with fright, gulped, pulled up my stockings under my breeches as I had when a child, and clutched the property hare. Heart, stop beating – speak up and be natural – remember the moon and the stars –

A rustle and a sweep, like a strong calm wind. The curtain was up.

EMLYN WILLIAMS, *GEORGE*

All rehearsal processes have much in common. Almost without exception the first day starts with a readthrough of the play. Edward Gordon Craig's description gives a fascinating sidelong glimpse of a great actor, Sir Henry Irving, going about his job.

We were all sitting round the Green Room (E.T. not there) while Irving read us his version of this play. It began at twelve o'clock, I see, and ended at two-fifteen. I and Ben Webster were seated side by side on some sort of a seat or bench which looked out through the window, across Burleigh Street, to the public house opposite. And as we settled into our places to listen to Irving reading, the vision of the public house came upon us. It made no immediate effect, but there it was.

Then Irving's voice began to inform us of the words of this play which, it occurred to me (looking at the public house), I could quite easily read to myself later on, without his taking all this trouble to read it to us. I began to puff and blow a little – gently. The words entered into my ears now and then, in a sort of corkscrew way which somehow irritated me – my eyes still on the public house. Those chaps in there, drinking beer … I began to move restlessly. Irving's voice went on and on. Ben Webster gave me a poke in the ribs with his elbow. What did he do that for? Men drinking beer … On goes the voice, on goes the beer. Something began to stir in me which I believe is called 'the devil'. But the result was not devilish, it was merely idiotic. I began to titter. Can one be drunk by thinking of beer and so lose control over some organ or other? My speech was all right, but I hadn't to use that. Looking was all right – I could see. I think it was the hearing that was troublesome. Irving's voice went on and on, and at last I was almost overcome by a desire to roar with laughter. The scene 'Public House' – the voice 'Irving doing the play' – these not of a piece. I bottled up the laughter with thoughts of the beer; but it became worse, and I let out a squeak with a pop. Irving, you know, was a saint: otherwise he would have risen up and told me to leave the room. I didn't laugh, but by this time I was gasping. Ben Webster gave me a kick on the leg, which didn't mend matters. I wanted to kick him back, but that would have meant catastrophe. Then I frowned. I frowned hard and in doing so, lowered my head and began to breathe heavily through my nose. My lips were sealed – no more squeaks. But I did not hear another word. All Irving's beautiful speech was lost on me, and the reading came to an end and I think I must have given him a glance out of the corner of my eye. And then he went out of the room, nobly – and I had no further desire to laugh – suicide was the thought then.

EDWARD GORDON CRAIG, *INDEX TO THE STORY OF MY DAYS*

The next two pieces deal with the bottom of the barrel. The second is an extract from one of Alan Bennett's justly famous television monologues, *Talking Heads*. In *'Her Big Chance'*, Lesley (originally played by Julie Walters) is a struggling actress thrilled to have landed a part in a film.

The first piece is again from John Osborne's autobiography, *A Better*

Class of Person. As a chronicler of the sleaze and tat of provincial theatre, Osborne has no peer – indeed he elevated it into a powerful metaphor for the state of post-war Britain in his play *The Entertainer.* Here, a season of weekly rep is staggering to its close. Actors are leaving, audiences are dwindling, Osborne is practically starving but the season continues.

之

We were left to find two more girls and a list of four-handed plays. The girl stage manager loyally decided to stay with us but she was unable to act at all. We continued until Christmas, never playing to more than a few dozen people every week. Our reserve profits were soon absorbed in paying the new girls their literal subsistence expenses. Anthony and I lived largely on evaporated milk and boiled nettles. We congratulated ourselves on discovering this reasonably agreeable diet. Our gypsy resourcefulness contrasted significantly with the bourgeois expectations of drama-school townies. The owners of the hotel seemed unaware of our presence in the building and had no interest in the matter of rent, even when I pointed it out to them. Anthony had rented his flat in Hammersmith, so apart from going back to Stoneleigh there was nowhere for me to go. Then the local Customs and Excise man caught up with us after months of profitable evasion. In the foyer, I handed him an unstamped ticket, along with maybe ten others. When he asked to see me privately, I knew I had been ambushed as surely as Pat Desmond behind the screens. The Excise achieved what Equity could never have done. The remnants of any godlike imaginings were hurled aside as my criminal activity was ransacked.

Within seconds, the Excise man seemed to be teetering with triumph at my discovered perfidy. The sounds of his conquest scarcely disturbed the other ticket holders as the curtains trickled apart for my entrance. His hysteria became reassuring, perhaps because of its familiarity. I wasn't able to make out a balance sheet but I thought I could smoke out a bully without looking up. He thought of himself as a personal servant of the King and accused me in the same terms as an Enemy of the King, which was flattering but was a clear sign of overheated impotence even to my unpreparedness. I pleaded the Nuremberg principle of obedience to orders from above. I had taken the instruction of my absent partner, David Payne, who had failed to supply me with the necessary stamps I had meticulously requested.

In fact, Dotty David had disappeared weeks before, on his way to Oberammergau. He had said something about being engaged, but Anthony and I decided that he had gone into some Retreat or a kind of

Catholic holiday camp. The Excise man began to be protective, in the way of policemen and gaolers. I said something idly about his interest in the theatre and was rewarded by confession. His daughter was a pupil at the Hayling Island School of Dancing. I said immediately that we would be wanting to cast the star role of the Good Fairy in our Christmas pantomime, *Aladdin*. His gratitude was as startling as his rage. The following day he brought her round for an audition. Anthony and I conferred, as if we, too, were servants of His Majesty, and told His Majesty's man that his daughter had been graciously given the job. For a while, I hoped, I had bought a blind eye.

On 12 December 1950, I spent my twenty-first birthday in Havant Magistrate's Court. Mr Cherry, the local grocer, had taken out a summons against us for a bill for fourteen pounds. We had begged him not to proceed, trying to persuade his never-festive spirit that the pantomime would bring in the locals where all else had failed. But he was eager for litigation as a career woman for alimony. We later based the character of Percy Elliot in *George Dillon* on him. Percy's lifetime ambition was to get the park gates closed long before dark so that no one could have any illicit pleasure. I denied any responsibility for these bills, saying that Dotty David was answerable for all company expenses. I believed this, thinking that just as I had provided work for actors, I had realized his own off-hand theatrical ambitions and my obligations were discharged. My own effort must be surely evident and my small reward undetectable. Convinced that no one would challenge me, except possibly Equity, I was disabused. Dotty David appeared in court, and was called into the witness box with his bank statements improbably to hand, which showed the sums of money he had paid out to us since the original £1,000. The magistrate was impressed by his vague but authoritative upper-class manner and his attitude changed at once. 'You are the company manager?' 'Yes,' I replied. 'I take it that you do keep properly audited books?' I hesitated. 'Yes.' Dotty David was dismissed from the case and Anthony and I were ordered to pay Mr Cherry's fourteen pounds as well as his legal costs.

The first and last night of *Aladdin*, was a cloud of unknowing nightmare. Through the innocent support of H.M. Customs, we had enlisted some volunteers to play small parts, a pianist and a dozen or so pupils of the Hayling Island School of Dancing. I had written the script and doubled as Abanaza and Dame. Anthony played Wishee Washee, ad-libbing enthusiastically and incomprehensibly throughout. We both sang 'J'attendrai' in the style of Flanagan and Allan, and attempted a comic lyric which I had written to the tune of 'Sabre Dance', which was then in Hayling Island's Top Ten. Barely rehearsed and unremembered by Anthony, it was a lot put by me into very little. I had a frontcloth act without front cloth, wearing my hat from *Springtime for Henry,* and I told all the cleaner Max Miller jokes I had ever heard. Most disastrous of all, we improvised what I could remember and Anthony had forgotten of Sid Field's golfing and painting sketches. Those who have never appeared on the stage will never know the living presence of silence. But that is familiar ground testified by more hardened pilgrims.

For someone who had scorned the sanctimonious conformity of Pat and Stella, I was fiercely derivative and plagiarist by now. The evening actually began to rouse feeling. Anthony's balding head was streaked with perspiration as I bullied and shouted at him through our halting charade. Our only hope of forgiveness from the audience lay in the girl playing Aladdin. She had quite beautiful legs and sang in an uncajoling, unpantomime, thin, apologetic way. She even persevered after our act which only the most true believers could have followed. She stood alone with a song-sheet lowered behind her trying to coax a few scattered rows of pensioners and parents to sing 'Hey, Little Hen' and 'Rudolph, the Red-Nosed Reindeer'. There was no doubt about their refusal or ill-feeling. I wished that she would kindly leave the stage, for my sake at least. It was magnificent or war even.

The opening of the second act was the Dancing School's big number, led by the Good Fairy. In the interval, His Majesty's man came round in the frenzy of the man moved only by the mole of his bureaucracy. The outrage he had suffered in watching his daughter taking part in such a disgraceful spectacle matched the perfidy of the King's unstamped tickets. 'I have never seen anything like it,' he screamed. 'You shan't have her.' He grabbed the Good Fairy and took her off like a snatched bride from the theatre. A dozen other angry parents followed, with their howling, protesting offspring. The Big Spectacular number of the show was cancelled. I took an uncaring look out front and saw that the audience had disappeared with the exception of the old man who had compared me to Benson. I explained to him that the performance was cancelled and he returned understandingly to the hotel's television room.

JOHN OSBORNE, *A BETTER CLASS OF PERSON*

❧

Come up on Lesley now in a bikini and wrap. An anonymous hotel room. Evening.

Please don't misunderstand me. I've no objection to taking my top off. But Travis as I was playing her wasn't the kind of girl who would take her top off. I said, 'I'm a professional, Nigel. Credit me with a little experience. It isn't Travis.'

I'd been sitting on the deck of the yacht all day as background while these two older men had what I presumed was a business discussion. One of them, who was covered in hair and had a real weight problem, was my boyfriend apparently. You knew he was my boyfriend because at an earlier juncture you'd seen him hit me across the face. Travis is supposed to be a good-time girl, though you never actually see me having a good time, just sat on this freezing cold deck plastering on the sun tan lotion. I said to Nigel, 'I don't know whether the cameraman's spotted it, Nigel, but would I be sunbathing? There's no sun.' Nigel said, 'No sun is favourite.' Nigel's first assistant, here there and everywhere. Gunther never speaks, not to me anyway. Just stands behind the camera with a little cap on. Not a patch on Roman. Roman had a smile for everybody.

Anyway, I'm sitting there as background and I say to Nigel, 'Nigel, am I right in thinking I'm a denizen of the cocktail belt?' He said, 'Why?' a bit guardedly. I said, 'Because to me, Nigel, that implies a cigarette-holder,' and I produced quite a modest one I happened to have brought with me. He went and spoke to Gunther, only Gunther ruled there was to be no smoking. I said, 'On grounds of health?' Nigel said, 'No. On grounds of it making continuity a bugger.' I'd also brought a paperback with me just to make it easier for props (which seemed to be Scott again). Only I'd hardly got it open when Nigel relieved me of it and said they were going for the sun tan lotion. I said, 'Nigel, I don't think the two are incompatible. I can apply sun tan lotion and read at the same time. That is what professionalism means.' He checked with Gunther again and he came back and said, 'Forget the book. Sun tan lotion is favourite.' I said, 'Can I ask you something else?' He said, 'Go on.' I said, 'What is my boyfriend discussing?' He said, 'Business.' I said, 'Nigel. Would I be right in thinking it's a drugs deal?' He said, 'Does it matter?' I said, 'It matters to me. It matters to Travis. It helps my character.' He said, 'What would help your character is if you took your bikini top off.' I said, 'Nigel. Would Travis do that?' I said, 'We know Travis plays chess. She also reads. Is Travis the type to go topless?' He said, 'Listen. Who do you think you're playing, Emily Brontë? Gunther wants to see your knockers.'

I didn't even look at him. I just took my top off without a word and applied sun tan lotion with all the contempt I could muster. They did the shot, then Nigel came over and said Gunther liked that and if I could give him a whisker more sensuality it might be worth a close-up. So we did it again and then Nigel came over and said Gunther was liking what I was giving them and in this next shot would I slip off my bikini bottom. I said, 'Nigel. Trust me. Travis would not do that.' Talks to Gunther. Comes back. Says Gunther agrees with me. The real Travis wouldn't. But by displaying herself naked before her boyfriend's business associate she is showing her contempt for his whole way of life. I said, 'Nigel. At last Gunther is giving me something I can relate to.' He says, 'Right! Let's shoot it! Elbow the bikini bottom!'

ALAN BENNETT, TALKING HEADS

Bennett's poor exploited actress is not an exaggeration, though his ear for the nuance of her speech makes us laugh. She is simply the late-twentieth-century heir to centuries of prejudice against and exploitation of actresses. Witness this entry from the Encyclopaedia Britannica of 1797.

There are some very agreeable and beautiful talents, of which the possession commands a certain sort of admiration; but of which the exercise for the sake of gain is considered, whether from reason or prejudice, as a sort of public prostitution. The pecuniary recompense, therefore, of those who exercise them in this manner, must be sufficient, not only to pay for the time, labour and expense, of acquiring the talents, but for the discredit which attends the employment of them as the means of subsistence. The exorbitant rewards of players, opera-singers, opera-dancers, &c are founded upon these two principles: the rarity and beauty of the talents, and the discredit of employing them in this manner. It seems absurd at first sight that we should despise their persons, and yet reward their talents with the most profuse liberality. While we do the one, however, we must of necessity do the other ... Such talents, though far from being common, are by no means so rare as imagined. Many people possess them in great perfection, who disdain to make this use of them; and many more are capable of acquiring them, if any thing could be made honourably by them.

ENCYCLOPAEDIA BRITANNICA, 1797

This association of actors (and actresses in particular) with vice, prostitution and general low-life is explored more fully in the next chapter, which takes a look at some peculiar situations within which the budding thespian has been required to practise his or her art.

CHAPTER 6
ODD JOBS

BROADWAY BABY
I'm just a Broadway baby
Walking off my tired feet
Pounding 42nd Street
To be in a show

Broadway Baby
Learning how to sing and dance
Waiting for that one big chance
To be in a show

Gee!
I'd like to be
On some marquee
All twinkling lights
A spark
To pierce the dark
From Battery Park
Way up to Washington Heights

Someday maybe
All my dreams will be repaid
Hell, I'd even play the maid
To be in a show

Say, Mr Producer
I'm talking to you sir
I don't need a lot
Only what I got
Plus a tube of greasepaint
and a follow-spot

I'm just a Broadway baby
If I stick it long enough
I may get to strut my stuff
Working for a nice man
Like a Ziegfeld or a Weissman
In a great
Big
Broadway
Show

STEPHEN SONDHEIM, *FOLLIES*

ಶಿ

B ut the Broadway show is an elusive prize. Nowadays the nearest thing to a steady job that a professional actor can ever hope to land is a part in a long-running TV soap. The perils and pitfalls are of course immense. The actor becomes public property in the street and in the tabloid press. His or her every peccadillo is slavered over even as it is criticized, and the dizzy heights of popularity are only a whisker away from disgrace and dismissal. The nearest historical equivalent I can think of is the medieval jester, who walked a similar professional tightrope over a pit of caprice. This is W. S. Gilbert's version of a jester's life from *The Yeomen of the Guard*.

ಶಿ

WILFRED. Aye, it's well for thee to laugh. Thou has a good post, and hast cause to be merry.
POINT *(bitterly)*. Cause? Have we not all cause? Is not the world a big butt of humour, into which all who will may drive a gimlet? See, I am a salaried wit; and is there aught in nature more ridiculous? A poor, dull,

heart-broken man, who must needs be merry, or he will be whipped; who must rejoice, lest he starve; who must jest you, jibe you, quip you, crank you, wrack you, riddle you, from hour to hour, from day to day, from year to year, lest he dwindle, perish, starve, pine, and die! Why, when there's naught else to laugh at, I laugh at myself till I ache for it!

WILFRED. Yet I have often thought that a jester's calling would suit me to a hair.

POINT. Thee? Would suit *thee,* thou death's head and cross-bones?

WILFRED. Aye, I have a pretty wit – a light, airy, joysome wit, spiced with anecdotes of prison cells and the torture chamber. Oh, a very delicate wit! I have tried it on many a prisoner, and there have been some who smiled. Now it is not easy to make a prisoner smile. And it should not be difficult to be a good jester, seeing that thou art one.

POINT. Difficult? Nothing easier. Nothing easier. Attend, and I will prove it to thee!

SONG – POINT.

Oh! a private buffoon is a light-hearted loon,
   If you listen to popular rumour;
From the morn to the night he's so joyous and bright,
   And he bubbles with wit and good humour!
He's so quaint and so terse, both in prose and in verse;
   Yet though people forgive his transgression,
There are one or two rules that all family fools
   Must observe, if they love their profession.
     There are one or two rules
      Half a dozen, maybe,
     That all family fools,
      Of whatever degree,
   Must observe, if they love their profession.

If you wish to succeed as a jester, you'll need
   To consider each person's auricular:
What is all right for B would quite scandalize C
   (For C is so very particular);
And D may be dull, and E's very thick skull
   Is as empty of brains as a ladle;
While F is F sharp, and will cry with a carp
   That he's known your best joke from his cradle!
     When your humour they flout,

You can't let yourself go;
And it *does* put you out
When a person says, 'Oh,
I have known that old joke from my cradle!'

If your master is surly, from getting up early
 (And tempers are short in the morning),
An inopportune joke is enough to provoke
 Him to give you, at once, a month's warning.
Then if you refrain, he is at you again,
 For he likes to get value for money;
He'll ask then and there, with an insolent stare,
 'If you know that you're paid to be funny?'
   It adds to the tasks
    Of a merryman's place,
   When your principal asks,
    With a scowl on his face,
 If you know that you're paid to be funny?

Comes a Bishop, maybe, or a solemn D.D. –
 Oh, beware of his anger provoking!
Better not pull his hair – don't stick pins in his chair;
 He don't understand practical joking.
If the jests that you crack have an orthodox smack,
 You may get a bland smile from these sages;
But should they, by chance, be imported from France,
 Half-a-crown is stopped out of your wages!
   It's a general rule,
    Though your zeal it may quench,
   If the family fool
    Tells a joke that's too French,
 Half-a-crown is stopped out of his wages!

Though your head it may rack with a bilious attack,
 And your senses with toothache you're losing,
Don't be mopy and flat – they don't fine you for that,
 If you're properly quaint and amusing!
Though your wife ran away with a soldier that day,
 And took with her your trifle of money;
Bless your heart, they don't mind – they're exceedingly kind –

They don't blame you – as long as you're funny!
　　It's a comfort to feel,
　　　　If your partner should flit,
　　Though you suffer a deal,
　　　　They don't mind it a bit –
They don't blame you – so long as you're funny!

W. S. GILBERT, THE YEOMEN OF THE GUARD

ᴈ

As the extract from the *Encyclopaedia Britannica* showed, a large section of society has always been all too inclined to blame you whether you were funny or not. Despite Sir Henry Irving's sterling efforts to drag the profession into respectability, 'occupation: actress' still cocks the odd eyebrow today and actors still find it almost impossible to get car insurance.

In Ben Jonson's *Bartholomew Fair*, the actor answers back. Zeal-of-the-Land Busy, a roving Puritan and guardian of public morals, has interrupted a puppet play and the puppeteer, Lantern Leatherhead, allows one of his wooden cast the right to reply.

ᴈ

[*Enter* BUSY.]

BUSY. Down with Dagon, down with Dagon! 'Tis I will no longer endure your profanations.

LEATHERHEAD. What mean you, sir?

BUSY. I will remove Dagon there, I say, that idol, that heathenish idol, that remains, as I may say, a beam, a very beam, not a beam of the sun, nor a beam of the moon, nor a beam of a balance, neither a house-beam nor a weaver's beam, but a beam in the eye, in the eye of the Brethren; a very great beam, an exceeding great beam; such as are your stage-players, rhymers, and morris-dancers, who have walked hand in hand in contempt of the Brethren and the Cause, and been borne out by instruments of no mean countenance.

LEATHERHEAD. Sir, I present nothing but what is licensed by authority.

BUSY. Thou art all license, even licentiousness itself, Shimei!

LEATHERHEAD. I have the Master of the Revels' hand for it, sir.

BUSY. The master of rebels' hand thou hast – Satan's! Hold thy peace; thy scurrility shut up thy mouth. Thy profession is damnable, and in pleading for it thou dost plead for Baal. I have long opened my mouth wide and gaped, I have gaped as the oyster for the tide, after thy destruction; but cannot compass it by suit or dispute; so that I look for a bickering

115

ere long, and then a battle.

KNOCKEM. Good Banbury-vapours.

COKES. Friend, you'd have an ill match on't if you bicker with him here; though he be no man o' the fist, he has friends that will go to cuffs for him. Numps, will not you take our side?

EDGWORTH. Sir, it shall not need; in my mind, he offers him a fairer course, to end it by disputation! Hast thou nothing to say for thyself, in defence of thy quality?

LEATHERHEAD. Faith, sir, I am not well studied in these controversies between the hypocrites and us. But here's one of my motion, Puppet Dionysius, shall undertake him, and I'll venture the cause on't.

COKES. Who? My hobby-horse? Will he dispute with him?

LEATHERHEAD. Yes, sir, and may a hobby-ass of him, I hope.

COKES. That's excellent! Indeed he looks like the best scholar of 'em all. Come, sir, you must be as good as your word, now.

BUSY. I will not fear to make my spirit and gifts known! Assist me, zeal; fill me, fill me, that is, make me full!

WINWIFE. What a desperate, profane wretch is this! Is there any ignorance or impudence like his? To call his zeal to fill him against a puppet?

GRACE. I know no fitter match than a puppet to commit with an hypocrite!

BUSY. First, I say unto thee, idol, thou hast no calling.

PUPPET DIONYSIUS. You lie; I am called Dionysius.

LEATHERHEAD. The motion says you lie, he is called Dionysius i' the matter, and to that calling he answers.

BUSY. I mean no vocation, idol, no present lawful calling.

PUPPET DIONYSIUS. Is yours a lawful calling?

LEATHERHEAD. The motion asketh if yours be a lawful calling.

BUSY. Yes, mine is of the spirit.

PUPPET DIONYSIUS. Then idol is a lawful calling.

LEATHERHEAD. He says, then idol is a lawful calling! For you called him idol, and your calling is of the spirit.

COKES. Well disputed, hobby-horse!

BUSY. Take not part with the wicked, young gallant. He neigheth and hinnyeth; all is but hinnying sophistry. I call him idol again. Yet, I say, his calling, his profession is profane, it is profane, idol.

PUPPET DIONYSIUS. It is not profane!

LEATHERHEAD. It is not profane, he says.

BUSY. It is profane.

PUPPET DIONYSIUS. It is not profane.

BUSY. It is profane.

PUPPET DIONYSIUS. It is not profane.

LEATHERHEAD. Well said, confute him with 'not', still. You cannot bear him down with your base noise, sir.

BUSY. Nor he me with his treble creaking, though he creak like the chariot wheels of Satan. I am zealous for the Cause –

LEATHERHEAD. As a dog for a bone.

BUSY. And I say it is profane, as being the page of pride and the waiting-woman of vanity.

PUPPET DIONYSIUS. Yea? What say you to your tire-women then?

LEATHERHEAD. Good.

PUPPET DIONYSIUS. Or feather-makers i' the Friars, that are o' your faction of faith? Are not they with their perukes and their puffs, their fans and their huffs, as much pages of pride and waiters upon vanity? What say you? What say you? What say you?

BUSY. I will not answer for them.

PUPPET DIONYSIUS. Because you cannot, because you cannot. Is a bugle-maker a lawful calling? or the confect-maker's? such you have there; or your French fashioner? You'd have all the sin within yourselves, would you not? would you not?

BUSY. No, Dagon.

PUPPET DIONYSIUS. What then, Dagonet! Is a puppet worse than these?

BUSY. Yes, and my main argument against you is that you are an abomination; for the male among you putteth on the apparel of the female, and the female of the male.

PUPPET DIONYSIUS. You lie, you lie, you lie abominably.

COKES. Good, by my troth, he has given him the lie thrice.

PUPPET DIONYSIUS. It is your old stale argument against the players, but it will not hold against the puppets; for we have neither male nor female amongst us. And that thou may'st see, if thou wilt, like a malicious purblind zeal as thou art!

THE PUPPET takes up his garment.

EDGWORTH. By my faith, there he has answered you, friend, by plain demonstration.

PUPPET DIONYSIUS. Nay, I'll prove, against e'er a rabbin of 'em all, that my standing is as lawful as his; that I speak by inspiration as well as he; that I have as little to do with learning as he; and do scorn her helps as much as he.

BUSY. I am confuted; the Cause hath failed me.

PUPPET DIONYSIUS. Then be converted, be converted.

LEATHERHEAD. Be converted, I pray you, and let the play go on!

BUSY. Let it go on. For I am changed, and will become a beholder with you!

COKES. That's brave i' faith. Thou hast carried it away, hobby-horse; on with the play!

BEN JONSON, *BARTHOLOMEW FAIR*

&a

As well as performing at large, loosely organized occasions like Bartholomew Fair, actors have always gone where the work was and sometimes to bizarre places. Oliver Goldsmith, author of *She Stoops to Conquer*, recalls meeting a strolling player in a pub who for a couple of free drinks and a meal was happy to discourse on life on the road.

&a

'Well, after travelling some days, whom should I light upon but a company of strolling players. – The moment I saw them at a distance, my heart warmed to them; I had a sort of natural love for everything of the vagabond order: they were employed in settling their baggage, which had been overturned in a narrow way; I offered my assistance, which they accepted; and we soon became so well acquainted, that they took me as a servant. This was a paradise to me; they sang, danced, drank, ate, and travelled, all at the same time. By the blood of the Mirabels, I thought I had never lived till then; I grew as merry as a grig, and laughed at every word that was spoken. They liked me as much as I liked them: I was a very good figure, as you see; and though I was poor, I was not modest.

'I love a straggling life above all things in the world; sometimes good, sometimes bad; to be warm to-day, and cold tomorrow; to eat when one can get it, and drink when (the tankard is out) it stands before me. We arrived that evening at Tenterden, and took a large room at the Greyhound; where we resolved to exhibit Romeo and Juliet, with the funeral procession, the grave, and the garden scene. Romeo was to be performed by a gentleman from the Theatre Royal in Drury Lane; Juliet, by a lady who never appeared on any stage before: and I was to snuff the candles: all excellent in our way. We had figures enough, but the difficulty was how to dress them. The same coat that served Romeo, turned with the blue lining outwards, served for his friend Mercutio: a large piece of crape sufficed at once for Juliet's petticoat and pall: a pestle and mortar from a neighbouring apothecary's answered all the purposes of a bell; and our landlord's own family, wrapped in white sheets, served to fill up the procession. In short, there were but three figures among us that might be said to be dressed with any propriety: I mean the nurse, the starved apothecary, and myself. Our performance gave universal satisfaction: the whole audience were enchanted with our powers.

'There is one rule by which a strolling player may be ever sure of success; that is, in our theatrical way of expressing it, to make a great deal of the character. To speak and act as in common life is not playing, nor is it what people come to see: natural speaking, like sweet white wine, runs glibly over the palate, and scarcely leaves any taste behind it; but being high in a part resembles vinegar, which grates upon the taste, and one feels it while he is drinking. To please in town or country the way is to cry, wring, cringe into attitudes, mark the emphasis, slap the pockets, and labour like one in the falling sickness; that is the way to work for applause; that is the way to gain it.

'As we received much reputation for our skill on this first exhibition, it was but natural for me to ascribe part of the success to myself: I snuffed the candles, and let me tell you that, without a candle-snuffer, the piece would have lost half its embellishments. In this manner we continued a fortnight, and drew tolerable houses, but the evening before our intended departure, we gave out our very best piece, in which all our strength was to be exerted. We had great expectations from this, and even doubled our prices, when behold one of the principal actors fell ill of a violent fever. – This was a stroke like thunder to our little company: they were resolved to go, in a body, to scold the man for falling sick at so inconvenient a time, and that too of a disorder that threatened to be expensive; I seized the moment, and offered to act the part myself in his stead. The case was desperate: they accepted my offer; and I accordingly sat down, with the part in my hand and a tankard before me (Sir, your health), and studied the character, which was to be rehearsed the next day, and played soon after.

'I found my memory excessively helped by drinking: I learned my part with astonishing rapidity, and bade adieu to snuffing candles ever after. I found that nature had designed me for more noble employments, and I was resolved to take her when in the humour. We got together in order to rehearse; and I informed my companions, masters now no longer, of the surprising change I felt within me. "Let the sick man," said I, "be under no uneasiness to get well again: I'll fill his place to universal satisfaction; he may even die if he thinks proper; I'll engage that he shall never be missed." I rehearsed before them, strutted, ranted, and received applause. They soon gave out that a new actor of eminence was to appear, and immediately all the genteel places were bespoke. Before I ascended the stage, however, I concluded within myself, that as I brought money to the house I ought to have my share in the profits. "Gentlemen," said I, addressing our company, "I don't pretend to direct you; far be it from me to treat you with so much ingratitude: you have published my name in the bills with the utmost good-nature, and as affairs stand, cannot act without me: so, gentlemen, to show you my gratitude, I expect to be paid for my acting as much as any of you, otherwise I declare off; I'll brandish my snuffers, and clip candles as usual." This was a very disagreeable proposal, but they found that it was impossible to refuse it; it was irresistible, it was adamant; they consented, and I went on in King Bajazet; my frowning brows bound with a stocking stuffed into a turban, while on my captive arms I brandished a jack-chain. Nature seemed to have fitted me for the part; I was tall, and had a loud voice; my very entrance excited universal applause; I looked round on the audience with a smile, and made a most low and graceful bow, for that is the rule among us. As it was a very passionate part, I invigorated my spirits with three full glasses (the tankard is almost out) of brandy. By Allah! it is almost inconceivable how I went through it. Tamerlane was but a fool to me; though he was sometimes loud enough too, yet I was still louder than he: but then, besides, I had attitudes in abundance: in general I kept my arms folded up thus, upon the pit of my stomach; it is the way at Drury Lane, and has always a fine effect. The tankard would sink to the bottom before I could get through the whole of my merits: in short, I came off like a prodigy; and such was my success, that I could ravish the laurels even from a sirloin of beef. The principal gentlemen and ladies of the town came to me, after the play was over, to compliment me upon my success; one praised my voice, another my person. "Upon my word," says the squire's lady, "he will make one of the finest actors in Europe; I say it, and I think I am something of a judge." – Praise in the beginning is agreeable enough, and we receive it as a favour; but when it comes in great quantities, we regard it only as a debt, which nothing but our merit could extort: instead of thanking them, I internally applauded myself. We were desired to give our piece a second time; we obeyed; and I was applauded even more than before.

'At last we left the town, in order to be at a horse-race at some distance from thence. I shall never think of Tenterden without tears of gratitude and respect. The ladies and gentlemen there, take my word for it, are very good judges of plays and actors. Come let us drink their healths, if you please, Sir. We quitted the town, I say; and there was a wide difference between my coming in and going out: I entered the town a candle-snuffer, and I quitted it a hero! – Such is the world; little to-day, and great to-morrow. I could say a great deal more upon the subject, something truly sublime upon the ups and downs of fortune; but it would give us both the spleen, and so I shall pass it over.'

OLIVER GOLDSMITH,
THE ADVENTURES OF A STROLLING PLAYER

🐝

Almost a century after Goldsmith, Mark Twain wrote *Huckleberry Finn*. He has his hero Huck and the runaway slave Jim fall in with some strolling players on their voyage down the Mississippi. The players in this case turn out to be conmen of near-genius.

🐝

It was after sun-up, now, but we went right on, and didn't tie up. The king and the duke turned out, by-and-by, looking pretty rusty; but after they'd jumped overboard and took a swim, it chippered them up a good deal. After breakfast the king he took a seat on a corner of the raft, and pulled off his boots and rolled up his britches, and let his legs dangle in the water, so as to be comfortable, and lit his pipe, and went to getting his Romeo and Juliet by heart. When he had got it pretty good, him and the duke begun to practise it together. The duke had to learn him over and over again, how to say every speech; and he made him sigh, and put his hand on his heart, and after while he said he done it pretty well; 'only,' he says, 'you mustn't bellow out *Romeo!* that way, like a bull – you must say it soft, and sick, languishy, so – Ro-o-meo! that is the idea; for Juliet's a dear sweet mere child of a girl, you know, and she don't bray like a jackass.'

Well, next they got out a couple of long swords that the duke made out of oak laths, and begun to practise the swordfight – the duke called himself Richard III; and the way they laid on, and pranced around the raft was grand to see. But by-and-by the king tripped and fell overboard, and after that they took a rest, and had a talk about all kinds of adventures they'd had in other times along the river.

After dinner, the duke says:

'Well, Capet, we'll want to make this a first-class show, you know, so I guess we'll add a little more to it. We want a little something to answer encores with, anyway.'

'What's onkores, Bilgewater?'

The duke told him, and then says:

'I'll answer by doing the Highland fling or the sailor's horn-pipe; and you – well, let me see – oh, I've got it – you can do Hamlet's soliloquy.'

121

'Hamlet's which?'

'Hamlet's soliloquy, you know; the most celebrated thing in Shakespeare. Ah, it's sublime, sublime! Always fetches the house. I haven't got it in the book – I've only got one volume – but I reckon I can piece it out from memory. I'll just walk up and down a minute, and see if I can call it back from recollection's vaults.

So he went to marching up and down, thinking, and frowning horrible every now and then; then he would hoist up his eyebrows; next he would squeeze his hand on his forehead and stagger back and kind of moan; next he would sigh, and next he'd let on to drop a tear. It was beautiful to see him. By-and-by he got it. He told us to give attention. Then he strikes a most noble attitude, with one leg shoved forwards, and his arms stretched away up, and his head tilted back, looking up at the sky; and then he begins to rip and rave and grit his teeth; and after that, all through his speech he howled, and spread around, and swelled up his chest, and just knocked the spots out of any acting ever *I* see before. This is the speech – I learned it, easy enough, while he was learning it to the king:

> To be, or not to be; that is the bare bodkin
> That makes calamity of so long life;
> For who would fardels bear, till Birnam Wood do come to Dunsinane,
> But that the fear of something after death
> Murders the innocent sleep,
> Great nature's second course,
> And makes us rather sling the arrows of outrageous fortune
> Than fly to others that we know not of.
> There's the respect must give us pause:
> Wake Duncan with thy knocking! I would thou couldst;
> For who would bear the whips and scorns of time,
> The oppressor's wrong, the proud man's contumely,
> The law's delay, and the quietus which his pangs might take,
> In the dead waste and middle of the night, when churchyards yawn
> In customary suits of solemn black,
> But that the undiscovered country from whose bourne no traveler
>   returns,
> Breathes forth contagion on the world,
> And thus the native hue of resolution, like the poor cat i' the adage,
> Is sicklied o'er with care,
> And all the clouds that lowered o'er our housetops,
> With this regard their currents turn awry,

And lose the name of action.
'Tis a consummation devoutly to be wished. But soft you, the fair
    Ophelia:
Ope not thy ponderous and marble jaws,
But get thee to a nunnery – go!

MARK TWAIN, *HUCKLEBERRY FINN*

쟈

The king and the duke, with Huck and Jim now in their company, continue down the river for a few days, rehearsing and arguing. They land by a little one-horse town – a violent place, full of ignorance and lynch mobs but aching for entertainment. When they see the huge success gained by a travelling circus, they decide to try their own luck.

쟈

Well, that night we had *our* show; but there warn't only about twelve people there; just enough to pay expenses. And they laughed all the time, and that made the duke mad; and everybody left, anyway, before the show was over, but one boy which was asleep. So the duke said these Arkansaw lunkheads couldn't come up to Shakspeare; what they wanted was low comedy – and may be something ruther worse than low comedy, he reckoned. He said he could size their style. So next morning he got some big sheets of wrapping-paper and some black paint, and drawed off some handbills and stuck them up all over the village. The bills said:

AT THE COURT HOUSE!
FOR 3 NIGHTS ONLY!
The World-Renowned Tragedians
DAVID GARRICK THE YOUNGER!
AND
EDMUND KEAN THE ELDER!
Of the London and Continental
Theatres,
In their Thrilling Tragedy of
THE KING'S CAMELOPARD
OR
THE ROYAL NONESUCH! !
Admission 50 cents.

Then at the bottom was the biggest line of all – which said:

123

LADIES AND CHILDREN NOT ADMITTED.

'There,' says he, 'if that line don't fetch them, I don't know Arkansaw!'

Well, all day him and the king was hard at it, rigging up a stage, and a curtain, and a row of candles for footlights; and that night the house was jam full of men in no time. When the place couldn't hold no more, the duke he quit tending door and went around the back way and come onto the stage and stood up before the curtain, and made a little speech, and praised up this tragedy, and said it was the most thrillingest one that ever was; and so he went on a-bragging about the tragedy and about Edmund Kean the Elder, which was to play the main principal part in it; and at last when he'd got everybody's expectations up high enough, he rolled up the curtain, and the next minute the king come a-prancing out on all fours, naked; and he was painted all over, ring-streaked-and-striped, all sorts of colors, as splendid as a rainbow. And – but never mind the rest of his outfit, it was just wild, but it was awful funny. The people most killed themselves laughing; and when the king got done capering, and capered off behind the scenes, they roared and clapped and stormed and haw-hawed till he come back and done it over again; and after that, they made him do it another time. Well, it would a made a cow laugh to see the shines that old idiot cut.

Then the duke he lets the curtain down, and bows to the people, and says the great tragedy will be performed only two nights more, on accounts of pressing London engagements, where the seats is all sold aready for it in Drury Lane; and then he makes them another bow, and says if he has succeeded in pleasing them and instructing them, he will be deeply obleeged if they will mention it to their friends and get them to come and see it.

Twenty people sings out:

'What, is it over? Is that *all*?'

The duke says yes. Then there was a fine time. Everybody sings out 'sold', and rose up mad, and was agoing for that stage and them tragedians. But a big fine-looking man jumps up on a bench, and shouts:

'Hold on! Just a word, gentlemen.' They stopped to listen. 'We are sold – mighty badly sold. But we don't want to be the laughing-stock of this whole town, I reckon, and never hear the last of this thing as long as we live. *No.* What we want, is to go out of here quiet, and talk this show up, and sell the *rest* of the town! Then we'll all be in the same boat. Ain't that sensible?' ('You bet it is! – the jedge is right!' everybody sings out.) 'All right, then – not a word about any sell. Go along home, and advise everybody to come and see the tragedy.'

Next day you couldn't hear nothing around that town but how splendid that show was. House was jammed again, that night, and we sold this crowd the same way. When me and the king and the duke got home to the raft, we all had a supper; and by-and-by, about midnight, they made Jim and me back her out and float her down the middle of the river and fetch her in and hide her about two mile below town.

The third night the house was crammed again – and they warn't new-comers, this time, but people that was at the show the other two nights. I stood by the duke at the door, and I see that every man that went in had his pockets bulging, or something muffled up under his coat – and I see it warn't no perfumery neither, not by a long sight. I smelt sickly eggs by the barrel, and rotten cabbages, and such things; and if I know the signs of a dead cat being around, and I bet I do, there was sixty-four of them went in. I shoved in there for a minute, but it was too various for me, I couldn't stand it. Well, when the place couldn't hold no more people, the duke he give a fellow a quarter and told him to tend door for him a minute, and then he started around for the stage door, I after him; but the minute we turned the corner and was in the dark, he says:

'Walk fast, now, till you get away from the houses, and then shin for the raft like the dickens was after you!'

I done it, and he done the same. We struck the raft at the same time, and in less than two seconds we was gliding down stream, all dark and still, and edging towards the middle of the river, nobody saying a word. I reckoned the poor king was in for a gaudy time of it with the audience; but nothing of the sort; pretty soon he crawls out from under the wigwam, and says:

'Well, how'd the old thing pan out this time, Duke?'

He hadn't been up town at all.

We never showed a light till we was about ten mile below that village. Then we lit up and had a supper, and the king and the duke fairly laughed their bones loose over the way they'd served them people. The duke says:

'Greenhorns, flatheads! *I* knew the first house would keep mum and let the rest of the town get roped in; and I knew they'd lay for us the third night, and consider it was *their* turn now. Well, it *is* their turn, and I'd give something to know how much they'd take for it. I *would* just like to know how they're putting in their opportunity. They can turn it into a picnic, if they want to – they brought plenty provisions.'

Them rapscallions took in four hundred and sixty-five dollars in that three nights. I never see money hauled in by the wagon-load like that, before.

MARK TWAIN, *HUCKLEBERRY FINN*

In the mid–1970s, after decades of successful and innovative work in the relatively safe and protected world of the subsidized theatre, Peter Brook decided to take his show on the road. The road he decided on was every bit as difficult and dangerous as Mark Twain's Mississippi. He took a company of actors to Africa with no stage but a carpet and no script but the actors' imaginations. The results are chronicled in John Heilpern's book *The Conference of the Birds*. Here, Brook's actors are about to perform to a Tuareg audience whose knowledge of theatre is so limited they have no word for 'play'.

➜

'What are you doing here?' a stranger asked in French.

'We've come to entertain you. *C'est une fête.*'

'Oh, that's okay.' The stranger looked pleased.

A small crowd gathered, no more than twenty or so at first, gazing at us round the carpet. Tamanrasset was a town of different temperaments. Life was calmer here. As we sat and waited for the crowd to grow, Brook put a scrappy piece of paper down on the carpet. It was *The Shoe Show*. I was very busy nervously pacing about in an imaginary silk dressing-gown and gay cravat. You must forgive me. I was comparatively young at the time, and over-excited. The actors gathered round. 'You might like to try a little of this,' said Brook, conjuring the rabbit out of the hat. The actors buzzed and seemed to look at me with a new respect. Or perhaps I imagined it. I had a new identity. 'It's nothing much,' I said to Mirren, reading the script with her.

Brook didn't explain anything. Most of the actors only had time to glance at the piece of paper.

If they only glanced at the paper, what was the point of having a script in the first place? Well, I was to ask that question many times – but not then. Not in the nerves and excitement of my first night. Or first afternoon. I'm always having first afternoons. The first play I ever had performed in a real theatre was at lunchtime. It takes the gloss off things. I mean people were really hungry.

Still, this was no time to quibble. Peter Brook doesn't direct my work, as a general rule. But he seemed to be convulsed with laughter at me. He yelled across the carpet that I looked like a terrified author in the crush bar before curtain-up. He said he didn't have time to send me flowers.

I ignored him, for I knew there was a post office. He could have sent me a telegram. 'Wishing you every success. Love and kisses. Peter and the gang.'

Curtain up! Swados and the seal act were on. They took the opening music gently, building confidence. Sometimes the crowd laughed at the strange music, though hushed itself into concentrated silence. It was good. Things were working. Michèle Collison fights Natasha Parry in sound. Others join them, taking sides: gang warfare of a special kind. No one wins the sound battle. There is no breath left. The Babylon song follows and, though sung in English, strikes a chord. An actor conducts the group, now a sound orchestra, builds rhythms, creating a melody. Instrumental work follows, simple, calm, together, taking off. Into a crazy burbling sound, burble ducts, a bizarre spectacle that has the actors laughing and the crowd in hysterics.

Why do audiences sit in darkness at the theatre? The whole convention seemed madness now. In the traditional theatre the actors don't even see their audience. And the members of the audience don't see each other. It's as if no one wants to meet. Whatever direction Brook's work took in the future I wouldn't believe it if a show of his ever played in darkness again.

'*Shoe Show!*' ordered Brook.

And Katsulas entered the carpet and placed his enormous shoes in the centre, his cartoon shoes. And Mirren was on her feet, bent double, ugly hag creeping and cursing her way round the fringes of the carpet. And I was so proud of this, it's ridiculous. But something dead on a scrap of paper had come to life. Life! And the crowd watched Mirren's every move because hag or no hag she's terrific to look at. And she found the shoes, grunting with pleasure. The crowd fell silent, watching. Veiled women peep round corners.

The old hag stared at the enormous shoes and everyone stared at the enormous shoes. She held them for a while. Was something wrong? She was taking her time. Slowly she put the shoes on. And then with a great shriek of triumph, Mirren grew and grew, and the old hag was young. Oh, fantastic! I just thought, fantastic. And cheered louder than anyone. No cute transformation this! There was violence there, and power. 'HANIKKA SHNIMIKKA SHNAP!' chanted Mirren, cribbing the words from a children's story she once read. 'HANIKKA SHNIMIKKA SHNIMIKKA SHNAP!' And the rest of the actors struck up the band as Ayansola got his drum talking and Mirren strode and strutted round that carpet in the amazing magic shoes. 'HANIKKA SHNIMIKKA SHNIMIKKA SHNAP! SHNAPAK SHNIMAK SHNIMIKKA MAAAAAAH!'

It wasn't anything you could join in. But the crowd were glad they came. And King Katsulas and a one-legged shoe polisher entered the carpet now on account of the fact that the two ridiculous thieves had missed their cue. 'This is what improvisation is all about,' I told myself. 'It's silly to have a heart attack.' But I couldn't believe what was happening on the carpet.

There seemed to be a rival Shoe Show going on.

King Katsulas was merrily cartwheeling round the place in the magic shoes when lovely mad Miriam Goldschmidt suddenly decided to enter with a rival shoe, which was dangling from a stick. I was following my script like the score of a concerto. I knew things had got a bit out of sequence. But I definitely didn't write the rival shoe scene. I was practically up on my feet slinging her off the carpet. Brook was helpless with laughter. King Katsulas looked stunned. There was a rival show dangling under his nose. But you could tell what was going on. She was a *wild* sorceress. All those wild sounds, she had to be. You could tell what she was saying. She was saying, 'You give me your shoes and I'll give you mine.' And it was so vivid and people were laughing so much I was already pretending I wrote it. I was the original inspiration, after all. But either way it didn't matter because I knew then that the show couldn't go wrong. We were laughing with the Tuaregs. Father de Foucauld was right. Laugh and the Tuaregs laugh with you.

The world comes later.

Well, in the end my precious script seemed to get a little lost in a thrilling tale about General Katsulas leading an army patrol through the jungle. It was a re-make of *The Snows of Kilimanjaro*. But what matter? In the simple beginnings to this journey there were simple failures, simple triumphs. The show had revived confidence. A start had been made. My début in Africa was a modest triumph. I may not have made it on Broadway yet, but I'm very big in the Sahara Desert. When Brook's critics say that he no longer cares about audiences, they mean something different. I think they unintentionally mean that he no longer cares about the 'right' audiences.

For myself, better a contented Tuareg than a miserable European.

Spirits were so high after the come-back that Brook thought a celebration would be in order. Several of us joined him on a visit to the local *hammam* – steam baths. We took a Land-Rover, bouncing and rattling through the back streets of the town as men knelt in the sand, praying. It was dusk. A small boy guided us for a small tip to a dark doorway. A sultan figure bowed and scraped us inside. Brook clapped his hands, ordering mint tea. But it wasn't exactly Arabian Nights. There wasn't any steam.

But there was water – water rediscovered! There was one hot-water tap.

As we stood shivering, Brook was reminded of Orson Welles' version of *Othello*, a film shot mostly in a Turkish bath in Morocco because the costumes didn't turn up. 'Wonderful improvisation,' said Brook, soaping himself down as cockroaches scattered across the floor.

Then we had the post-show conference.

'We must learn to *train* the audience,' said Brook, whispering to a group of naked actors in his urgent voice. 'If you meet a stranger, you don't pour out your heart to him in the first five minutes. We must learn to build a real relationship. Did you notice how quickly we were able to touch and disturb the children? You see, they don't have television to create thick skins. There's a lot to learn. Still, an hour of theatre without sex or violence,' added Brook, who's no prude, 'is truly remarkable. Anyone seen the soap?'

JOHN HEILPERN, *THE CONFERENCE OF THE BIRDS*

❧

Many more conventional actors were forced into playing under unusual circumstances by the Second World War. ENSA and its equivalents catapulted unwary thespians into unlikely places. The outstanding chronicler of these collisions is Peter Nichols. As well as his play *Privates on Parade*, his autobiography, *Feeling You're Behind*, has many hilarious passages about his experience with Combined Services Entertainments in 1940s Malaya. Here we meet for the first time the model for Nichols's famous creation Captain Terri Dennis.

❧

The Major had no say in the production of our shows which was, strictly speaking, in the limp hands of Fl-Lieut. Lawson. No one could have expected these two officers, so different in every way, to be at anything but daggers drawn. In fact, they seemed the best of friends and formed a more profound partnership than any of us knew at the time. Now spare and fit for odd jobs, we actors were put on scene-shifting duties for Lawson's latest revue, *Over to You*, part of which I'd seen in rehearsal when I gave my reading. The bohemian-looking blond I referred to then was the star of this production, Barri Chatt, a dancer and drag-artiste who'd lately arrived from England with his female partner. The presence of several girls in the troupe gave Barri no excuse for drag, though his off-stage gear was so androgynous that his costumes in the show looked almost butch. To me he seemed immensely old but was probably in his forties. His hair was dyed peroxide yellow, his eyebrows were plucked and pencilled in and all his other body hair shaved to a baby's smoothness. He wore what he called 'the full slap' (new word) which could be either day or night. After dark the cupid's bow lipstick was more emphatic, the eye-liner a darker blue. Silk scarves flopped at his neck, sandals displayed his painted toe-nails, at the pool his trunks were provocatively laced down the side.

The air of Shaftesbury Avenue sophistication, culled from people he called Binkie, Binnie and Boo, was belied by the accent of his native Yorkshire. The story of his arrival in Singapore has long since entered the Chatt mythology. Some high-ranking officers had met one morning for a top-level briefing in the Victoria Theatre and were waiting for staff cars to take them to chota pegs at Raffles when a taxi drew up and Barri stepped out. Making straight for the astonished generals and air marshals, he waved his cigarette-holder and greeted them: 'Tell them to put the kettle on, loves, your aunty's arrived!'

Barri was put up at Raffles, then the premier hotel, now a haunted house for package-tours. Coward's description of Singapore as a second-rate city for third-rate people was never more apt than in the prompt out-of-bounds on other ranks reintroduced as soon as the war years were over. Had Barri known he would not be allowed to entertain able seamen in his room, he might have stayed elsewhere.

'Luckily my room had a balcony with an easy climb from the garden,' says Terri Dennis in *Privates on Parade*, 'and most naval ratings are very nimble nipping up the rigging after weeks afloat doing the Captain Bligh stint. Well, it didn't say anything in my contract about setting an example. There was no work in England, the panto season was over and life under Clementina Attlee wasn't exactly the Roman Empire. So I signed on for sun and fun.'

Barri got plenty of both, more than most of us get in a lifetime. He was bold (new word – or new nuance) and free to do as he liked among an army, an air force and above all a navy of sex-starved men.

'Oh, doockie,' he said one day beside a swimming-pool, varnishing his toe-nails, 'sex – it's becooming an obsession.'

All the same, he was an artiste and prided himself on Knowing The Business and Being A True Pro. This side of him showed itself at the dress-rehearsal of *Over to You* in the garrison theatre. We were stagehands, Lawson was the director and Major Cotton, with the help of a bottle of Scotch, was working out the lighting-plot. The first rehearsal began at eight and he was drunk by midnight. He blundered about repositioning the spots, floods and gelatines while the rest of us kept our tempers. At last began a run of the first half, starting with the opening chorus, sung to the tune of 'Plenty of money and you'.

We're all coming over to you-oo-who!
To make you forget that you're blue-oo-who!
With plenty of laughter and songs and jokes –
So sit back and relax and just be happy folks.

This went well enough until Barri's big dance number announced in his best Showbiz Yorkshire: 'Well, you've seen a little of Costa Rica, we've shown you something of a negro's life – its trials and tribulations, its sorrows and its joys – and now we bring you a choreographic fantasia from the much-loved legend of Faust and Marguerite. Thank you!'

A Lawsonesque introduction from the band brought on Barri's partner, dancing her love in tight bolero and full skirt.

'Lift up your skirt, dear,' shouted Lawson from one of the front rows.

She paused, mystified, then went on dancing.

'I said, raise your skirt and show us the petticoats.'

She stopped and stared out, shielding her eyes. The music died away and Barri came on, half into his Faust togs.

'Now, now, doockie, it's not a can-can, it's choreography.'

'I'm not asking to see her legs, only the sumptuous underskirts that have been provided at great public expense.'

'That I never asked for!' Barri snapped.

'The boys want colour, glamour, spectacle!'

'I know very well what the boys want, luv.'

The laughter was interrupted by Cotton lurching down the aisle.

'Look here, Barri, no more argument. She'll show the underskirt – that's an order!'

'It's not that kind of dance.'

Kenneth and I and the rest of our company sat watching from the dim hall while at every window transit personnel craned for a view.

'These costumes have been paid for out of taxpayers' money. I shouldn't need to remind you of that. The boys up-country must be given their money's worth.'

'Nobody told us this was going to be a mannequin parade!'

'Do as I say!' shouted Cotton, stumbling on the steps from hall to stage.

'Right, dear,' said Barri to his partner, 'parade round once with your skirt up, show your undies, then start the music and go into the dance!'

'Wait a minute, wait a minute –'

'Barri, don't be tiresome,' droned Lawson.

But Barri had left the stage.

'Come back here at once!' ordered Cotton, trying again to climb the steps.

'Don't you dare talk to Barri like that,' said his partner through her tears.

'I'll talk to him how I damn well like,' said Cotton, his diction slurred by Scotch, 'I'm his commanding officer.'

He turned to us.

'And you lot – close the shutters!'

At every window were the faces of transit squaddies, finding more entertainment in this rehearsal than they ever did in the shows. Before we'd finished, Barri walked into the darkened house, threw the can-can dress at Lawson and shouted 'Take your bleedin' frock and I hope it suits you.'

Cotton followed him out, then Lawson, slowly, as though honing an epigram. Moments later, the Major returned to announce that the rehearsal was over and we could all go home.

'Parade tomorrow ten hundred hours,' he rapped out in a last attempt military order, mopping his brow with a white handkerchief.

'Look,' said Kenneth quietly, 'vada the powder-brownish on her hankie.'

'The what?'

'The Leichner brownish. She wears it to make her seem more butch, more the grizzled campaigner.'

'Parade,' shouted Cotton, 'dismiss!'

But before we could, from out of a great shouting backstage came a beserk sergeant electrician.

'Lock me up, sir, please, sir,' he demanded, his mad face close to the major's ear, 'before I punch you in the face, sir. I've had enough of you and your lighting cues!'

'Now simmer down, sergeant, back to your mess with the others, there's a good lad.'

'No, sir, put me under close arrest, sir,' the man insisted, his fists clenching and spreading with fury.

Baxter had come from backstage too and told us he'd seen the sergeant try to hit the CO once already.

'If you don't put me in the guard-house, sir, under lock and key, sir, I swear I'll smash you in the face, sir, and that would be an offence punishable under King's Regulations and I'm group 56, sir, coming up for release. I want to be on that boat, sir, when it sails, so lock me up, you must, sir.'

'Oh, very well,' said Cotton, and turned to the nearest sergeants, a conjurer and impersonator, 'you two, arrest this sergeant and escort him to the guard-room.'

'They can't,' insisted the frantic sergeant, 'they're not substantive sergeants, they're only privates.'

'Oh, for God's sake – what about Sergeants Moore and Whittle – will they do?'

'No, sir, we can't,' said Whittle, 'we're in civilian clothes.'

An understatement – they were in the frilly blouses of a South American band.

'Well, for God's sake, which of you is a properly dressed substantive sergeant?'

Two volunteers stepped one pace forward.

'Then take charge of this man.'

'This man? This man, sir?' raved the demented Sparks. 'You should call me "sergeant", sir, that's in King's Regulations too.'

He was finally taken off and subdued, we were dismissed and the show opened the next night with Barri doing the number as he wished.

'That's the theatre, doockies,' said Barri later, when we reminded him. 'It's Life, The Drama, let's face it!'

PETER NICHOLS, FEELING YOU'RE BEHIND

Eventually, Nichols and such colleagues as Kenneth Williams and Stanley Baxter compiled their own show. His description will ring a bell with any fan of the long-running TV sitcom *It Ain't Half Hot Mum*.

At Your Service opened before my discharge came and my visitors reported a great success. I got out in time to join it on its tour of Singapore island. My solo, a cod-dramatic monologue called 'The Condemned Cell', which Kenneth remembers better than I, had been replaced by a hefty lad singing and dancing 'Happy Feet', a song that surfaced later in *Joe Egg*. Cotton offered me a choice of waiting at Nee Soon for something to turn up or going on the road as chorus and stagehand. This I quickly took, though I wrote home: 'my talents would be wasted in such a capacity'. Evidently my resentment showed because Lawson told me I was to be Returned to Unit for being truculent. I pleaded with Cotton and watched with relief while the orderly-room sergeant tore up my movement order. From then on, I knuckled under, carting props, operating colour-wheels and appearing in one or two concerted numbers.

My dim memory of the show has been refreshed by Stanley Baxter, who became a stand-in director during the tour, as Lawson remained at Nee Soon preparing more touring extravaganzas, one so grandiose that it could not be played anywhere but the Victoria Theatre. *At Your Service* began with our full company of ten (or, depending on the size of the stage, nine, eight or less) wearing blue-and-gold uniforms, all no doubt exorbitantly priced, like so many tin soldiers, standing in a line-up and doing square-bashing movements as we sang:

'We're *men* of the service –'

('It had been *boys* at first,' said Stanley, 'but Cotton said it wasn't butch enough.')

'We're at your service entertaining – YOU!

(Ten fingers pointed at audience, ten right feet stamping on the word.)

> We'll bring you songs both old and new –
> Fun and laughter – if you're blue!
> Men of the service,
> We're at your service,
> Snappy, smart and – gay!
> So be happy and bright as we're with you tonight,
> We're at your service now.'

('Salute,' said Stanley, 'smart left turn and march off, ten bodies piling up in whatever we were using for wings or backstage, by which time, of course, the howls of hairy-arsed derision had to be heard to be believed. Luckily Kenneth showed a stroke of genius to save us from disaster. Instead of marching off on the end of the line, he let us go, gave a disgusted gesture and said "Oh, I can't be doing with all that", turned back and went straight into his impersonations.')

These I *do* remember – lightning flashes of Nellie Wallace, Bette Davis, and Felix Aylmer.

'Feel who?' asked bewildered squaddies, already reeling from the rich bouquet, but he whirled them into

> This above all, to thine own self be true
> And it must follow as the night the day
> Thou canst not then be false to any man

and, avoiding applause or mockery, got off pronto with Harry Champion's 'Any Old Iron'.

Somewhere in the first half, the entire company appeared on a blacked-out stage (not easy during matinées), our faces lit by individual torches held beneath chins, to sing a current favourite, 'Pedro the fisherman'. It told how Pedro had left his sweetheart to find wealth, how she'd been forcibly betrothed to 'swarthy Miguel' and was standing beside him at the altar, another chance for Kenneth to do his Felix Aylmer:

> Will you take this maid to be
> Your lawful wife eternallee?

And the rest of us:

> When through the open doorway there
> A sudden sound disturbs the air

and a full chorus whistling the theme should have announced the return of Pedro, rich and just in time. Kenneth, however, had spent much of the bridge passage running up and down the two rows goosing us all. You cannot laugh and whistle at the same time and most nights the pianist had to bash out the theme without any whistles from the stage. We were busy laughing or goosing Kenneth in return.

The pianist was our only civilian, Leo Conriche, whom I'd probably seen in the variety halls of my childhood accompanying people like Ronald Frankau and Stanley Holloway. He had in his fifties the sour, tortoise face of the middle-aged Maugham but his air of weary resignation was a relief among so much vitality. 'And now,' he would say, standing at the piano to announce his own solo, 'I should like to play a lovely piece you all know and love: "The Swan" by Saint-Saëns.' And, as he sat, an aside to no one but himself: 'Never 'eard of it.' Unrest would grow while he played, lifting his right hand high above the keys, until at the end he stood to the ironic cheers and whistles of the soldiers.

'Are they sending me up?' he would ask himself.

From Rae Hammond's magic act I filched most of the lines for Young-Love in *Privates on Parade*. 'This is called the Russian shuffle because the cards are Russian from one hand to the other.' 'You will observe that during this trick my hand never leaves the end of my arm.' It was Rae, not I, who remembered being sent to a Burmese unit by mistake with a show called *Chinese Crackers*. The orchestra-pit was awash with monsoon rain and no one in the audience understood English. 'And now,' Leo announced from his piano, 'Saint-Saëns's absolutely adorable "Swan", which will be much more at home than usual in all this water.'

The item that had come straight from Lawson's heart was a series of patriotic tableaux, in which tabs were drawn back to show members of the company posing in Allied uniforms while Leo played a medley of anthems and Stanley Baxter recited jingo verse.

'I don't remember that at all,' I said when he tried to remind me, 'didn't they send you up?'

'Through the roof. Can you imagine what your average peacetime conscript thought of lines like "Britain kneels in pledge to you"? As soon as we got away from Nee Soon, we dropped it but Lawson would sneak out to see the show in some unlikely spot, there'd be hell to pay and we'd have to put it back in.'

With this anthology of garbage, we toured Singapore.

PETER NICHOLS, *FEELING YOU'RE BEHIND*

CHAPTER 7
SUCCESS

Success. The glittering prizes, the world at your feet, slippers squelchy with champagne. Success, particularly in a notionally 'glamorous' profession such as acting, is worshipped and envied in about equal measure. For some, it is almost a religion. However, it is difficult to analyse. In Henry Fielding's *Tom Jones*, Tom and Mrs Miller take the naïve Mr Partridge to see David Garrick play Hamlet – one of the most successful performances ever. Partridge has never seen the play, heard of Garrick or been inside a London theatre.

≥

In the first row then of the first gallery did Mr Jones, Mrs Miller, her youngest daughter, and Partridge, take their places. Partridge immediately declared, it was the finest place he had ever been in. When the first musick was played, he said, 'It was a wonder how so many fiddlers could play at one time, without putting one another out.' While the fellow was lighting the upper candles, he cried out to Mrs Miller, 'Look, look, madam, the very picture of the man in the end of the Common-Prayer Book, before the Gunpowder-Treason service.' Nor could he help observing, with a sigh, when all the candles were lighted, 'That here were candles enough burnt in one night, to keep an honest poor family for a whole twelve-month.'

As soon as the play, which was *Hamlet Prince of Denmark*, began, Partridge was all attention, nor did he break silence till the entrance of the ghost; upon which he asked Jones, 'What man that was in the strange dress; something,' said he, 'like what I have seen in a picture. Sure it is not armour, is it?' Jones answered, 'That is the ghost.' To which Partridge replied with a smile, 'Persuade me to that, sir, if you can. Though I can't say I ever actually saw a ghost in my life, yet I am certain I should know one, if I saw him, better than that comes to. No, no, sir, ghosts don't appear in such dresses as that, neither.' In this mistake, which caused much laughter in the neighbourhood of Partridge, he was suffered to continue, 'till the scene between the ghost and Hamlet, when Partridge gave that credit to Mr Garrick, which he had denied to Jones, and fell into so violent a trembling, that his knees knocked against each other, Jones asked him what was the matter, and whether he was afraid of the warrior upon the stage? 'O la! sir,' said he, 'I perceive now it is what you told me. I am not afraid of anything; for I know it is but a play: and if it was really a ghost, it could do no harm at such a distance, and in so much company; and yet if I was frightened, I am not the only person.' 'Why, who,' cries Jones, 'dost though take to be such a coward here besides thyself?' 'Nay, you may call me coward if you will; but if that little man there upon the stage is not frightened, I never saw any man frightened in my life. Ay, ay; *go along with you!* Ay, to be sure! Who's fool then? Will you? Lud have mercy upon such fool-hardiness! – Whatever happens it is good enough for you. – *Follow you?* I'd follow the devil as soon. Nay, perhaps, it is the devil – for they say he can put on what likeness he pleases. – Oh! here he is again. – *No farther!* No, you have gone far enough already; farther than I'd have gone for all the King's dominions.' Jones offered to speak, but Partridge cried, 'Hush, hush, dear sir, don't you hear him!' And during the whole speech of the ghost, he sat with his eyes fixed partly on the ghost, and partly on Hamlet, and with his mouth open; the same passions which succeeded each other in Hamlet, succeeding likewise in him.

When the scene was over, Jones said, 'Why, Partridge, you exceed my expectations. You enjoy the play more than I conceived possible.' 'Nay, sir,' answered Partridge, 'if you are not afraid of the devil, I can't help it; but to be sure it is natural to be surprized at such things, though I know there is nothing in them: not that it was the ghost that surprized me neither; for I should have known that to have been only a man in a strange dress: but when I saw the little man so frightned himself, it was that which took hold of me.' 'And dost thou imagine then, Partridge,' cries Jones, 'that he was really frightned?' 'Nay, sir,' said Partridge, 'did not you yourself observe afterwards, when he found out it was his own father's spirit, and how he was murdered in the garden, how his fear forsook him by degrees, and he was struck dumb with sorrow, as it were, just as I should have been, had it been my own case. – But hush! O la! What noise is that? There he is again. – Well, to be certain, though I know there is nothing at all in it, I am glad I am not down yonder, where those men are.' Then turning his eyes again upon Hamlet, 'Ay, you may draw your sword; what signifies a sword against the power of the devil?'

During the second act, Partridge made very few remarks. He greatly admired the fineness of the dresses; nor could he help observing upon the king's countenance. 'Well,' said he, 'how people may be deceived by faces? *Nulla fides fronti* is, I find a true saying. Who would think, by looking in the king's face, that he had ever committed a murder?' He then enquired after the ghost; but Jones, who intended he should be surprized, gave him no other satisfaction, than 'that he might possibly see him again soon, and in a flash of fire.'

Partridge sat in fearful expectation of this; and now, when the ghost made his next appearance, Partridge cried out, 'There, sir, now; what say you now? Is he frightned now or no? As much frightned as you think me, and, to be sure, nobody can help some fears, I would not be in so bad a condition as what's his name, Squire Hamlet, is there, for all the world. Bless me! What's become of the spirit? As I am a living soul, I thought I saw him sink into the earth.' 'Indeed, you saw right,' answered Jones. 'Well, well,' cries Partridge, 'I know it is only a play; and besides, if there was any-thing in all this, Madame Miller would not laugh so: for as to you, sir, you would not be afraid, I believe, if the devil was here in person. – There, there – Ay, no wonder you are in such a passion; shake the vile wicked wretch to pieces. If she was my own mother I should serve her so. To be sure, all duty to a mother is forfeited by such wicked doings. – Ay, go about your business: I hate the sight of you.'

Our critic was now pretty silent till the play, which Hamlet introduces before the king. This he did not at first understand, 'till Jones explained it to him; but he no sooner entered into the spirit of it, than he began to bless himself that he had never committed murder. Then turning to Mrs Miller, he asked her, 'If she did not imagine the king looked as if he was touched; though he is,' said he, 'a good actor, and doth all he can to hide it. Well, I would not have so much to answer for, as that wicked man there hath, to sit upon a much higher chair than he sits upon. – No wonder he run away; for your sake I'll never trust an innocent face again.'

The grave-digging scene next engaged the attention of Partridge, who expressed much surprize at the number of skulls thrown upon the stage. To which Jones answered, 'That it was one of the most famous burial-places about town.' 'No wonder then,' cries Partridge, 'that the place is haunted. But I never saw in my life a worse grave-digger. I had a sexton, when I was clerk, that should have dug three graves while he is digging one. The fellow handles a spade as if it was the first time he had ever had one in his hand. Ay, ay, you may sing. You had rather sing than work, I believe.' – Upon Hamlet's taking up the skull, he cried out, 'Well, it is strange to see how fearless some men are: I never could bring myself to touch anything belonging to a dead man on any account. – He seemed frightened enough too at the ghost I thought. *Nemo omnibus horis sapit.*'

Little more worth remembring occurred during the play; at the end of which Jones asked him, 'which of the players he had liked best?' To this he answered, with some appearance of indignation at the question. 'The king without doubt.' 'Indeed, Mr Partridge,' says Mrs Miller, 'you are not of the same opinion with the town; for they are all agreed, that Hamlet is acted by the best player who was ever on the stage.' 'He the best player!' cries Partridge, with a contemptuous sneer, 'Why I could act as well as he myself. I am sure if I had seen a ghost, I should have looked in the very same manner, and done just as he did. And then, to be sure, in that scene, as you called it, between him and his mother, where you told me he acted so fine, why, Lord help me, any man, that is, any good man, that had had such a mother, would have done exactly the same I know you are only joking with me; but, indeed, madam, though I was never at a play in London, yet I have seen acting before in the country; and the king for my money; he speaks all his words distinctly, half as loud again as the other. – Anybody may see he is an actor.'

While Mrs Miller was thus engaged in conversation with Partridge, a lady came up to Mr Jones, whom he immediately knew to be Mrs Fitzpatrick. She said, she had seen him from the other part of the gallery, and had taken that opportunity of speaking to him, as she had something to say, which might be of great service to himself. She then acquainted him with her lodgings, and made him an appointment the next day in the morning; which, upon recollection, she presently changed to the afternoons at which time Jones promised to attend her.

Thus ended the adventure at the playhouse; where Partridge had afforded great mirth, not only to Jones and Mrs Miller, but to all who sat within hearing, who were more attentive to what he said, than to anything that passed on the stage.

He durst not go to bed all that night, for fear of the ghost; and for many nights after, sweat two or three hours before he went to sleep, with the same apprehensions, and waked several times in great horrors, crying out, 'Lord have mercy upon us! there it is.'

HENRY FIELDING, TOM JONES

🙠

Rose, the heroine of Pinero's *Trelawny of the 'Wells'*, is a successful actress, the toast of London. She becomes engaged to an aristocratic young gentleman and leaves the stage. To see if she will 'fit into society' she lives for a time with her fiancé's grandfather Sir William Gower in his Cavendish Square mansion. She feels impossibly stifled and runs back to her theatrical friends. The stricken fiancé disappears. Sir William tracks Rose down for news of his grandson and finds her downcast and dejected. Her friend Avonia Bunn explains what has gone wrong:

🙠

AVONIA. You've brought her to beggary, amongst you! You've broken her heart; and, what's worse, you've made her genteel. She can't act, since she left your mansion; she can only mope about the stage with her eyes fixed, like a person in a dream – dreaming of him, I suppose, and of what it is to be a lady.

(*SIR WILLIAM gets above table to R. of it.*)

And first she's put upon half-salary; and then, to–day, she gets the sack – (*she leans over table to him*) the entire sack, Sir Gower! So there's nothing left for her but to starve, or to make artificial flowers. Miss Trelawny I'm speaking of ! (*Crossing to ROSE, who rises and stands above basket, and embracing her.*) Our Rose! our Trelawny! (*To ROSE, breaking down.*) Excuse me for interfering, ducky. (*Retiring, in tears.*) Good day, Sir Gower.

(*She goes out, c. door. SIR WILLIAM puts stick quietly on table and stands L.C. in front of chair.*)

SIR WILLIAM (*after a pause, to Rose*). Is this – the case?
ROSE (*standing, R.C. – in a low voice*). Yes. As you have noticed, fortune has turned against me, rather.
SIR WILLIAM (*penitently*). I – I'm sorry, ma'am. I – I believe ye've kept your word to us concerning Arthur. I – I –
ROSE (*not heeding him, looking before her, dreamily*). My mother knew how fickle fortune could be to us gipsies. One of the greatest actors that ever lived warned her of that –

141

SIR WILLIAM. Miss Gower will also feel extremely – extremely –

ROSE *(as before)*. Kean once warned mother of that.

SIR WILLIAM *(in an altered tone)*. Kean? Which Kean?

ROSE. Edmund Kean. My mother acted with Edmund Kean, when she was a girl.

SIR WILLIAM *(approaching her slowly, speaking in a queer voice)*. With Kean? with Kean!

ROSE. Yes.

SIR WILLIAM *(at her side, in a whisper)*. My dear, I – *I've* seen Edmund Kean.

ROSE. Yes?

SIR WILLIAM. A young man then, I was; quite different from the man I am now – impulsive, excitable. Kean! *(Drawing a deep breath.)* Ah, he was a *splendid* gipsy!

ROSE *(looking down at the dress-basket)*. I've a little fillet in there that my mother wore as Cordelia to Kean's Lear –

SIR WILLIAM. I may have seen your mother also. I was somewhat different in those days –

ROSE *(kneeling at the basket and opening it)*. And the Order and chain, and the sword, he wore in Richard. He gave them to my father; I've always prized them.

(She drags to the surface a chain with an Order attached to it, and a sword-belt and sword – all very theatrical and tawdry – and a little gold fillet.)

(Handing him the chain.) That's the Order.

SIR WILLIAM *(handling it tenderly)*. Kean! God bless me!

ROSE *(holding up the fillet)*. My poor mother's fillet.

SIR WILLIAM *(looking at it)*. I may have seen her. *(Thoughtfully, gazing in front.)* I was a young man then. *(Looking at Rose steadily.)* Put it on, my dear.

(She looks at him inquiringly and crosses to the mirror L. and puts on the fillet.)

(Examining the Order.) Lord bless us! How he stirred me! how he –!

(He puts the chain over his shoulders. Rose turns to him.)

ROSE *(advancing to him)*. There!

SIR WILLIAM *(looking at her)*. Cordelia! Cordelia – with Kean!

ROSE *(adjusting the chain upon him)*. This should hang so. *(Returning to front of the basket and taking up the sword-belt and sword.)* Look!

SIR WILLIAM *(handling them)*. Kean! *(To her, in a whisper.)* I'll tell ye! I'll tell ye! When I saw him as Richard – I was young and a fool – *(he goes a step or two to L., then returns to her)* I'll tell ye – he almost fired me with an ambition to – to *(Fumbling with the belt.)* How did he carry this?

ROSE *(fastening the belt, with the sword, round him).* In this way – *(She gets L. of him as she does so.)*

SIR WILLIAM. Ah!

(He paces the stage, growling and muttering, and walking with a limp and one shoulder hunched. He goes down round basket, up to R.C., muttering, 'Now is the winter of our discontent,' etc. She watches him, seriously, standing L.)

(Up R., partly to himself) Ah! he was a little man too! *(Going up L., muttering, then returning to C. and drawing sword.)* I remember him, as if it were last night! I remember – *(Pausing, C., sword in hand, looking at her fixedly.)* My dear, your prospects in life have been injured by your unhappy acquaintanceship with my grandson.

ROSE *(gazing into the fire).* Poor Arthur's prospects in life – what of them?

SIR WILLIAM *(testily, flourishing sword).* Tsch, tsch, tsch!

ROSE. If I knew where he is –!

SIR WILLIAM. Miss Trelawny, if you cannot act, you cannot earn your living. *(Taps on table with point of sword.)*

ROSE. How is he earning *his* living!

SIR WILLIAM. And if you cannot earn your living, you must be provided for.

ROSE *(turning to him).* Provided for?

SIR WILLIAM *(R.C.).* Miss Gower was kind enough to bring me here in a cab. She and I will discuss plans for making provision for ye, while driving home.

ROSE *(advancing to him).* Oh, I beg you will do no such thing, Sir William.

SIR WILLIAM *(R.C.).* Hey!

ROSE. I could not accept any help from you or Miss Gower.

SIR WILLIAM. You must! You shall!

ROSE. I will not.

SIR WILLIAM *(touching the order and the sword).* Ah – ! Yes, I – I'll buy these of ye, my dear –

ROSE. Oh, no, no ! not for hundreds of pounds! Please take them off !

ARTHUR PINERO, *TRELAWNY OF THE 'WELLS'*

❧

Sir William's memory of seeing Kean act thaws his heart. He doesn't particularly try to analyse the actor's technique or describe his effects, but we know he was profoundly moved by the experience. Edward

Gordon Craig was similarly knocked out by Isadora Duncan, with two important differences: he was an analyst of the theatrical process and he was her lover.

❧

The world raved about her for several years, as it will rave – and often ignorantly – and then it forgot her. People called her a great artist – a Greek goddess – but she was no such thing. She was something quite different from anyone and anything else. I always thought how Irish she was – which means, how full of a natural genius which defies description – but she had more than that. Yet there was the tip-tilted nose and the little firm chin and the dream in her heart of the Irish who are so sweet to know. And in her eye was California, and this eye looked out over Europe and thought fairly well of what it saw.

What more she had, no one will ever describe. She was a forerunner. All she did was done with great ease – or so it seemed – this it was which gave her an appearance of power. She projected the dance into this world of ours in full belief that what she was doing was right and great. And it was. She threw away ballet skirts and ballet thoughts. She discarded shoes and stockings too. She put on some bits of stuff which when hung upon a peg looked more like torn rags than anything else; when she put them on they became transformed. Stage dresses usually transform the performers – but in her case it was these bits that became transformed by her putting them on. She transformed them into marvels of beauty, and at every step she took they spoke.

I do not exaggerate.

Some of you will have read a book on this lady, in which it is stated that the first time I saw her dance I was bereft of the artist's heart which all artists possess and which, when it is touched by beauty in anything, is greatly moved. It prompts us all to silence, to be reverent. Now that book states that after seeing this lady dance, I went to speak with her in her rooms. I did. No one else was there, and I went in and found her lying down tired after her dancing, and I sat facing her. I did not say one word. I looked at her. We shared in this silence. And some fool in a book asks the world to believe that I grew angry and said all sorts of stupid, rude things to her. No one being present but we two, the writer of that paragraph tries to assert that Isadora herself wrote it. That can only be a lie. She died before that book came out: had she seen that lie, how she would have grieved.

I shall never forget the first time I saw her come on to an empty platform to dance. Berlin – the year 1904, the month December. Not on a theatre stage was this performance given, but in a concert-hall, and you may recall what the platforms of concert-halls were like in 1904.

She came through some little curtains which were not much taller than she was herself – she came through and walked down to where a musician, his back to us, was seated at a large piano – he had just finished playing a short prelude by Chopin when in she came, and in some five or six steps was standing by the piano, quite still and, as it were, listening to the hum of the last notes ... Quite still – you might have counted five or eight, and then there sounded the voice of Chopin in a second prelude or étude – it was played through gently and came to an end – she had not moved at all. Then one step back or sideways, and the music began again as she went moving on before or after it. Only just moving – not pirouetting or doing any of those things which a Taglioni or a Fanny Elssler would have certainly done. She was speaking in her own language, not echoing any ballet master, and so she came to move as no one had ever seen anyone move before.

The dance ended, she again stood quite still. No bowing, no smiling – nothing at all. Then again the music is off, and she runs from it – it runs after her then, for she has gone ahead of it.

How is it that we know she is speaking her own language? We know it, for we see her head, her hands, gently active, as are her feet, her whole person.

And if she is speaking, what is she saying? No one would ever be able to report truly, yet no one present had a moment's doubt. Only this can we say – that she was telling to the air the very things we longed to hear and till she came we had never dreamed we should hear; and now we heard them, and this sent us all into an unusual state of joy, and I – I sat still and speechless.

I remember that when it was over I went rapidly round to her dressing-room to see her – and there too I sat still and speechless for a while. She understood my silence very well – all talk being unnecessary. No one else came to see her, so far as I remember, so far as she remembered – afar off we heard applause going on and on. She put on a cloak, shoes and we went out into the streets of Berlin where the snow looked friendly and shops were still lighted up, the Xmas trees all spangled and lighted – and we walked and talked the shops. The shops – the Xmas trees – the crowd – no one heeds us.

Later on she thought she could found a school of such dance; or she said she thought so. She had forgotten what her much-loved poet Whitman

145

had said: 'I charge you that you found no school after me … ' Cautious was that wild and lovely poet, and he often uses the word 'Caution' in his books.

Isadora caused the rash enthusiasts to imitate her – to do it well or badly – but she laboured very long to create a school – talking much for many years about it all, getting girls into a school-house and putting her sister Elizabeth to train them.

The first result of this showed well – I saw this first showing at a matinée at Kroll's Opera House in Berlin, where after dancing her own dances she called her little pupils to come with her and please the public with their little leapings and runnings. As they did – and with her leading them the whole troupe became irresistibly lovely.

I suppose some people even then and there began reasoning about it all, trying to pluck out the heart of the mystery, but I and hundreds of others who saw this first revelation did not stop to reason … for we too had all read what the poets had written of life and love and nature, and we had not reasoned then – we had read, and wept, and laughed for joy; and so was it at Kroll's Opera House that day – we all wept and laughed for joy.

And to see her shepherding her little flock, keeping them together and especially looking after one very small one of four years old, Erika was her name, I believe, was a sight no one there had ever seen before or would ever see again.

This is something she did towards forming a school – only something – just as Blake's first two verses in the *Songs of Innocence* are but something – the whole great singing follows. And as surely did the whole great dancing of Isadora follow after these first wild lovely steps. Unlike weeds, schools are things of peculiar slow growth: but in this way for ten or more years she projected *the Dance* for us to carry with us ever after in our heart's heart, Horatio.

Was it art? No, I should not call it that.

It was something which inspires those men who labour in the narrower fields of the arts, harder and more lasting. It released the minds of hundreds of such men: one had but to see her dance for one's thoughts to wing their way, as it were, with the fresh air. It rids us of all the nonsense one had been pondering so long. How's that? – she said nothing. On the contrary, she said everything that was worth hearing – and everything that everyone else but the poets had forgotten to say. Yet hers was a divine accident.

How did she do it? Ask a poet how he makes his verse – he answers:

'I made it out of a mouthful of air.'

You may find that an unpractical answer, but do you get any further if he tells you, like Baudelaire, 'I made it by always reading the dictionary'? 'Words, words, words' – it's about all the poet has to work with; so give your son a dictionary if he fancies he will write verse. But tell him, too, what Yeats said.

But do you think that by sending your girl to a ballet school you will help her to dance? You won't – you will hinder her. What must she do, then? Why, what Isadora did – learn what it is to *move*: to step, to walk, to run; few people can do these things. First the thought – then the head – then the hands and feet a little – just move, and *look around, watch all which moves*. Tell that to your daughter. For Dance comes with movement – but there are no 1st, 2nd and 3rd positions unless you are drilling for a soldier, though after all each dancer will make his 1st, 2nd and 3rd positions if he wants to – but *his own*.

How long did it take Isadora to move?

Five minutes (that is no answer, yet it is the only true one anyone can give) and then she taught herself how to move this way, that way, every way. But not according to the teaching of Noverre, or of Blasis or Petipa or any of the famous Ballet masters. This took her many years to learn. But I believe that Delsarte helped her to some extent through his book. I found a copy in her room when I was looking for a trunkful of books I had lent her. I didn't find the trunkful, so I took this one. It seems that many thousands of people in America and France studied this book by Delsarte, and yet very few of these thousands ever gleaned any secret from its pages. A word or two to a genius like Isadora is always enough, whereas 100,000 are thrown away on duffers.

What is it she lacked?

What was it she had?

She had calm –

No vanity –

No cleverness – by which I mean no clever little tricks of the trade – little or no understanding of the arts – a great comprehension of nature and perhaps overmuch ambition.

I have heard Christian Bérard say that he only saw her dance once – in 1925, when she was no longer slim – 'fat,' he said, without a shade of contempt or criticism – 'quite big – fat – but I never saw such movement in my life – a transformation took place when she began to move.'

EDWARD GORDON CRAIG, *INDEX TO THE STORY OF MY DAYS*

&

W ith a very few exceptions, filmed records of stage performances kill the very pieces they are intended to immortalize. Bernhardt appears jerky and ludicrous, Olivier's Othello seems mannered and overblown, and the circus tricks and acrobatics of Peter Brook's *A Midsummer Night's Dream* are transmuted into mere hollow trendiness. We rely on the written word for memories of theatrical performances. Many critics are a joy to read – Shaw, Agate, Tynan and Dorothy Parker, for instance – but I have decided not to include critics in this anthology. This is not out of prejudice – I just feel I would be retreading old ground and repackaging material that is readily available elsewhere. Instead, here are a couple of actors writing about their colleagues' work.

ᕦ

29 June 1964
My dear John,
    ... What a marvellous city you live in. The bars and the parties and the excitement. Everything seems colourless here by comparison. Did I tell you that I went to see *Othello* at the National? – Maggie [Smith] got me two seats and I was v. curious to see what she did with Desdemona and I am here to tell you that it is quite stunning. It must be the best Desdemona in the history of the English theatre. She has increased in stature so much, she astonished me. The performance is superb vocally and physically. Not one of her gestures comes from the elbow; when an arm is raised, it is raised totally, and with an authority that is classic. The costumes are wonderfully authentic, and richly Venetian; when she appears, with yards and yards of heavy silk brocade trailing behind her, and that magnificent red hair braided, she walks downstage for the first part of the speech and then turns in a great sweeping movement, so every fold in the umber and gold material undulates under the lights; the rest of the court are in those heavy long velvets, and the entrance of Olivier in a simple white linen tunic is in perfect juxtaposition. He gives a performance of soaring grandeur. He goes from simple dignity and gentleness into vexation and terrible anger, and then – heartrending despair. I think it will be a milestone in my theatre going. The performance stayed with me for days afterwards. I wrote him a fan letter. I told him that twentieth century spontaneity was out of place: that one needed eighteenth century precision and formality to convey one's thanks. He is a giant, John, really, and I think he is the last of a breed that is almost extinct in this country. Who else has got this hugeness in all the senses? – this fantastic generosity of spirit that comes pouring over the footlights and envelops you – and encompasses you in a world where the

artist's vision is complete, and leaves you richer for seeing him. I would work for him ANY day. I can tell you that. The rest of the company does not match these two. The Iago of Frank Finlay is simply too ordinary for poetic drama. He is hewn out of OUR world, not the world of poetic drama. He splits the speeches into 'points' which make a kind of sense, but the sense is one of prosody. You are never swept into the iambic pentameter, and it is strangely worthy and dull.

Last weekend there were eight shows closed in the London theatre. Audiences are dwindling to the merest trickle. The Phoenix had eleven people out front on Saturday night, and Eli Wallach at the Globe had five for one matinee. It is all so frightening that the London Theatre Managers have appealed to the owners to reduce the theatre rents. I predict the closing of a lot of theatres. Soon there will only be a coterie audience for the serious play – and theatres will house only musicals and light stuff.

love,

[K]

KENNETH WILLIAMS, *LETTER TO NOEL WILLMAN*

❧

The rehearsal room at the Vic – too hot in summer and too cold in winter – has witnessed some remarkable scenes. Unlike so many rehearsal rooms, it seems to take on the character of the actors who are at work in it.

During the rehearsals of *As You Like It*, its walls resounded to the cascade of merriment which was Edith Evans's voice. Her voice was very particular to her. She had studied with Elsie Fogerty, the great teacher-healer. (Much could be written of Fogerty's ability to divine the source of an actor's problems. Once, when in trouble with a part, Edith went to Fogerty, who said, 'Well, of course you can't act it in those shoes.' 'So,' said Edith, 'I took them off and that was all there was to it. I had no more trouble after that.')

Each day she had lunch in her dressing-room. She was dieting to reduce her weight. She was a sturdily-built woman, and now she needed to do what she had done so successfully as Millamant in *The Way of the World*, when she is reputed to have said to some admirer, 'I just say to myself, "You are the most beautiful woman in London"' – and so, for the nonce, she was. Unkind critics, not the professional ones, would remark that the three best actresses in London were 'Bosseye', 'Popeye', and 'Dropeye'. 'Dropeye', of course, referred to Edith, whose drooping eyelid can be seen in Sickert's portrait of her. She didn't follow fashion. The works of Schiaparelli and company had no allure for her. At first glance, indeed, one could describe her manner of dressing truthfully, if not charitably, as dowdy. And now that she was forty-eight, even her most devoted admirers feared that she had left it too late to play Rosalind again.

The Country Wife had been as big a success as it promised to be, and was still playing to packed houses. The advance bookings for *As You Like It* seemed, by comparison, thin. Even some of Edith's closest friends had not booked seats for the first night.

None of these perilous thoughts seemed to touch her. Only in the first scenes were her fears evident. As Rosalind the girl, she was less than persuasive. But when she changed into a boy her whole being seemed transformed. It was not that she looked in the least like a boy. The Watteau style which the designer had imposed upon the play was most unbecoming to her. But nothing mattered except her spell – even when, once, she 'dried'. She simply laughed, in the most assured way, and one could have sworn that the word that eluded her mattered far less than the music of her laughter. She waltzed across to the prompt corner, took her prompt, and waltzed back, laughing.

I had fallen under this spell when we were half-way through rehearsals. We had worked together all morning. When we came to the exit in Act Three – 'Will you go?' says Rosalind. 'With all my heart, good youth,' says Orlando. 'Nay, you must call me Rosalind' – at this point, when we were sitting close to each other on the ground, I leant forwards and, taking her in my arms, kissed her.

For several days Edith made no reference to the incident in the rehearsal room. Then, one morning, during a break, she asked me to have dinner with her at the Café Royal, a place which still offered an atmosphere of bohemianism.

'Tell me,' she said that night, 'why did you kiss me?'

I tried to shrug it off with a laugh. 'Because I wanted to. Did you mind?'

'That makes me feel quite sick.'

I felt like a man who goes out to paddle at the water's edge, and finds himself up to his neck in deep waters. We were silent for several moments. 'Is that a new hat?'

'Yes.' She smiled. 'Do you like it?'

I realized that I was completely out of my depth. Still I floundered on. 'You have a farm? Where is it?'

She told me about the farm. Thirteenth century. Moated. Guy's pride and joy. 'You must come down and see it one weekend. What about next weekend?'

'I'd love to.'

She had surprised me again by referring to her husband. I had no idea she had been married. Very few people knew of her marriage to George (Guy) Booth, a childhood friend, who had died tragically the year before.

The following day at rehearsal I asked her, 'Would you care to try the Café Royal again?'

'I was hoping you'd say that. Why not come to my flat? What do you like to eat?'

'Scrambled eggs would be very nice.'

That night after the show we went to her flat in West Halkin Street. 'There's something I wanted to show you.'

On the mantelpiece was a photograph of Guy pruning an apple tree.

'You see, I was in New York when he died. Playing the nurse in *Romeo* with Kit Cornell. I knew nothing of his illness until after his death. But it's there, do you see? There's death in that face.'

She asked me about my family – Mother, Andy, Peggy. She was particularly interested in my Portsmouth relations. I asked her about her Welsh origins.

'I'm not really,' she said. 'Not *really* Welsh. I just let them think that because of the name.'

'I do hope that you have no notion whatever of living your life without me,' she wrote. 'You simply couldn't do it. We have such beautiful things in common. Oh – so very common. Rice pudding on the hearth rug and coats over the back of the chair. Darling, please don't alter. I love you shamelessly.'

What with rehearsals of *As You Like It* by day and performances of *The Country Wife* at night, we hoped to conceal major indiscretions with a host of minor fibs and prevarications. When, in response to her invitation that night at the Café Royal, I went to stay for the weekend at her farm in Biddenden, Alec Guinness accompanied us. A photo, taken by her chauffeur, shows Guinness, a very young man, with a few sparse curls still lingering on his crown, arm in arm with Edith on her left hand; I, windblown, laughing, a head taller than my companions, arm in arm on Edith's right; and Edith, between us, her slacks tucked into woollen socks, like a land-girl, is smiling triumphantly as if saying, 'Aha! Look what I've got!'

That evening, after our walk on the Romney Marshes, Edith asked us both, 'What is your idea of a theatre?' Alec, answering first, talked gently but cogently about a company, like the Moscow Arts Theatre, working together, developing its own repertoire and style. And I answered in similar terms.

Both of us had been inspired by the theatre of Jacques Copeau and La Compagnie des Quinze. A theatre without stars. 'But what,' asked Edith, 'would there be for me in such a theatre?'

I fell head over heels in love with Edith, and she with me. She had chosen me, a young actor floundering helplessly in his first leading role, to play Orlando to her Rosalind.

Esmé Church, our producer, was of the 'Yes, dear, that'll be lovely, let's do it again' school. I cannot for the life of me recall a single note she gave me during our four weeks' rehearsal, or whether she gave me a note at all. Nor do I think it mattered. I can think of one prescription only for any young actor who is to play Orlando: fall in love with your Rosalind. And if that should fail? Try again ...

'Isn't love extraordinary,' [Edith] wrote, 'the way it releases energy?' It was so, for her. She took up riding and then, having been chauffeured for years, learned to drive and passed her test. And her dress, very ordinary and everyday before, became distinctly smart and fashionable.

Though I never learned to ride nor to drive – I had given over driving to Rachel ever since our honeymoon. – I nevertheless felt immeasurably strengthened by Edith's love. She had accepted me at a very early, critical stage in my career. One day, at the start of rehearsals for *As You Like It*, she had asked me, 'What do you want in the theatre? Everyone knows what Larry stands for, and what Peggy and John and I stand for. But what sort of an actor do you want to be?' Suddenly I realized that she was suggesting that I might, if I chose, and applied myself, and put thought and passion into it, find my place in such company. It took my breath away.

Her remarks about my acting, and acting in general, were brief, but illuminating. 'I am told you are going to be most excellent as Sir Andrew. (It was the summer of 1938 and I was rehearsing in Michel Saint-Denis's production of *Twelfth Night* at the Phoenix.) 'It doesn't surprise me. I saw all the seeds of your acting when we were so much together. A look here, a look there, told me all I wanted. I just knew that you required stability of character to hold your talents in place.' Written in pencil, these last words are scored in so heavily as almost to break the pencil lead. 'If you want things enough, you can't compromise. To like them enough you must have passion. If you want to be first-class you must grow in loving and passion.'

Years later, in America, I gave an interview to Lillian Ross of *The New Yorker*, in which I spoke about Edith. It conveys, I think, the absence of our relationship:

For me, Edith Evans has the authentic magic. Claptrap word though 'magic' may be, it's the only word for the stage. When she comes onstage, the stage lights up. She's a very strict person about her own profession and is without any of the nonsense. She's a real and dedicated artist. Her art is her life. Everything she does on the stage is interpreted through her own morality. It's the way Picasso paints. It's the way Beethoven composed. It's the thing the great artist has that makes him different from other people. I don't mean morality in a pettifogging way. I mean moral values, without which nothing is achieved, and nothing created. Part of it is caring enough about what you do to achieve something beyond the mundane.

Acting with Edith Evans was heaven. It was like being in your mother's arms, like knowing how to swim, like riding a bicycle. You're safe. The late Michael Chekhov said once that there were three ways to act: for yourself, for the audience, and to your partner. Some of the newer theorists say that if it's true for yourself, it's truthful, which is not so. The majority of actors act for themselves or for the audience. I believe that the only way to act is to your partner. As a partner Edith Evans was like a great conductor who allows a soloist as much latitude as is needed, but always keeps everything strict. It's strict but free. Never is anything too set, too rigid. The stage relationship always leaves enough room to improvise. For the first time in my life, acting in *As You Like It*, I felt completely unselfconscious. Acting with her made me feel, oh, it's so easy. You don't start acting, she told me, until you stop *trying* to act. It doesn't leave the ground until you don't have to think about it. The play and our stage relationship in it always had the same shape. It was entirely well-proportioned and yet, in many respects, it was all fluid. In the forest scenes between Orlando and Rosalind, she would encourage me to do almost anything that came into my head. Yet, if I had done anything excessive she would have stopped it by the simplest means. Somehow it didn't occur to me to do anything excessive. For the first time, onstage or off, I felt completely free.

After *As You Like It*, we saw each other only infrequently. It was Edith who ended it. Rachel and I, for what reason I forget, had had an argument and I, in a fit of temper, stayed out all night. Rachel rang Edith in desperation. She came round immediately and spent the night with Rachel, comforting her. Days later she wrote me a letter of farewell. She was incapable of jealousy and hated deception. And she was very fond of

Rachel. She would always write, at the end of her letters, 'My love to your two ladies.'

MICHAEL REDGRAVE, *IN MY MIND'S EYE*

❧

Michael Redgrave's other lady, of course, was his daughter Vanessa, who went on to be the critically acclaimed Rosalind of her generation. She writes here of the experience, and particularly of the first night.

❧

It was spring 1961. I had my own flat now, off Gloucester Road, on the ground floor with a door that led down some iron steps into a communal garden. The telephone rang and Peter Hall asked me to come to Stratford to play Rosalind in *As You Like It*. Over the next weeks I studied and learned all my lines. I tramped along the soggy, springing paths in the woods around Wilks Water, the cottage in Hampshire given to my mother by Cousin Lucy, thinking over the play. Denne Gilkes had made the Studio at 18, The High Street, Stratford available for me again. Before going up for rehearsals I listened to an old recording of Dame Edith Evans and Michael playing one of the love scenes from *As You Like It*. Rosalind has long, incredibly quick-thinking, quick-witted speeches. Like a driver about to set off on a complicated cross-country drive to an unknown destination, I needed a really good map. Dame Edith, one might say, had recorded an Ordnance Survey of the Forest of Arden, if only for one scene. Her tempo, her phrasing, her through line on the dialogue, were superb. I copied everything I could, and committed it to memory. Next, I read every piece of Elizabethan prose I could lay my hands on, including the short stories of the time, particularly the story of Dick Whittington. I have never dared tell a journalist that I prepared for Shakespeare's *As You Like It* by reading 'Dick Whittington', but that is exactly what I did. The prose, which was the nearest window into the actual vocabulary and style of speaking in everyday life in the late sixteenth century made it possible for me to understand how a lively, interesting man or woman might talk.

Michael Elliott, our director, took me to lunch on the day of the first night. We had rehearsed for six weeks. I was nervous and keyed up, anxious about the first night, but looking forward to it. Michael was looking at me with the same grave eyes as my father. I thought he was going to thank me for my hard work, offer me words of encouragement. What he said shocked me.

'Vanessa, the whole production is going to be a failure. You won't give yourself up to the play and to what is happening. You are refusing to give *yourself* over, you are holding back. You've held back all though rehearsals, and if you don't go on stage tonight and give *all* of yourself to the play, the actors and the audience, we will have failed totally.'

The grilled plaice turned to sticky cotton wool in my mouth. My jaws continued to munch, but the saliva had stopped totally and I couldn't swallow, I was terrified. Then he said: 'That's all I have to say: if you can't do that there's no meaning to the play.'

John Barton, Peter Hall's co-director, gave me one of his notorious massages. It hurt horribly as I was so tense, his fingers were like steel rods punching away at my shoulders, back and neck. My mind was racing. I wanted to run after Michael and say 'Why now? Why do you tell me all this now, after six weeks?' But I couldn't. I respected Michael and trusted his direction of the play absolutely. Rosalind, which is one of the longest and most complex of Shakespeare's parts for an actress, longer than Cleopatra, had been making me more nervous than I realized. I was cautiously trying to control my performance, to get it right. With Michael's words burnt into my brain I realized that I had absolutely nothing to lose and everything to gain by going with the immediacy of the moment and the audience. It goes back to Jani Strasser's advice – if you keep controlling your poodles they can do so much and no more, you've got to let them off the leash. This isn't something you can suddenly do unless somebody gives you a very big jolt as Michael did. I dressed, went down to the wings, and took a leap into the unknown. All mental control and calculation vanished, all precautions, *how* I do this, *how* I say that. I threw myself into the moment of Rosalind's life, into Orlando's eyes, into the Forest of Arden. Around the giant oak in the dapple-shadowed clearing we danced in a chain, four men and four women, celebrating their love for each other. With *As You Like It* I rediscovered on a new level and in a different way the same sheer enjoyment and living of my parts that I'd felt in *A Touch of the Sun*, and that alertness and immediacy has stayed with me in my acting to this day.

I doubt whether any other director would have had the courage, or the wisdom, to speak to me as he did only hours before the first performance. Only a director who had won the total confidence of his actors could have said such things, and only a man who cared so deeply about his work would have dared to take such a risk. There are people who will be important to work with throughout a career but if, as I did with Michael, you are

lucky enough to work with them at a very important moment of development it will prove decisive. Michael was the same person with everybody,
he loved his work and respected the theatre. He saw so much in *As You
Like It*, and combined a complete conviction and thoughtfulness in trying
to bring out what he saw in the play that I found absolutely inspiring. He
was very direct but when he gave advice or encouragement I trusted it
completely which is very rare. Working with him so early in my professional life, and on a classic was crucial, and I certainly could not have
played the part as I did without him. A great Italian actress once said to me
about the director who found her and cast her in three of his films: 'He is
my husband, my lover, my father, my son, and my brother.' I felt that way
about Michael Elliott, with whom I worked three times. He changed my
life.

Ian Bannen played Orlando, and I was, as every Rosalind becomes with
her Orlando, in love with him. *As You Like It* was praised beyond praise.
Michael Elliott's production struck a deep, responsive chord with audiences
and critics, for there was not a shadow of cynicism in it, and that was
already rare among directors of his generation. The word was that 'upstairs'
in the offices of the administration the production was thought too sentimental. It was not in the least sentimental. Michael had understood the
essence of the play. The dream of Orlando's older brother, which changes
him, is the allegorical form of the story for all the characters, who discover
their essential, true human nature, at odds with the inhuman world of the
Court and Frederick, the usurper.

VANESSA REDGRAVE, *VANESSA REDGRAVE*

To complete an *As You Like It* trilogy, here is another wonderful
Rosalind, Juliet Stevenson, discussing the process of finding out
about the character. This comes from Carol Rutter's book of interviews
with contemporary Shakespearean actresses, *Clamorous Voices*. The itali-
cized passages are Rutter's commentary.

*Finally, having dispatched everyone else's love affairs, Rosalind gets back to her own.
Orlando at last appears in IV, i and she lambasts him.*

The teacher has been waiting for her pupil to show up: Ganymede is supposed to be giving a wooing lesson. But the woman in love has been
waiting too, and that woman is very vulnerable, very exposed. Rosalind,
unlike the audience, doesn't know the end of the play. Orlando may never

show up! By now she's spent most of the play talking to other people. there's the scariness of having slipped herself into love with someone, and, having tumbled, it can be terrifying.

And yet, fortunately, she has this structure, this Ganymede, to make it possible to deal with the chaos of feeling that's overwhelming her. Ganymede affords her the control that might otherwise be beyond her. That is not to say that the 'man' Rosalind can control things, the 'woman' can't. Because it's always only Rosalind. It's just that the disguise, and the perceived role imposed upon her by the disguise, force her to detach just sufficiently to be able to free the mind from the trammels of the heart. What she's experiencing emotionally is very real, but she's channelling it, through role-play, into something controllable. And that way she doesn't expose too much. She doesn't do too much damage. She can quickly and lightly restore the scene to harmony. And she can use this structure to explore Orlando's response.

I'll tell you what it's like: it's like acting. You go on stage and you're two people: you are yourself, the actress, but you are also a character; you are bound by the dictates of playing somebody else within a fiction, a piece of make-believe. So you may be feeling all manner of things about what a fellow actor is doing, but you don't have the means in the fiction to express that. What you do have at your disposal, as the actress, is a variety of choices by which you can make those feelings manifest, without destroying the fiction.

What is wonderful about the beginning of the wooing scene is the scale of the chastisement. The scale of her thought is always commensurate with the rhythms of her language. And it's very funny. Because it's a completely over-the-top reaction. I don't think Orlando had a clue. I think he thought it was going to be really charming, wooing games under cherry blossoms, and what does he get? The biggest roasting of his life! Rosalind rails at him, tears him to shreds, rages. She will not let him off the hook. She's a love guerrilla!

> Break an hour's promise in love? He that will divide a minute into a
> thousand parts, and break but a part of the thousandth part of a
> minute in the affairs of love, it may be said of him that Cupid hath
> clapped him o'th'shoulder, but I'll warrant him heart-whole.

It has the protection and qualification of role-play, but it isn't a spoof. Rosalind isn't burlesquing some archetype of female behaviour in love, she's not sending up the idea that women in love are volatile, difficult. Women *are* volatile in love – whether we approve of it or not, we are. She is allowing him to see the complexity, the perversity, the contradictions he will find inherent in female nature. The object is not to expose those contradictions so he can avoid them or get rid of them, it's so he can take them on board, because they are inevitably going to be there. Those contradictions are going to be a part of his future.

What is also glorious is that this is the scene when Rosalind is able to play Rosalind, because now the conceit is in place, that she will play a woman. So for the first time since she put the trousers on Rosalind can directly use her own responses. She doesn't have to conceal them because she has the role-play as a framework inside which she can be herself. And she's there with this person she's madly in love with, basking in mutual discovery, but always having a safety catch on the door.

They give each other such energy in the scene. And they go on such a long journey together. She discovers as she goes along, as she tests him, as she explores his reactions again and again, that the lettering goes all the way through the rock: Orlando is the real thing.

But she is also discovering and testing herself. She isn't a know-all; if she becomes knowing, she becomes closed. I don't think she *knows* any more about love than Orlando does. But, being a woman, her relationship to it is different. Perhaps because she knows what it costs. It can cost women their lives. And for some reason she has that knowledge: she knows that right from the start of the play. The stakes are often higher for women. But the reality of loving is as new for her as for him – it's just that because she plays the role of teacher, she has to articulate the discoveries.

The centre of Rosalind's instruction is surely this: Orlando, ready to die for love, should 'die by attorney', since in all six thousand years of the world's history no man has 'died in his own person, videlicet, in a love cause': 'men have died from time to time, and worms have eaten them, but not for love.' Juliet's director thought the line should be played sorrowfully, a mournful reflection that romantic love is merely a posture. But Juliet couldn't agree.

It was one of those examples when you find in a rehearsal room that the male and female experience of loving are in some ways different. It was difficult to compromise. Either I played it Adrian's way, against what I felt to be my own experience, or I played it my way and denied him his interpretation, his experience. In the end I chose my own interpretation. Rosalind isn't *regretting* that romanticism doesn't exist; she is debunking the whole myth of romanticism, and saying, 'These romantic myths persist, but they are lies.' She's being iconoclastic again.

That scene with Phebe shows what happens when you put women on a pedestal. It can't be in any woman's interest to be the object of idealized love, because the same instinct that elevates her this week may well dump her in the gutter next week. Contrary to all those conventions in pulp romance magazines, it is often men, not women, who are the conservers of romantic idealism, and who then re-write history to authorize these distorted perceptions.

It's so modern, it's what the feminist movement has been doing for the past twenty odd years, taking sacredly held myths and beginning to prise them open. And 'open' is the operative word, because Rosalind's iconoclasm isn't destructive, she isn't just wantonly smashing Orlando's illusions, she's breaking through a carapace of expectation and prejudgement to liberate the woman – warts and all. Rosalind is telling Orlando that it is of no use to women if men do not see the warts. Women have to be allowed their fallibility, their flaws, their human-ness; and that's a process of opening up, for both men and women.

(What Rosalind has to say is also very funny. Troilus didn't die for Cressida, he had 'his brains dashed out with a Grecian club'; Leander didn't die for Hero, he was 'taken with a cramp and drowned'. Her revisionist obituaries are so deeply unglamorous!)

Orlando is attentive to this astonishing lesson, yet Juliet thinks his appalled response teaches Rosalind something:

Rosalind is at her most acerbic, her most percipient, her wittiest in these exchanges, but Orlando's reaction, 'I would not have my right Rosalind of this mind, for I protest her frown might kill me,' utterly disarms her. Orlando somehow doesn't seem to have absorbed the content of her speech quite yet. But she doesn't reject him. She replies with one of the tenderest lines of the play, which isn't repealing her former statement but is making space for something quite different from that witty alienation. She says, 'By this hand, it will not kill a fly.' Love breathes through those open vowels! It's so wonderfully gentle.

JULIET STEVENSON IN CAROL RUTTER (ED.), *CLAMOROUS VOICES*

☙

A hundred years earlier, Ellen Terry jotted this down in her copy of *Romeo and Juliet*. There does not seem that wide a gulf between the Victorian and the new Elizabethan actresses.

☙

Get the words into your remembrance first of all. Then, (as you have to convey the meaning of the words to *some* who have ears, but don't hear, and eyes, but don't see) put the words into the simplest vernacular. Then exercise your judgment about their sound.

So many different ways of speaking words! Beware of sound and fury signifying nothing. Voice unaccompanied by imagination, dreadful. Pomposity, rotundity.

Imagination and intelligence absolutely necessary to realize and portray high and low imaginings. Voice, yes, but not mere voice production. You must have a sensitive ear, and a sensitive judgment of the effect on your audience. But all the time you must be trying to please *yourself*.

Get yourself into *tune*. Then you can let fly your imagination, and the words will seem to be supplied by yourself. Shakespeare supplied by one-self! Oh!

Realism? Yes, if we mean by that real feeling, real sympathy. But people seem to mean by it only the realism of low-down songs.

To act, you must make the thing written your own. You must steal the words, steal the thought, and *convey* the stolen treasure to others with great art.

ELLEN TERRY, *MEMO*

Another two actresses now, also a century apart, each talking about a successful performance. Eleonora Duse, Bernhardt's great rival and by all accounts a profoundly moving tragedienne, and Fiona Shaw, whose devastating performance of naked grief in *Electra* will stay for a long time with anyone who saw it.

I have read certain letters ... or studies on our Art that ... shall I tell you. They brought back my blissful childhood: the time cranky Grandpa gave me the beautiful Pulcinella with the movable arms and legs and the laugh-ing, shrivelled up face that we – restless children that we were – had to break, in order to find out how he was put together. Is it of Art that you wanted me to speak to you? It seems to me that it is ... unless the successes of Rome have beclouded my brain ... it seems to me that it is. And does it seem to you that it is possible to speak of Art? It would be the same as explaining love! Along that Way of the Cross we all have travelled; we all have talked about it, but absolutely no one has defined it *completely*. One loves, or is an artist, according to one's ability. Precepts, customs, conven-tions, are worthless, especially in art. The ways of love and of art are equally various. There is the love that ennobles and leads to goodness, and

there is the love that obliterates all will, all strength, all intelligent channelling. This, as far as I am concerned, is the more true, but there is no
doubt that it is fatal.

It is that way in Art … which sometimes reveals itself as the *expression*
and *expansion* of a soul, with the result that it soars to such heights that it is
imprinted with feeling and passion.

He who claims to teach Art understands nothing whatsoever about it.

And since you will lose your way if you keep following me down all
these strange passageways, I shall be brief and begin speaking with you by
way of a bit of reportage.

Without posing (because it is important to me that you know I am no
poser; I am not yet at that stage of imbecility), I tell you that I never dared
hope for a season as successful as this one in Rome has been. It all fills me
with a happiness and an optimism that – to put it mildly – do me so much
good! And should someone tell you that success ruins the artist, you must
respond with a firm contradiction. Success is without doubt a tonic, and it
is success that provides the enthusiasm indispensable to the continuance of
the daily struggle, that burden of years and years of toil required to achieve
repose, the repose that lives on memories.

As for me, when that time arrives, and my youth is passed, and I must
write *fine* beneath all my successes, both the ones I achieved and the ones I
only hoped for, I shall retire from my career in silence, and with a strong
and sweet conviction I shall know: that it was in Art – both the inward
thought and the outward expression – in Art that I placed all my soul. It
shall be a compensation …

Act? What a nasty word! If acting were all there was to it; I feel that I have
never known nor *shall I ever know how to act!* Those poor women in my plays
have entered so totally into my heart and head, that while I am striving as
best I can to make the audience understand them, I almost feel like comforting them … but it is they who, little by little, end up by comforting
me!

How – and why, and at what point – this affectionate, inexplicable, and
undeniable 'exchange' takes place between those women and me … it
would take too long and be too difficult to relate precisely. The fact
remains that, while everybody else is suspicious of the women, I get along
beautifully with them! I pay no attention if they have lied, if they have
betrayed, if they have sinned, if they were born crooked, as long as I feel
that they have wept, that they have suffered as a result of lying or betraying
or loving … I put myself with them, and I ransack their emotions not out

of any mania for suffering, but because the *communal lamentation* among women is greater and more detailed, is sweeter and more complete, than that which is granted to them by men.

ELEONORA DUSE IN ACTORS ON ACTING

🥀

There's a wonderful bit at the end of *Antony and Cleopatra* – my favourite line in all of Shakespeare really – when Cleopatra dies, and the soldier comes in, some little thug from Italy, and says to Charmian: 'Charmian, is this well done?' and she says, 'It is well done and fitting for a princess descended of so many royal kings. Ah, soldier!' It feels like the tide goes out all over the world for me when I hear that, 'Ah, soldier'. The combination of those two words says everything Charmian can't even begin to say, and the air in the silent half of the sentence opens a crack in the imagination of the hearer for history and sorrow to fill.

That's why I loved doing *Electra*. I found it very moving to start with someone who's been twelve years grieving. On top of this state is a very precise argument. Her world is so reduced, a bit like Beckett's. There is only one subject. She hasn't gone to university or lived at all. She has only gone in ever shrinking circles. At the moment at which life is so unbearable, it should go into song or opera and it doesn't quite. The emotion ferments and explodes finally, perversely, without any kind of catharsis.

I don't think we could have played it with more intensity or more precisely. There's very little room to manoeuvre, you're just hanging on to the thought on top of this grief. Deborah Warner nearly conducted it, really. It was very hard because it was taking the pinnacle of what you can do with Shakespeare, which is distilling the notion that thought and feeling are the same thing. And there was no relief. I used to dread it as though it was bad for me. I'd stand in a darkened shower, just before the performance, getting ready for the onslaught. But I got to like Electra tremendously. You have to go with her, why she feels so strongly about things – not judge her.

I saw a clip of *Electra* on television. There's a bit where she was throwing herself down on to the circle and so I stopped the machine to see what happened when the body just fell. I was very entertained by it but I felt it was somebody else completely which reminded me that if you take yourself too seriously, you're lost.

Very few actors really feel the emotions. We perceive things at about six different levels at one time. I can be playing Electra and knowing that I'm down on this little bit there even whilst doing it. You're lifting things and adjusting, whilst absolutely being in it at the same time. That's how self-conscious we are as people.

Every now and then though, actors play a part that really says something about who they are. I went into acting because of comedy so I was very surprised that Electra seemed to be the thing that was much nearer who *I* was when I played it.

I always told myself I could do tragedy. That's why I didn't have any interest in doing it, because, I thought, 'I know what it is; it's about being very upset, making yourself very unhappy'. Comedy interested me much more. But, of course, I'm avoiding something.

I think tragedy is expensive. After the *Electra* run, I was in a terrible state for many months, utterly worn out. I went walking in Greece to try and recover. I didn't realize it was going to be like that. I was very depressed and upset, like going to the moon – it's very hard to know what has meaning afterwards.

What interested me about the whole experience was that this play, after 2,000 years, got an audience to grieve in some way in a country that has lost almost all ritual of grief.

Literature, I think, is humanity's dialogue with itself and an actor is the interpreter of the text of the *writer*, who is tapping the soul of who we all are. The best one does is to give it expression – the key being one's own grief that reveals a very dark pool of basic grief that everybody has. The actor allows it out specifically in the moment. In the end, I suspect, that dark pool is a very similar pool to everybody else's pool.

FIONA SHAW IN CAROLE WOODIS (ED.), *SHEER BLOODY MAGIC*

ક

A great performance can and should cause a thrill of absolute recognition in each member of the audience. Sometimes this feeling is so intense that we feel we know the actor or actress personally. In extreme cases this can lead to obsession, even to love. In Oscar Wilde's novel *The Picture of Dorian Gray* the Faustian hero with the famous secret falls completely in love with an unknown actress. Here, he is telling his friend, Lord Henry Wotton, about his chance visit to the theatre.

ક

'I went in and paid a whole guinea for a stage-box. To the present day I can't make out why I did so; and yet if I hadn't I should have missed the greatest romance of my life. I see you are laughing. It is horrid of you!'

'I am not laughing, Dorian; ... But you should not say the greatest romance of your life. You should say the first romance of your life. You will always be loved, and you will always be in love with love. A *grande passion* is the privilege of people who have nothing to do. That is the one use of the idle classes of a country. Don't be afraid. There are exquisite things in store for you. This is merely the beginning.'

'Do you think my nature so shallow?' cried Dorian Gray, angrily.

'No; I think your nature so deep.'

'How do you mean?'

'My dear boy, the people who love only once in their lives are really the shallow people. What they call their loyalty, and their fidelity, I call either the lethargy of custom or their lack of imagination. Faithfulness is to the emotional life what consistency is to the life of the intellect – simply a confession of failures. Faithfulness! I must analyse it some day. The passion for property is in it. There are many things that we would throw away if we were not afraid that others might pick them up. But I don't want to interrupt you. Go on with your story.'

'Well, I found myself seated in a horrid little private box, with a vulgar drop-scene staring me in the face. I looked out from behind the curtain, and surveyed the house. It was a tawdry affair, all Cupids and cornucopias, like a third-rate wedding cake. The gallery and pit were fairly full, but the two rows of dingy stalls were quite empty, and there was hardly a person in what I suppose they called the dress-circle. Women went about with oranges and ginger-beer, and there was a terrible consumption of nuts going on.'

'It must have been just like the palmy days of the British Drama.'

'Just like, I should fancy, and very depressing. I began to wonder what on earth I should do, when I caught sight of the play-bill. What do you think the play was, Harry?'

'I should think "The Idiot Boy, or Dumb but Innocent". Our fathers used to like that sort of piece, I believe. The longer I live, Dorian, the more keenly I feel that whatever was good enough for our fathers is not good enough for us. In art, as in politics, *les grand-pères ont toujours tort.*'

'This play was good enough for us, Harry. It was "Romeo and Juliet". I must admit that I was rather annoyed at the idea of seeing Shakespeare done in such a wretched hole of a place. Still, I felt interested, in a sort of way. At any rate, I determined to wait for the first act. There was a dreadful orchestra, presided over by a young Hebrew who sat at a cracked piano, that nearly drove me away, but at last the drop-scene was drawn up, and the play began. Romeo was a stout elderly gentleman, with corked eyebrows, a husky tragedy voice, and a figure like a beer-barrel. Mercutio was almost as bad. He was played by the low-comedian, who had introduced gags of his own and was on most friendly terms with the pit. They were both as grotesque as the scenery, and that looked as if it had come out of a country-booth. But Juliet! Harry, imagine a girl, hardly seventeen years of age, with a little flower-like face, a small Greek head with plaited coils of dark-brown hair, eyes that were violet wells of passion, lips that were like the petals of a rose. She was the loveliest thing I had ever seen in my life. You said to me once that pathos left you unmoved, but that beauty, mere beauty, could fill your eyes with tears. I tell you, Harry, I could hardly see this girl for the mist of tears that came across me. And her voice – I never heard such a voice. It was very low at first, with deep mellow notes, that seemed to fall singly upon one's ear. Then it became a little louder, and sounded like a flute or a distant hautbois. In the garden-scene it had all the tremulous ecstasy that one hears just before dawn when nightingales are singing. There were moments, later on, when it had the wild passion of violins. You know how a voice can stir one. Your voice and the voice of Sibyl Vane are two things that I shall never forget. When I close my eyes, I hear them, and each of them says something different. I don't know which to follow. Why should I not love her? Harry, I do love her. She is everything to me in life. Night after night I go to see her play. One evening she is Rosalind, and the next evening she is Imogen. I have seen her die in the gloom of an Italian tomb, sucking the poison from her lover's lips. I have watched her wandering through the forest of Arden, disguised as a pretty boy in hose and doublet and dainty cap. She has been mad, and has come into the presence of a guilty king, and given him rue to wear, and bitter herbs to taste of. She has been innocent, and the black hands of jealousy have crushed her reed-like throat. I have seen her in every age and in every costume. Ordinary women never appeal to one's imagination. They are limited to their century. No glamour ever transfigures them. One knows their minds as easily as one knows their bonnets. One can always find them. There is no mystery in any of them. They ride in the Park in the morning, and chatter at tea-parties in the afternoon. They have their stereotyped smile, and their fashionable manner. They are quite obvious. But an actress! How different an actress is! Harry! why didn't you tell me that the only thing worth loving is an actress?'

'Because I have loved so many of them, Dorian.'

'Oh, yes, horrid people with dyed hair and painted faces.'

'Don't run down dyed hair and painted faces. There is an extraordinary charm in them, sometimes,' said Lord Henry.

'I wish now I had not told you about Sibyl Vane.'

'You could not have helped telling me, Dorian. All through your life you will tell me everything you do.'

'Yes, Harry, I believe that is true. I cannot help telling you things. You have a curious influence over me. If I ever did a crime, I would come and confess it to you. You would understand me.'

'People like you – the wilful sunbeams of life – don't commit crimes, Dorian. But I am much obliged for the compliment, all the same. And now tell me – reach me the matches, like a good boy: thanks – what are your actual relations with Sibyl Vane?'

Dorian Gray leaped to his feet, with flushed cheeks and burning eyes. 'Harry! Sibyl Vane is sacred!'

'It is only the sacred things that are worth touching, Dorian,' said Lord Henry, with a strange touch of pathos in his voice. 'But why should you be annoyed? I suppose she will belong to you some day. When one is in love, one always begins by deceiving one's self, and one always ends by deceiving others. That is what the world calls a romance.'

OSCAR WILDE, *THE PICTURE OF DORIAN GRAY*

CHAPTER 8
FAILURE

Dorian Gray meets Sibyl Vane and she falls in love with him. Alas for her, having a real emotion in her heart renders her joyfully incapable of acting. God knows what a psychiatrist (or an actress, come to that) would make of such a transformation, but Wilde's description of Sibyl's failure is nonetheless extraordinary. Dorian has brought Sir Henry and Basil Hallward, his painter friend, to see Sibyl play Juliet.

৯

The heat was terribly oppressive, and the huge sunlight flamed like a monstrous dahlia with petals of yellow fire. The youths in the gallery had taken off their coats and waistcoats and hung them over the side. They talked to each other across the theatre, and shared their oranges with the tawdry girls who sat beside them. Some women were laughing in the pit. Their voices were horribly shrill and discordant. The sound of the popping of corks came from the bar.

'What a place to find one's divinity in!' said Lord Henry.

'Yes!' answered Dorian Gray. 'It was here I found her, and she is divine beyond all living things. When she acts you will forget everything. These common, rough people, with their coarse faces and brutal gestures, become quite different when she is on the stage. They sit silently and watch her. They weep and laugh as she wills them to do. She makes them as responsive as a violin. She spiritualizes them, and one feels that they are of the same flesh and blood as one's self.'

'The same flesh and blood as one's self! Oh, I hope not!' exclaimed Lord Henry, who was scanning the occupants of the gallery through his opera-glass.

'Don't pay any attention to him, Dorian,' said the painter. 'I understand what you mean, and I believe in this girl. Anyone you love must be marvellous, and any girl that has the effect you describe must be fine and noble. To spiritualize one's age – that is something worth doing. If this girl can give a soul to those who have lived without one, if she can create the sense of beauty in people whose lives have been sordid and ugly, if she can strip them of their selfishness and lend them tears for sorrows that are not their own, she is worthy of all your adoration, worthy of the adoration of the world. The marriage is quite right. I did not think so at first, but I admit it now. The gods made Sibyl Vane for you. Without her you would have been incomplete.'

'Thanks, Basil,' answered Dorian Gray, pressing his hand. 'I knew that you would understand me. Harry is so cynical, he terrifies me. But here is the orchestra. It is quite dreadful, but it only lasts for about five minutes. Then the curtain rises, and you will see the girl to whom I am going to give all my life, to whom I have given everything that is good in me.'

A quarter of an hour afterwards, amidst an extraordinary turmoil of applause, Sibyl Vane stepped on to the stage. Yes, she was certainly lovely to look at – one of the loveliest creatures, Lord Henry thought, that he had ever seen. There was something of the fawn in her shy grace and startled eyes. A faint blush, like the shadow of a rose in a mirror of silver, came to her cheeks as she glanced at the crowded, enthusiastic house. She stepped back a few paces, and her lips seemed to tremble. Basil Hallward leaped to his feet and began to applaud. Motionless, and as one in a dream, sat Dorian Gray, gazing at her. Lord Henry peered through his glasses, murmuring, 'Charming! charming!'

The scene was the hall of Capulet's house, and Romeo in his pilgrim's dress had entered with Mercutio and his other friends. The band, such as it was, struck up a few bars of music, and the dance began. Through the crowd of ungainly, shabbily-dressed actors, Sibyl Vane moved like a creature from a finer world. Her body swayed, while she danced, as a plant sways in the water. The curves of her throat were the curves of a white lily. Her hands seemed to be made of cool ivory.

Yet she was curiously listless. She showed no sign of joy when her eyes rested on Romeo. The few words she had to speak:

> Good pilgrim, you do wrong your hand too much,
> Which mannerly devotion shows in this;
> For saints have hands that pilgrims' hands do touch,
> And palm to palm is holy palmers' kiss –

with the brief dialogue that follows, were spoken in a thoroughly artificial manner. The voice was exquisite, but from the point of view of tone it was absolutely false. It was wrong in colour. It took away all the life from the verse. It made the passion unreal.

Dorian Gray grew pale as he watched her. He was puzzled and anxious. Neither of his friends dared to say anything to him. She seemed to them to be absolutely incompetent. They were horribly disappointed.

Yet they felt that the true test of any Juliet is the balcony scene of the second act. They waited for that. If she failed there, there was nothing in her.

She looked charming as she came out in the moonlight. That could not be denied. But the staginess of her acting was unbearable, and grew worse as she went on. Her gestures became absurdly artificial. She over-emphasized everything that she had to say. The beautiful passage:

> Thou knowest the mask of night is on my face,
> Else would a maiden blush bepaint my cheek
> For that which thou hast heard me speak tonight –

was declaimed with the painful precision of a schoolgirl who has been taught to recite by some second-rate professor of elocution. When she leaned over the balcony and came to those wonderful lines:

> Although I joy in thee,
> I have no joy of this contract tonight:
> It is too rash, too unadvised, too sudden,
> Too like the lightning, which doth cease to be
> Ere one can say, 'It lightens.' Sweet, goodnight!
> This bud of love by summer's ripening breath
> May prove a beauteous flower when next we meet –

she spoke the words as though they conveyed no meaning to her. It was not nervousness. Indeed, so far from being nervous, she was absolutely self-contained. It was simply bad art. She was a complete failure.

Even the common, uneducated audience of the pit and gallery lost their interest in the play. They got restless, and began to talk loudly and to whistle.

The Jew manager, who was standing at the back of the dress-circle, stamped and swore with rage. The only person unmoved was the girl herself.

When the second act was over there came a storm of hisses, and Lord Henry got up from his chair and put on his coat. 'She is quite beautiful, Dorian,' he said, 'but she can't act. Let us go.'

'I am going to see the play through,' answered the lad, in a hard, bitter voice. 'I am awfully sorry that I have made you waste an evening, Harry. I apologize to you both.'

'My dear Dorian, I should think Miss Vane was ill,' interrupted Hallward. 'We will come some other night.'

'I wish she were ill,' he rejoined. 'But she seems to me to be simply callous and cold. She has entirely altered. Last night she was a great artist. This evening she is merely a commonplace, mediocre actress.'

'Don't talk like that about anyone you love, Dorian. Love is a more wonderful thing than Art.'

'They are both simply forms of imitation,' remarked Lord Henry. 'But do let us go. Dorian, you must not stay here any longer. It is not good for one's morals to see bad acting. Besides, I don't suppose you will want your wife to act. So what does it matter if she plays Juliet like a wooden doll? She is very lovely, and if she knows as little about life as she does about acting, she will be a delightful experience. There are only two kinds of people who are really fascinating – people who know absolutely everything, and people who know absolutely nothing. Good heavens, my dear boy, don't look so tragic! The secret of remaining young is never to have an emotion that is unbecoming. Come to the club with Basil and myself. We will smoke cigarettes and drink to the beauty of Sibyl Vane. She is beautiful. What more can you want?'

'Go away, Harry,' cried the lad. 'I want to be alone. Basil, you must go. Ah! can't you see that my heart is breaking?' The hot tears came to his eyes. His lips trembled, and, rushing to the back of the box, he leaned up against the wall, hiding his face in his hands.

'Let us go, Basil,' said Lord Henry, with a strange tenderness in his voice; and the two young men passed out together.

A few moments afterwards the footlights flared up, and the curtain rose on the third act. Dorian Gray went back to his seat. He looked pale, and proud, and indifferent. The play dragged on, and seemed interminable. Half of the audience went out, tramping in heavy boots, and laughing. The whole thing was a *fiasco*. The last act was played to almost empty benches. The curtain went down on a titter, and some groans.

As soon as it was over, Dorian Gray rushed behind the scenes into the greenroom. The girl was standing there alone, with a look of triumph on her face. Her eyes were lit with an exquisite fire. There was a radiance about her. Her parted lips were smiling over some secret of their own.

When he entered, she looked at him, and an expression of infinite joy came over her. 'How badly I acted tonight, Dorian!' she cried.

'Horribly!' he answered, gazing at her in amazement – 'horribly! It was dreadful. Are you ill? You have no idea what it was. You have no idea what I suffered.'

The girl smiled. 'Dorian,' she answered, lingering over his name with long-drawn music in her voice, as though it were sweeter than honey to the red petals of her mouth – 'Dorian, you should have understood. But you understand now, don't you?'

'Understand what?' he asked, angrily.

'Why I was so bad tonight. Why I shall always be bad. Why I shall never act well again.'

He shrugged his shoulders. 'You are ill, I suppose. When you are ill you shouldn't act. You make yourself ridiculous. My friends were bored. I was bored.'

She seemed not to listen to him. She was transfigured with joy. An ecstasy of happiness dominated her.

'Dorian, Dorian,' she cried, 'before I knew you, acting was the one reality of my life. It was only in the theatre that I lived. I thought that it was all true. I was Rosalind one night, and Portia the other. The joy of Beatrice was my joy, and the sorrows of Cordelia were mine also. I believed in everything. The common people who acted with me seemed to me to be godlike. The painted scenes were my world. I knew nothing but shadows, and I thought them real. You came – oh, my beautiful love! – and you freed my soul from prison. You taught me what reality really is. Tonight, for the first time in my life, I saw through the hollowness, the sham, the silliness of the empty pageant in which I had always played. Tonight, for the first time, I became conscious that the Romeo was hideous, and old, and painted, that the moonlight in the orchard was false, that the scenery was vulgar, and that the words I had to speak were unreal, were not my words, were not what I wanted to say. You had brought me something higher, something of which all art is but a reflection. You had made me understand what love really is. My love! my love! Prince Charming! Prince of life! I have grown sick of shadows. You are more to me than all art can ever be. What have I to do with the puppets of a play? When I came on tonight, I could not understand how it was that everything had gone from me. I thought that I was going to be wonderful. I found that I could do nothing. Suddenly it dawned on my soul what it all meant. The knowledge was exquisite to me. I heard them hissing, and I smiled. What could they know of love such as ours? Take me away, Dorian – take me away with you, where we can be quite alone. I hate the stage. I might mimic a passion that I do not feel, but I cannot mimic one that burns me like fire. Oh, Dorian, Dorian, you understand now what it signifies? Even if I could do it, it would be profanation for me to play at being in love. You have made me see that.'

He flung himself down on the sofa, and turned away his face. 'You have killed my love,' he muttered.

She looked at him in wonder, and laughed. He made no answer. She came across to him, and with her little fingers stroked his hair. She knelt down and pressed his hands to her lips. He drew them away, and a shudder ran through him.

Then he leaped up, and went to the door. 'Yes,' he cried, 'you have killed my love. You used to stir my imagination. Now you don't even stir my curiosity. You simply produce no effect. I loved you because you were marvellous, because you had genius and intellect, because you realized the dreams of great poets and gave shape and substance to the shadows of art. You have thrown it all away. You are shallow and stupid. My God! how mad I was to love you! What a fool I have been! You are nothing to me now. I will never see you again. I will never think of you. I will never mention your name. You don't know what you were to me, once. Why ... Oh, I can't bear to think of it! I wish I had never laid eyes upon you! You have spoiled the romance of my life. How little you can know of love, if you say it mars your art! Without your art you are nothing. I would have made you famous, splendid, magnificent. The world would have worshipped you, and you would have borne my name. What are you now? A third-rate actress with a pretty face.'

The girl grew white and trembled. She clenched her hands together, and her voice seemed to catch in her throat. 'You are not serious, Dorian?' she murmured. 'You are acting.'

'Acting! I leave that to you. You do it so well,' he answered bitterly.

She rose from her knees, and, with a piteous expression of pain in her face, came across the room to him. She put her hand upon his arm, and looked into his eyes. He thrust her back. 'Don't touch me!' he cried.

A low moan broke from her, and she flung herself at his feet, and lay there like a trampled flower. 'Dorian, Dorian, don't leave me!' she whispered. 'I am so sorry I didn't act well. I was thinking of you all the time. But I will try – indeed, I will try. It came so suddenly across me, my love for you. I think I should never have known it if you had not kissed me – if

172

we had not kissed each other. Kiss me again, my love. Don't go away from me. I couldn't bear it. Oh! don't go away from me. My brother ... No; never mind. He didn't mean it. He was in jest ... But you, oh! can't you forgive me for tonight? I will work so hard, and try to improve. Don't be cruel to me because I love you better than anything in the world. After all, it is only once that I have not pleased you. But you are quite right, Dorian. I should have shown myself more of an artist. It was foolish of me; and yet I couldn't help it. Oh, don't leave me, don't leave me.' A fit of passionate sobbing choked her. She crouched on the floor like a wounded thing, and Dorian Gray, with his beautiful eyes, looked down at her, and his chiselled lips curled in exquisite disdain. There is always something ridiculous about the emotions of people whom one has ceased to love. Sibyl Vane seemed to him to be absurdly melodramatic. Her tears and sobs annoyed him.

'I am going,' he said at last, in his calm, clear voice. 'I don't wish to be unkind, but I can't see you again. You have disappointed me.'

She wept silently, and made no answer, but crept nearer. Her little hands stretched blindly out, and appeared to be seeking for him. He turned on his heel, and left the room. In a few moments he was out of the theatre.

OSCAR WILDE, *THE PICTURE OF DORIAN GRAY*

ঽ

The actor's great dread is the audience 'turning nasty'. This they do, fairly comprehensively, in the next two extracts. In the first, the hapless performer maintains a ghastly cheerfulness. In the second, from Dickens's *Great Expectations*, the victim contrives to rise above it all.

ঽ

THE NIGHT I APPEARED AS MACBETH
A Song

'Twas at a YMCA concert
I craved a desire for the stage.
In Flanders one night I was asked to recite,
Gadzooks, I was quickly the rage.
They said I was better than Irving,
And gave me some biscuits and tea.
I know it's not union wages,
But that was the usual fee.
Home I came, bought a dress,
Appeared in your Theatre and what a success!

173

I acted so tragic the house rose like magic,
The audience yelled 'You're sublime!'
They made me a present of Mornington Crescent,
They threw it a brick at a time.
Someone threw a fender which caught me a bender,
I hoised a white flag and tried to surrender.
They jeered me, they queered me,
And half of them stoned me to death.
They threw nuts and sultanas, fried eggs and bananas,
The night I appeared as Macbeth.

The play tho' ascribed to Bill Shakespeare,
To me lacked both polish and tone,
So I put bits in from Miss Elinor Glyn,
Nat Gould and some bits of my own.
The band played *The Barber of Seville*
And being too long they made cuts,
Then I entered somewhere in Scotland
And finished in Newington Butts.
Oh, the flowers, what a feast!
They threw it in bagfuls, self-raising and yeast.

I acted so tragic the house rose like magic,
I improved the part with a dance.
The pit had a relapse, so RAMC chaps
Were wired for to come back from France.
I withdrew my sabre, and started to labour,
Cried 'Lay on Macduff' to my swash-buckling neighbour,
I hollared 'I'm collared,
I must reach the bridge or it's death!'
But they altered my journey, I reached the infirmary,
The night I appeared as Macbeth.

The advertised time for the curtain
Was six forty-five on the sheet;
The hall-keeper he having mislaid the key
We played the first act in the street.
Then some-body called for the author,
'He's dead' said the flute player's wife.
The news caused an awful commotion

And gave me the shock of my life.
Shakespeare dead? Poor old Bill!
Why I never knew the poor fellow was ill.

I acted so tragic the house rose like magic,
They wished David Garrick could see,
But he's in the Abbey, then someone quite shabby
Suggested that's where I should be.
Lloyd George and Clemenceau they both carried on so
The King of the Belgians rushed in with Alfonso.
They pleaded unheeded
And all of them cried in one breath
'There another war coming if you don't stop humming,'
The night I appeared as Macbeth.

I acted so tragic the house rose like magic,
I gave them such wonderful thrills,
My tender emotion caused so much commotion
The dress circle made out their wills;
The gallery boys straining dropped tears uncomplaining,
The pit put umbrellas up, thought it was raining.
Some floated, some boated,
And five of the band met their death,
And the poor programme women sold programmes while
    swimming,
The night I appeared as Macbeth.

William Hargreaves

❧

As we contemplated the fire, and as I thought what a difficult vision to realize this same Capital sometimes was, I put my hands in my pockets. A folded piece of paper in one of them attracting my attention, I opened it and found it to be the playbill I had received from Joe, relative to the celebrated provincial amateur of Roscian renown. 'And bless my heart,' I involuntarily added aloud, 'it's to-night!'

This changed the subject in an instant, and made us hurriedly resolve to go to the play. So, when I had pledged myself to comfort and abet Herbert in the affair of his heart by all practicable and impracticable means, and when Herbert had told me that his affianced already knew me by reputation and that I should be presented to her, and when we had warmly shaken hands upon our mutual confidence, we blew out our candles, made up our fire, locked our door, and issued forth in quest of Mr Wopsle and Denmark.

On our arrival in Denmark, we found the king and queen of that country elevated in two arm-chairs on a kitchen-table, holding a Court. The whole of the Danish nobility were in attendance; consisting of a noble boy in the wash-leather boots of a gigantic ancestor, a venerable Peer with a dirty face who seemed to have risen from the people late in life, and the Danish chivalry with a comb in its hair and a pair of white silk legs, and presenting on the whole a feminine appearance. My gifted townsman stood gloomily apart, with folded arms, and I could have wished that his curls and forehead had been more probable.

Several curious little circumstances transpired as the action proceeded. The late king of the country not only appeared to have been troubled with a cough at the time of his decease, but to have taken it with him to the tomb, and to have brought it back. The royal phantom also carried a ghostly manuscript round its truncheon, to which it had the appearance of occasionally referring, and that, too, with an air of anxiety and a tendency to lose the place of reference which were suggestive of a state of mortality. It was this, I conceive, which led to the Shade's being advised by the gallery to 'turn over!' – a recommendation which it took extremely ill. It was likewise to be noted of this majestic spirit that whereas it always appeared with an air of having been out a long time and walked an immense distance, it perceptibly came from a closely contiguous wall. This occasioned its terrors to be received derisively. The Queen of Denmark, a very buxom lady, though no doubt historically brazen, was considered by the public to have too much brass about her; her chin being attached to her diadem by a broad band of that metal (as if she had a gorgeous toothache), her waist being encircled by another, and each of her arms by another, so that she was openly mentioned as 'the kettledrum.' The noble boy in the ancestral boots, was inconsistent; representing himself, as it were in one breath, as an able seaman, a strolling actor, a grave-digger, a clergyman, and a person of the utmost importance at a Court fencing-match, on the authority of whose practised eye and nice discrimination the finest strokes were judged. This gradually led to a want of toleration for him, and even – on his being detected in holy orders, and declining to perform the funeral service – to the general indignation taking the form of nuts. Lastly, Ophelia was a prey to such slow musical madness, that when, in course of time, she had taken off her white muslin scarf, folded it up, and buried it, a sulky man who had been long cooling his impatient nose against an iron bar in the front row of the gallery, growled, 'Now the baby's put to bed let's have supper!' Which, to say the least of it, was out of keeping.

Upon my unfortunate townsman all these incidents accumulated with playful effect. Whenever that undecided Prince had to ask a question or state a doubt, the public helped him out with it. As for example; on the question whether 'twas nobler in the mind to suffer, some roared yes, and some no, and some inclining to both opinions said 'toss up for it;' and quite a Debating Society arose. When he asked what should such fellows as he do crawling between earth and heaven, he was encouraged with loud cries of 'Hear, hear!' When he appeared with his stocking disordered (its disorder expressed, according to usage, by one very neat fold in the top, which I suppose to be always got up with a flat iron), a conversation took place in the gallery respecting the paleness of his leg, and whether it was occasioned by the turn the ghost had given him. On his taking the recorders – very like a little black flute that had just been played in the orchestra and handed out at the door – he was called upon unanimously for Rule Britannia. When he recommended the player not to saw the air thus, the sulky man said, 'And don't *you* do it, neither; you're a deal worse than *him*!' And I grieve to add that peals of laughter greeted Mr Wopsle on every one of these occasions.

But his greatest trials were in the churchyard: which had the appearance of a primeval forest, with a kind of small ecclesiastical wash-house on one side, and a turnpike gate on the other. Mr Wopsle in a comprehensive black cloak, being descried entering at the turnpike, the gravedigger was admonished in a friendly way, 'Look out! Here's the undertaker a coming, to see how you're a getting on with your work!' I believe it is well known in a constitutional country that Mr Wopsle could not possibly have returned the skull, after moralizing over it, without dusting his fingers on a white napkin taken from his breast; but even that innocent and indispens-able action did not pass without the comment 'Wai-ter!' The arrival of the body for interment (in an empty black box with the lid tumbling open), was the signal for a general joy which was much enhanced by the discov-ery, among the bearers, of an individual obnoxious to identification. The joy attended Mr Wopsle through his struggle with Laertes on the brink of the orchestra and the grave, and slackened no more until he had tumbled the king off the kitchen-table, and had died by inches from the ankles upward.

We had made some pale efforts in the beginning to applaud Mr Wopsle; but they were too hopeless to be persisted in. Therefore we had sat, feeling keenly for him, but laughing, nevertheless, from ear to ear. I laughed in spite of myself all the time, the whole thing was so droll; and yet I had a latent impression that there was something decidedly fine in Mr Wopsle's elocution – not for old associations' sake, I am afraid, but because it was very slow, very dreary, very up-hill and down-hill, and very unlike any way in which any man in any natural circumstances of life or death ever expressed himself about anything. When the tragedy was over, and he had been called for and hooted, I said to Herbert, 'Let us go at once, or perhaps we shall meet him.'

We made all the haste we could down-stairs, but we were not quick enough either. Standing at the door was a Jewish man with an unnatural heavy smear of eyebrow, who caught my eyes as we advanced, and said, when we came up with him:

'Mr Pip and friend?'

Identity of Mr Pip and friend confessed.

'Mr Waldengarver,' said the man, 'would be glad to have the honour.'

'Waldengarver?' I repeated – when Herbert murmured in my ear, 'Probably Wopsle.'

'Oh!' said I. 'Yes. Shall we follow you?'

'A few steps, please.' When we were in a side alley, he turned and asked, 'How did you think he looked? – I dressed him.'

I don't know what he had looked like, except a funeral; with the addition of a large Danish sun or star hanging round his neck by a blue ribbon, that had given him the appearance of being insured in some extraordinary Fire Office. But I said he had looked very nice.

'When he come to the grave,' said our conductor, 'he showed his cloak beautiful. But, judging from the wing, it looked to me that when he see the ghost in the queen's apartment, he might have made more of his stockings.'

I modestly assented, and we all fell through a little dirty swing door, into a sort of hot packing-case immediately behind it. Here Mr Wopsle was divesting himself of his Danish garments, and here there was just room for us to look at him over one another's shoulders, by keeping the packing-case door, or lid, wide open.

'Gentlemen,' said Mr Wopsle, 'I am proud to see you. I hope, Mr Pip, you will excuse my sending round. I had the happiness to know you in former times, and the Drama has ever had a claim which has ever been acknowledged, on the noble and the affluent.'

Meanwhile, Mr Waldengarver, in a frightful perspiration, was trying to get himself out of his princely sables.

'Skin the stockings off, Mr Waldengarver,' said the owner of that property, 'or you'll bust 'em. Bust 'em, and you'll bust five-and-thirty shillings. Shakspeare never was complimented with a finer pair. Keep quiet in your chair now, and leave 'em to me.'

With that, he went upon his knees, and began to flay his victim; who, on the first stocking coming off, would certainly have fallen over backward with his chair, but for there being no room to fall anyhow.

I had been afraid until then to say a word about the play. But then, Mr Waldengarver looked up at us complacently, and said:

'Gentlemen, how did it seem to you, to go, in front?'

Herbert said from behind (at the same time poking me), 'capitally.' So I said 'capitally.'

'How did you like my reading of the character, gentlemen?' said Mr Waldengarver, almost, if not quite, with patronage.

Herbert said from behind (again poking me), 'massive and concrete.' So I said boldly, as if I had originated it, and must beg to insist upon it, 'massive and concrete.'

'I am glad to have your approbation, gentlemen,' said Mr Waldengarver, with an air of dignity, in spite of his being ground against the wall at the time, and holding on by the seat of the chair.

'But I'll tell you one thing, Mr Waldengarver,' said the man who was on his knees, 'in which you're out in your reading. Now mind! I don't care who says contrairy; I tell you so. You're out in your reading of Hamlet when you get your legs in profile. The last Hamlet as I dressed, made the same mistakes in his reading at rehearsal, till I got him to put a large red wafer on each of his shins, and then at that rehearsal (which was the last) I went in front, sir, to the back of the pit, and whenever his reading brought him into profile, I called out "I don't see no wafers!" And at night his reading was lovely.'

Mr Waldengarver smiled at me, as much as to say 'a faithful dependent – I overlook his folly;' and then said aloud, 'My view is a little classic and thoughtful for them here; but they will improve, they will improve.'

Herbert and I said together, Oh, no doubt they would improve.

'Did you observe, gentlemen,' said Mr Waldengarver, 'that there was a man in the gallery who endeavoured to cast derision on the service – I mean, the representation?'

We basely replied that we rather thought we had noticed such a man. I added, 'He was drunk, no doubt.'

'Oh dear no, sir,' said Mr Wopsle, 'not drunk. His employer would see to that, sir. His employer would not allow him to be drunk.'

'You know his employer? said I.

Mr Wopsle shut his eyes, and opened them again; performing both ceremonies very slowly. 'You must have observed, gentlemen,' said he, 'an ignorant and a blatant ass, with a rasping throat and a countenance expressive of low malignity, who went through – I will not say sustained – the rôle (if I may use a French expression) of Claudius King of Denmark. That is his employer, gentlemen. Such is the profession!'

Without distinctly knowing whether I should have been more sorry for Mr Wopsle if he had been in despair, I was so sorry for him as it was, that I took the opportunity of his turning round to have his braces put on – which jostled us out at the doorway – to ask Herbert what he thought of having him home to supper? Herbert said he thought it would be kind to do so; therefore I invited him, and he went to Barnard's with us, wrapped up to the eyes, and we did our best for him, and he sat until two o'clock in the morning, reviewing his success and developing his plans. I forget in detail what they were, but I have a general recollection that he was to begin with reviving the Drama, and to end with crushing it; inasmuch as his decease would leave it utterly bereft and without a chance of hope.

CHARLES DICKENS, *GREAT EXPECTATIONS*

The unfortunate Wopsle clearly makes up in self-deception what he lacks in ability. However, failure is not the sole province of the untalented – witness Peter O'Toole's disastrous and headline-grabbing performance as Macbeth at the Old Vic in 1980. Failure can pop up from anywhere – as Rosalind says of woman's wit: 'Make the door [upon it] and it will out at the casement; shut that, and 'twill out at the keyhole; stop that, 'twill fly with the smoke out at the chimney.' You can blame the play, the part, the company, the audience, even the weather. Very rarely do you blame yourself. Here is a salutary little anecdote from the American actor Joseph Jefferson.

... The great value of art when applied to the stage is that it enables the performer to reproduce the gift [of acting] and so move his audience night after night even though he has acted the same character a thousand times. In fact, we cannot act a character too often, if we do not lose interest in it. But when its constant repetition palls on the actor it will as surely weary his audience. When you lose interest – stop acting.

This loss of interest on the part of the actor may not be visible in the action or pantomime; but unless care and judgment are observed it will assuredly betray itself in the delivery of the language, and more particularly in the long speeches and soliloquies. In dialogue the spirit of the other actors serves to stimulate and keep him up; but when alone, and unaided by the eye and presence of a companion, the old story fails to kindle the fire. An anecdote of [William Charles] Macready that I heard many years ago throws a flood of light upon this subject; and as I think it too important a one to remain in obscurity I will relate it as I got it from Mr Couldock, and then refer to its influence upon myself and the means I used to profit by it. The incident occurred in Birmingham, England, some forty years ago. The narrator was present and naturally listened with interest to a conversation upon art between two such able exponents of it as Mr Macready and Mrs Warner. What they said referred to an important scene in the tragedy of *Werner*, which had been acted the evening before.

Mr Macready, it seems, had much respect for Mrs Warner's judgment in matters relating to the stage, and desired to consult her on the merits and demerits of the preceding evening's performance. As nearly as can be remembered, his question and her reply were as follows:

'My dear madam,' said Macready, you have acted with me in the tragedy of *Werner* for many years, and naturally must be very familiar with it and with my manner of acting that character. I have noticed lately, and more particularly last evening, that some of the passages in the play do not produce the effect that they formerly did. There is a certain speech especially that seems to have lost its power. I refer to the one wherein Werner excuses himself to his son for the "petty plunder" of Stralenheim's gold. In our earlier performances, if you remember, this apology was received with marked favour, and, as you must have observed, last evening it produced no apparent effect; can you form any idea why this should be? Is it that the audience has grown too familiar with the story? I must beg you to be candid with me. I shall not be offended by any adverse criticism you may make, should you say that the fault is with me.'

'Well, Mr Macready, since you desire that I should speak plainly,' said Mrs Warner, 'I do not think it is because your audience is too familiar with the story, but because you are too familiar with it yourself.'

'I thank you, madam,' said Macready; 'but how does this mar the effect of the speech?'

'Thus,' said Mrs Warner. 'When you spoke that speech ten years ago there was a surprise in your face as though you then only realized what you had done. You looked shocked and bewildered, and in a forlorn way seemed to cast about the words that would excuse the crime; and all this with a depth of feeling and sincerity that would naturally come from an honest man who had been for the first case in his life accused of theft.'

'That is as it should be given,' said Macready. 'And now, madam?'

'You speak it,' said his frank critic, 'like one who has committed a great many thefts in his life, and whose glib excuses are so pat and frequent that he is neither shocked, surprised, nor abashed at the accusation.'

'I thank you, madam,' said the old actor. 'The distinction may appear at first as a nice one, but there is much in it.'

When I heard the story from Mr Couldock it struck me with much force. I knew then that I had been unconsciously falling into the same error, and I felt that the fault would increase rather than diminish with time if I could not hit upon some method to check it. I began by listening to each important question as though it had been given for the first time, turning the query over in my mind and then answering it, even at times hesitating as if for want of words to frame the reply. I will admit that this is dangerous ground and apt to render one slow and prosy; in fact, I was accused, and I dare say quite justly, of pausing too long. This, of course, was the other extreme and had to be looked to, so that it became necessary that the pauses should, by the manner and pantomime, be made sufficiently interesting not to weary an audience; so I summed it up somewhat after the advice of Mr [George Henry] Lewes to take time without appearing to take time.

It is the freshness, the spontaneity, of acting that charms. How can a weary brain produce this quality? Show me a tired actor and I will show you a dull audience. They may go in crowds to see him, and sit patiently through his performance. They have heard that he is great, they may even know it from past experience; so they accept the indifferent art, thinking, perhaps, that they are to blame for a lack of enthusiasm.

JOSEPH JEFFERSON IN ACTORS ON ACTING

❧

Of course, the best actor in the world cannot function without an audience. Sir John Gielgud has pointed out that acting is the only art that cannot be practised in private. In Tom Stoppard's play *Rosencrantz and Guildenstern Are Dead*, the heroes have encountered a troupe of strolling players en route to Elsinore Castle, but have given them the slip while they prepare for a performance.

❧

PLAYER *(Bitterly.)* You left us.

GUILDENSTERN: Ah! I'd forgotten – you performed a dramatic spectacle on the way. Yes, I'm sorry we had to miss it.

PLAYER (*bursts out*): We can't look each other in the face! (*Pause, more in control.*) You don't understand the humiliation of it – to be tricked out of the single assumption which makes our existence viable – that somebody is *watching* ... The plot was two corpses gone before we caught sight of ourselves, stripped naked in the middle of nowhere and pouring ourselves down a bottomless well.

ROSENCRANTZ: Is *that* thirty-eight?

PLAYER (*lost*): There we were – demented children mincing about in clothes that no one ever wore, speaking as no man ever spoke, swearing love in wigs and rhymed couplets, killing each other with wooden swords, hollow protestations of faith hurled after empty promises of vengeance – and every gesture, every pose, vanishing into the thin unpopulated air. We ransomed our dignity to the clouds, and the uncomprehending birds listened. (*He rounds on them.*) Don't you see?! We're *actors* – we're the opposite of people! (*They recoil nonplussed, his voice calms.*) Think, in your head, *now*, think of the most ... *private* ... *secret* ... *intimate* thing you have ever done secure in the knowledge of its privacy ... (*He gives them – and the audience – a good pause. Rosencrantz takes on a shifty look.*) Are you thinking of it? (*He strikes with his voice and his head.*) Well, I saw you do it! (*Rosencrantz leaps up, dissembling madly.*)

ROSENCRANTZ: You never! It's a lie! (*He catches himself with a giggle in a vacuum and sits down again.*)

PLAYER: We're actors ... We pledged our identities, secure in the conventions of our trade; that someone would be watching. And then, gradually, no one was. We were caught, high and dry. It was not until the murderer's long soliloquy that we were able to look around; frozen as we were in profile, our eyes searched you out, first confidently, then hesitantly, then desperately as each patch of turf, each log, every exposed corner in every direction proved uninhabited, and all the while the murderous King addressed the horizon with his dreary interminable guilt ... Our heads began to move, wary as lizards, the corpse of unsullied Rosalinda peeped through his fingers, and the King faltered. Even then, habit and a stubborn trust that our audience spied upon us from behind the nearest bush, forced our bodies to blunder on long after they had emptied of meaning, until like runaway carts they dragged to a halt. No one came forward. No one shouted at us. The silence was unbreakable, it imposed itself upon us; it was obscene. We took off our crowns and swords and cloth of gold and moved silent on the road to Elsinore.

TOM STOPPARD, *ROSENCRANTZ AND GUILDENSTERN ARE DEAD*

The most moving portrait of a failed actor I know is in Chekhov's *The Seagull*. Nina has been full of dreams and enthusiasm, but her life, like most lives, has not gone the way she planned. In the last act of the play Dr Dorn asks Konstantin (Trepliov) for news of her.

☙

DORN. By the way, where is Zaryechnaia now? Do you know how she is?
TREPLIOV. I suppose she's all right.
DORN. Someone told me she's been leading a rather peculiar kind of life. What's been happening?
TREPLIOV. Well, Doctor, it's a long story.
DORN. Never mind, you can make it short.

[A pause.]

TREPLIOV. She ran away from home and had an affair with Trigorin. You knew that, didn't you?
DORN. Yes, I did know.
TREPLIOV. She had a child. It died. Trigorin fell out of love with her and went back to his former attachments, as might have been expected. In fact he never gave them up, but in his spineless way he somehow managed to keep them all going. As far as I can make it out from what I've heard, Nina's personal life turned out a complete failure.
DORN. And what about the stage?
TREPLIOV. That was worse still, I believe. She started acting in a small theatre at some holiday place near Moscow, then went to the provinces. I never lost sight of her at that time, and wherever she went, I followed. She would always take on big parts, but she acted them crudely, without distinction – with false intonations and violent gestures. There were moments when she showed talent – as when she uttered a cry, or died on the stage – but they were only moments.
DORN. Then she has some talent, after all?
TREPLIOV. It's very hard to tell. I believe she has. I saw her, of course, but she refused to see me, and the servants wouldn't let me go up to her room at the hotel. I understood her state of mind and did not insist on seeing her.

[A pause.]

What more can I tell you? Afterwards, when I got back home, I had letters from her, intelligent, warm, interesting letters ... She did not complain, but I could feel that she was profoundly unhappy, every line was like an exposed, aching nerve ... Her imagination seemed to be confused, too. She signed herself 'Seagull'. You remember, in Pushkin's play *The River Nymph* the miller says he's a raven. So in the same way she kept calling herself 'the seagull' in her letters.

ANTON CHEKHOV, *THE SEAGULL*

Nina is in fact nearby. She has followed Trigorin back to the estate. In the following scene Konstantin hears a noise at the window and goes to look. As a sympathetic portrait of lost love and failed lives this scene has no equal.

TREPLIOV. What's that? *[Looks through the window.]* I can't see anything ... *[Opens the french window and looks out into the garden.]* Someone ran down the steps. *[Calls.]* Who's there? *[Goes out and is heard walking rapidly along the terrace, then returns half a minute later with Nina Zaryechenaia.]* Nina! Nina!

[Nina leans her head against his breast and sobs quietly]

TREPLIOV. *[deeply moved]*. Nina! Nina! It's you ... you ... I seem to have had a presentiment, my heart's been aching terribly all day ... *[Takes off her cape and hat.]* Oh, my sweet, my precious girl, she's come at last! Don't let us cry, don't!
NINA. There's someone here.
TREPLIOV. There isn't anyone.
NINA. Please lock the doors, or someone will come in.
TREPLIOV. No one will come in.
NINA. I know Irena Nikolayevna is here. Lock the doors.
TREPLIOV. *[locks the door on right, then crosses to the left.]* There's no lock on this one. I'll put a chair against it. *[Puts an armchair against the door.]* Don't be afraid, no one will come in.
NINA. *[looks intently at his face]*. Let me look at you for a little while. *[Looking round.]* How warm, how nice it is here! ... This used to be a drawing-room. Have I changed a lot?
TREPLIOV. Yes ... You are thinner and your eyes have grown bigger. Nina, it's so strange to be seeing you! Why wouldn't you let me see you? Why haven't you come here before now? I know you've been in the town almost a week ... I've been to your place everyday, several times a day: I stood under your window like a beggar.

185

NINA. I was afraid that you might hate me. Every night I dream that you look at me and don't recognize me. If only you knew! Ever since I came I've been walking round here ... beside the lake. I've been near this house many times, but I dared not come in. Let us sit down.

[They sit down.]

Let us sit and talk, talk ... It's nice here, warm and comfortable ... Do you hear the wind? There's a passage in Turgenev: 'Fortunate is he who on such a night has a roof over him, who has a warm corner of his own.' I am a seagull ... No, that's not it. *[Rubs her forehead.]* What was I saying? Yes ... Turgenev ... 'And Heaven help the homeless wayfarers' ... Never mind ... *[Sobs.]*

TREPLIOV. Nina, you're crying again! ... Nina!

NINA. Never mind, it does me good ... I haven't cried for two years. Yesterday, late in the evening I came into the garden to see whether our stage was still there. And it is still standing! I began to cry for the first time in two years, and it lifted the weight from my heart, and I felt more at ease. You see, I'm not crying now. *[Takes his hand.]* And so you've become a writer ... You are a writer and I'm an actress. We've been drawn into the whirlpool, too. I used to live here joyously, like a child – I used to wake up in the morning and burst into song. I loved you and dreamed of fame ... And now? Tomorrow morning early I have to go to Yelietz in a third-class carriage ... with the peasants; and at Yelietz, upstart business men will pester me with their attentions. Life is coarse!

TREPLIOV. Why do you have to go to Yelietz?

NINA. I've changed an engagement for the whole winter. It's time to go.

TREPLIOV. Nina, I used to curse you: I hated you, I tore up your letters and photographs, but all the time I knew that I was bound to you heart and soul, and for ever! It's not in my power to stop loving you, Nina. Ever since I lost you, ever since I began to get my work published, my life's been untolerable. I'm wretched ... I feel as if my youth has been suddenly torn away from me, as if I've been inhabiting this world for ninety years. I call out your name, I kiss the ground where you've walked; wherever I look I seem to see your face, that sweet smile that used to shine on me in the best years of my life ...

NINA *[bewildered]*. Why does he talk like this, why does he talk this?

TREPLIOV. I am lonely. I've no-one's love to warm me, I feel as cold as if I were in a cellar – and everything I write turns out lifeless and bitter and gloomy. Stay here, Nina, I entreat you, or let me come with you!

186

[Nina quickly puts on her hat and cape.]

TREPLIOV. Nina, why – for Heaven's sake, Nina ...

[Looks at her as she puts on her clothes.]
[A pause.]

NINA. The horses are waiting for me at the gate. Don't see me off, I'll go
   by myself ... *[Tearfully.]* Give me some water.
TREPLIOV *[gives her water].* Where are you going now?
NINA. To the town. *[A pause.]* Irena Nikolayevna's here, isn't she?
TREPLIOV. Yes ... My uncle had an attack on Thursday, so we telegraphed
   for her.
NINA. Why did you say you kissed the ground where I walked? Someone
   ought to kill me. *[Droops over the table.]* I am so tired. Oh, I wish I could
   rest ... just rest! *[Raising her head.]* I'm a seagull ... No, that's not it. I'm
   an actress. Oh, well! *[She hears Arkadina and Trigorin laughing off-stage, lis-
   tens, then runs to the door at left and looks through the keyhole.]* So he is here
   too! ... *[Returning to Trepliov.]* Oh, well! ... Never mind ... Yes ... He
   didn't believe in the theatre, he was always laughing at my dreams, and
   so gradually I ceased to believe too, and lost heart ... And then I was so
   preoccupied with love and jealousy, and a constant fear for my baby ...
   I became petty and common, when I acted I did it stupidly ... I didn't
   know what to do with my hands or how to stand on the stage, I could-
   n't control my voice ... But you can't imagine what it feels like – when
   you know that you are acting abominably. I'm a seagull. No, that's not it
   again ... Do you remember you shot a seagull? A man came along by
   chance, saw it and destroyed it, just to pass the time ... A subject for a
   short story ... That's not it. *[Rubs her forehead.]* What was I talking
   about? ... Yes, about the stage. I'm not like that now ... Now I am a
   real actress, I act with intense enjoyment, with enthusiasm; on the stage
   I am intoxicated and I feel that I am beautiful. But now, while I'm living
   here, I go for walks a lot ... I keep walking and thinking ... thinking
   and feeling that I am growing stronger in spirit with every day that
   passes ... I think I now know, Kostia, that what matters in our work –
   whether you act on the stage or write stories – what really matters is not
   fame, or glamour, not the things I used to dream about – but knowing
   how to endure things. How to bear one's cross and have faith. I have
   faith now and I'm not suffering quite so much, and when I think of my
   vocation I'm not afraid of life.
TREPLIOV *[sadly].* You have found your right path, you know which way

187

you're going – but I'm still floating about in a chaotic world of dreams and images, without knowing what use it all is … I have no faith, and I don't know what my vocation is.

NINA [listening]. Sh-sh! … I'm going now. Good-bye. When I become a great actress, come and see me act. Promise? And now … [Presses his hand.] It's late. I can hardly stand up … I'm so tired and hungry …

TREPLIOV. Do stay, I'll give you some supper.

NINA. No, no … Don't see me off, I'll go by myself … My horses are not far off … So she brought him with her? Oh, well, it doesn't matter … When you see Trigorin don't tell him anything … I love him. I love him even more than before. A subject for a short story … Yes I love him, I love him passionately, I love him desperately! How nice it all used to be, Kostia! Do you remember? How tranquil, warm, and joyous, and pure our life was, what feelings we had – like tender, exquisite flowers … Do you remember? … [Recites.] 'The men, the lions, the eagles, the partridges, the antlered deer, the geese, the spiders, the silent fishes of the deep, starfishes and creatures unseen to the eye – in short all living things, all living things, all living things, having completed their mournful cycle, have been snuffed out. For thousands of years the earth has borne no living creature, and this poor moon now lights its lamp in vain. The cranes no longer wake up in the meadows with a cry, the May beetles are no longer heard humming in the groves of lime trees.' …
[Impulsively embraces Trepliov and runs out through the french window.]

TREPLIOV [after a pause]. It won't be very nice if someone meets her in the garden and tells Mamma. It might upset Mamma … [He spends the next two minutes silently tearing up all his manuscripts and throwing them under the table, then unlocks the door at right and goes out.]

DORN [trying to open the door at left] That's strange. The door seems to be locked … [Comes in and puts the arm-chair in its place.] Quite an obstacle race.

[Enter Arkadina and Polena, followed by Yakov carrying drinks, then Masha, Shamrayev and Trigorin.]

ARKADINA. Put the red wine and the beer on the table here for Boris Aleksyeevich. We'll drink as we play. Let us sit down, friends.

POLENA [to Yakov]. Bring the tea in as well. [Lights the candles and sits down at the card table.]

SHAMRAYEV [leads Trigorin to the cupboard]. Here is the thing I was telling you about just now … [Takes the stuffed seagull out of the cupboard]. This is what you ordered.

TRIGORIN [*looking at the seagull*]. I don't remember [*Musing.*] No, I don't remember!

    [*There is a sound of a shot off-stage on right. Everyone starts.*]

DORN. That's nothing. It must be something in my medicine chest that's gone off. Don't worry. [*Goes out through door at right, returns in half a minute.*] Just as I thought. A bottle of ether has burst. [*Hums.*] 'Again I stand before you, enchanted.' ...

ARKADINA [*sitting down to the table*]. Ough, how it frightened me! It reminded me of how ... [*Covers her face with her hands.*] Everything went dark for a moment.

DORN [*turning over the pages of a magazine, to Trigorin*]. There was an article here about two months ago ... a letter from America, and I wanted to ask you ... [*Puts his arm round Trigorin's waist and leads him to the footlights.*] Because I'm very much interested in this question ... [*Dropping his voice, in a lower tone.*] Take Irena Nikolayevna away from here somehow. The fact is, Konstantin Gavrilovich has shot himself ...

        curtain

               ANTON CHEKHOV, *THE SEAGULL*

CHAPTER 9
MONSTERS

Monsters. We all love 'em. Even the most lemon-lipped art worshipper can crack up at an anecdote involving appaling behaviour or a withering one-liner from one or other of our leading players. We gasp and disapprove and revel in it, each generation, and probably each address book, yielding its own favourites. Here is a short and random collection, loosely in chronological order. We start with Edmund Kean – diminutive and demoniacal, especially towards the end.

છે

He was killing himself as much by overwork as by drink. It seemed as he knew the end could not be long delayed, and for the sake of a final fling, was prepared to throw away heedlessly his last reserves of strength. And yet when he *was* at Richmond, his life was more sheltered than it had ever been before. He had a home. He assumed an invalid's role. And he was well protected from the blasts of the world by a devoted entourage.

There was John Lee, who looked after his business interests. He was a young ex-actor, and had only recently taken up Phillips' duties. But he had worshipped Edmund long before he had even known him. Five years ago, when Edmund had arrived in America – an outcast from his own country – John Lee had stood on the quay, a solitary Englishman, to welcome him.

There was James Smith, a local physician, who was Edmund's medical attendant. He visited him daily, and liked him so well that he consistently refrained from sending in an account. He considered himself sufficiently rewarded by Edmund's friendship.

And lastly there was 'Aunt' Tid. She was an old lady now, in her seventy-first year, but she had come from her retreat in Chelsea (she had at last left Tavistock Row) to nurse her nephew, who needed nursing, and to keep house for him. According to Dr Smith she was 'tall, erect, grey haired and exceedingly well conducted.' She often used to be seen with Edmund walking on the green, and he looked small and bent beside her. Her fondness for Edmund puzzled Dr Smith. One day he asked her outright whether she was 'Mr Kean's mother.' She answered that she was not, but she had known him since he was a little boy. 'And it's hard, very hard,' she added, 'to see him fading away like this in the best part of life.' Then she burst into tears.

He was, in truth, fading away. From his very appearance – so old and pallid – it was obvious that death was closing in upon him and would not be kept at bay. He had about him an air of mystery and not be kept at bay. He had about him an air of mystery and other-earthliness which usually belongs only to men who have reached a great age. There was something almost miraculous in the fact that Edmund Kean was alive at all. Those of the new generation who were at the outset of their stage careers regarded him as a kind of oracle and made pilgrimages to Richmond to seek his advice while it could yet be given. 'Can you starve?' he said to one of them.

It was impossible to suppose now that he would ever recover his health and fortune. He was still prodigiously extravagant, still spent money as fast as he earned it and was still wildly generous. It became known in Richmond that he was incapable of turning a deaf ear to any hard-luck story, however fanciful or far-fetched. And there were several who abused his charity.

He survived on brandy. Neither 'Aunt' Tid nor Doctor Smith could persuade him to eat solid food. He had no appetite. While he was under their care he did behave otherwise in a sensible, dignified way. He never left his house unless the weather was fine when he went, well wrapped up, for a walk on the green or for a row on the river. But the moment he was out of their sight, fulfilling provincial engagements, he became again the carousing, gallivanting vulgarian, a prey to all his weaknesses.

From some town in the Midlands he wrote to John Lee on April 10th, 1831:

'DEAR LEE,

'What a day do I open in Cheltenham. The stupid son of a bitch has not dated his letter, write me Birmingham. Get as much money as you can and save it for me, I shall send you – money as soon as I get it – I won't say – I wish her dead but I'll be damned if I don't.

'Yours truly,

'EDMUND KEAN.'

To this letter he added a playful little postscript for 'Aunt' Tid's benefit: 'Tiddy no sausages out of season capitol [sic] cigars & grog.'

The sharp contrasts in his character persisted to the end. And nothing reveals them more clearly than the distinct impression of two celebrated figures of the Victorian stage, Samuel Phelps and Helen Faucit, who in their youth both had the privilege of a single meeting with him.

Samuel Phelps remembered him professionally. 'He was,' he said, 'like thunder and lightning, wild and extravagant and frequently incorrect. But … terribly in earnest. He lifted you off your feet.'

Phelps was a young member of the resident company at a theatre in York, and when Edmund came there to star as Shylock he was cast as Tubal. Edmund did not bother to attend rehearsal, and though Phelps had been put through his paces by John Lee, he was a trifle puzzled at the actual performance, for Edmund 'prowled about the stage like a caged tiger.' However, he did his best. 'He dodged him up and down, and crossed when he crossed.' Everything seemed to be going smoothly, when Edmund hissed into his ear: 'Get out of my focus – blast you – get out of my focus. Phelps looked into the wings, where John Lee was standing. Lee motioned him to stand higher up. He had committed the unpardonable sin of blocking the floats' light from shining into Edmund's face.

After the play was over Phelps was summoned to Edmund's dressing-room. He found him drinking copiously of brandy with Bill Anderton, a well-known provincial actor and a notorious dipsomaniac. (Apparently Edmund spent most of his time during this engagement drinking with Bill Anderton, whom he had known in his strolling player days. They got up drunk. And when they appeared together on the stage they were both 'more than half seas over.') Edmund welcomed Phelps: 'Have a glass of grog, young stick-in-the-mud. You'll be an actor one of these days, sir, but mind, the next time you play with me, for God's sake steer clear of my focus.' Phelps never had occasion to heed this advice. And no doubt he was glad to see the last of Mr Kean.

GILES MAYFAIR, EDMUND KEAN

Mrs Patrick Campbell was a radiant beauty, a fine actress and anecdote heaven. People repeat the stories without having the slightest notion of who she was, or that she created many of Shaw's greatest roles, including Eliza Doolittle. Emlyn Williams met her in old age.

ఇ∂

One night I arrived later and the one caller still there was spread on the sofa: a stout old lady in a rag-bag of a black evening dress ornamented with what looked like jet. Her hair, an improbable black, was done in old-fashioned loops above a face to which, earlier in the evening, make-up had been applied, hastily and liberally. She looked like a grand theatrical landlady on a night out, who had herself once trod the boards.

'Stella dear, this is Emlyn Williams – Mrs Patrick Campbell.'

'Oh, he won't recognize the name of an old has-been … '

She would anyway have been identified by a voice imitated in a hundred anecdotes: throaty and over-articulated, sounding anxious to please until you realize that the humble pie was flavoured with arsenic.

It was my first and last meeting with a sacred monster who so perfectly lived up to herself that next day I wrote it down. I waited for the darts, and they came.

John said, 'Emlyn has a great success at the St James's, with Edith [Evans] and Cedric.' I wondered if the mention of the foremost contemporary actress was the happiest of strokes.

'*Do* tell me more, but you look a *child*, did you write it all by yourself?'

She cannot have known how lethal that dart was. John looked nervous. 'He's adapted it from the French.'

The black eyes fixed on me with horror and there was a weightlift of beringed fingers. 'Oh, you poor dear, a *translation*?' She made it sound like a dirty book. 'Translations remind me of those short-sighted spinsters slaving over their abominable copies in the Louvre. John, dear, do you remember our *Ghosts*, the programme should have read "*Mangled* from the Norwegian by William What-was-his-name … " Bowmen? Arrowsmith? *Archer*, that was it … '

She turned to me again, 'Now I've got a *spiffing* idea, why not write a play out of your *very own head*, for a penniless old harridan who can still act? Goodbye dear John, such lovely costumes, and goodbye you naughty *cribber*, goodbye … '

EMLYN WILLIAMS, *EMLYN*

ఇ∂

John Barrymore is more renowned for his drunkenness and temper than for his talent. But he must have been prodigiously gifted to have recovered from the following outburst of fury.

Some weeks afterward, and in another city, he lost his temper entirely. It was at the end of the first act. At this point in the play Peter picked up the Duchess of Towers' bouquet. After looking at it tenderly for a long moment, he pressed the flowers to his lips. Then he murmured, *'L'amour.'* It was one of the most touching scenes in the play. It sent the ladies into near-swoons.

On this particular evening some girl in the gallery, hysterical with delight, giggled. Jack called out: 'Damn it! If you think you can play this better than I can, come on down and do it.'

He hurled the bouquet into the audience. It struck a woman in the face. The curtain fell. Barrymore stomped off-stage to his dressing-room to lock himself inside it.

Sounds of outrage came from the audience. Miss [Constance] Collier was dismayed to hear high-pitched voices filtering through the curtain. The actors stood in their places on the stage as if paralyzed. Then the manager of the theatre, purple and blowing, charged round from the pass-door.

'I'll bring a damage suit against you!' he shouted at Miss Collier. 'Barrymore has ruined the reputation of my theatre. I'll not allow you to fulfil your engagement for the remainder of the week. My God! Nobody is safe with this man. I'll have him barred from every ... '

He paused to regain his wind. The actress took this opportunity to beg the manager to allow the curtain to rise for the second act. He said no. The audience would throw things.

'They're sitting out there now, desperate and waiting,' he said. 'Peek out at 'em. You'll see. They're like a sheriff's posse.'

Miss Collier did peer out to observe the audience waiting as if to exercise some terrible judgment. She finally persuaded the manager to allow the curtain to rise. He recommended that Miss Collier make a speech of apology and offer to return all box-office moneys to the patrons. She declined to do this.

'All right then,' the manager warned, 'but if you're killed, don't say I didn't tell you.'

There had been half an hour's delay. Jack refused to come out of his dressing-room. No threats could move him. Finally Miss Collier informed him that he really had injured an inoffensive woman in the audience, and that the victim's eye had been bandaged.

'In that case,' Barrymore said, 'ring up the curtain.'

The curtain rose for the second act. It seemed remarkable that so few persons had left the theatre or asked for their money back. There was the type of quietness that obtains before a prison riot. The slight plop of a moth against a spotlight slide sounded like a howitzer shell in the challenging silence.

Jack's entrance did not occur until halfway through the second act. Ordinarily, before this appearance of Peter, there were moments of laughter or hand-clapping. Tonight there was no laughter, no applause. Silence.

The cast was terrified. The suspense led Miss Collier to issue whispered instructions of an 'abandon ship' nature. She admonished the crew to lower the curtain the moment the audience began to tear Jack apart.

The moment arrived, and Jack arrived with the moment. He entered with profound self-assurance. He was casual. He might have been on his way to a church, so poised was he. And now the presence that mysteriously was his on any stage, and always would be strangely his, spread its electric influence over the whole house.

He received the wildest sort of applause. Cheers even, and the waving of women's kerchiefs.

It is said that the manager of the theatre sank to his knees, either to pray or to keep from collapsing on his face. No one was sued. The play could have gone on for weeks to capacity business in that city.

GENE FOWLER, GOODNIGHT SWEET PRINCE

Martita Hunt's performance as Miss Haversham in David Lean's film of *Great Expectations* haunted my nightmares as a child. Alec Guinness knew her for many years and, while remaining a close friend, was not blind to her eccentricities.

I was still in uniform, but about to be demobbed, when I did a screen test for David Lean's film of *Great Expectations*. Having got the part I did a further test, for make-up, wig and clothes, at Denham Studios, and David invited me to sit next to him to see the 'rushes' of the previous day's work, which was the scene of Miss Havisham showing the young Estella her ancient wedding-cake, covered in cobwebs and nibbled by mice. I watched it fascinated but was troubled, at the back of my mind, about something in Martita's performance; and when David turned to me happily, saying

'Well?', I could only mutter, 'It's marvellous; but I didn't realize you put the sound on afterwards.' 'What do you mean?' he asked, suddenly worried. 'It's in perfect sync!' I had no knowledge at all of filming and didn't want to make a fool of myself so I just said, 'It's just that I couldn't see Martita's mouth move when she was speaking. It looked as if she had a stiff upper lip.' He obviously thought I was mad. Then it dawned on me; a week or two earlier, when I had told Martita I was going to play Herbert Pocket, she had said, 'My darling, I have at last found the secret of acting on the screen, it is *never* to move the upper lip.' What price all that lip muscle, I had thought. It was great nonsense, of course, and typical of her to be always pinning her faith on some new theory, of breathing, speaking, meditating, tooth-brushing, bowel movement or just living. She was always seeking new knowledge. On one occasion I discovered her near tears with the great tome of *Mathematics for the Million* open on her lap. 'Darling,' she said, looking up sorrowfully, 'I wanted to learn how to work out twelve percent and now I'm lost in logarithms.'

In 1951 my wife and I bought a ten-acre field near Petersfield in Hampshire, and built a modest house which we intended to use as a weekend cottage but which eventually became our permanent home. One of the first people we invited down for a couple of nights was Martita, in spite of the fact that Merula said the prospect of cooking for her was too alarming. The answer to that was to suggest that Martita should be asked to cook dinner, something she always enjoyed doing, and accordingly a splendid chicken was bought and everything we thought she might need. A Rolls-Royce arrived – loaned by a friend of hers complete with chauffeur – and Martita descended in leopard-skin coat, chic hat, with white hide luggage and a flurry of little parcels of expensive luxuries none of which she could possibly afford. I had explained the house was small and simple but that at least she would have her own bathroom. One look and she knew she was in for a weekend of slumming, but she rallied at the idea of cooking dinner. The chicken was pinched and prodded with an approving, greedy smile. 'Darlings,' she informed us, 'I think it would be good to it in a French way I am sure you will like very much.' Pans and apron and all the equipment for a special operation were put on display; seasonings and spice ready to hand, the oven explained, and she all ready to go when, quite casually, she said, 'Chéri, all I need now is six pounds of butter.' There were only four pounds in the house, Sunday to get through and the shops shut. I explained the butter situation, which until that moment I hadn't looked on as a shortage. She flew into a rage, picked up the chicken and threw it on the kitchen floor, tore off her apron and rushed to the living-room, where she flung herself full length along a window-seat. Merula and I were aghast. 'Fools! Fools! Where's the telephone?' She dialled for her friend's Rolls to collect her as soon as possible – which it wasn't able to do until the following morning. I can't remember the rest of the evening except for the fact that it was extremely uncomfortable and Merula turned out a perfectly respectable roast chicken and I poured out several whiskies and uncorked quite a lot of wine. It took Merula years to recover from the shock of knowing you *could* require six pounds of butter to cook a chicken and I don't think she or Martita ever saw eye to eye again.

Wimpole Street was exchanged for a ground-floor studio flat in a quiet little corner of Primrose Hill. Quite a lot of film work came her way, largely due to the great kindness and generosity of Jimmy Woolf, who ran Romulus Films, and had become a close friend, and life continued in much the same old way, with manicures, expensive hair-dos and higher irrigation. Jimmy saw to it that she was supplied with the little luxuries that were so essential to her and when her flat was badly burned – she and the curtains went up in the flames of a guttering candle, not unlike Miss Havisham – he arranged and paid for redecoration while she was recovering in hospital. When filming she took to having a little mid-morning tea tray provided for her on the set, which led to difficulties. The tea wasn't hot; what came down the spout of the elegant pot was a neat Highland brew. 'No, chérie! No milk. No lemon. Just a little tea; that's all the stimulant I need.' It was a sad habit which deceived no one; brought on, I think, by the wartime air raids, when she was so often alone and frightened in her Wimpole Street eyrie, and it was a habit which was intensifying with the years.

A mild flutter on the horses became one her major pleasures. She studied form, in an amateur way, and had a few horsy friends who advised her on bets and accepted, too often I suspect, 'surefire' tips from George or Harry or whoever the current favourite taxi-driver might be. Not that I disapproved in any way, but she never took me in her confidence where racing was concerned. Watching her wield a pencil over a tipster's column in an evening paper I couldn't resist a wry smile which she caught. 'You, my darling, have no sportin' instincts,' she said: which was true; except for my periodic passion for roulette.

We were together in Peter Glenville's marvellous production of Feydeau's *Hotel Paradiso* at the Winter Garden Theatre and had adjacent dressing-rooms. Every evening, while making up, I could hear her doing her vocal exercises, 'Ho! Ho! Ho-ho! Hi! Hum, um, oom. Aha! A-a-h-h!' (Larry Olivier does a brilliant imitation of this.) One night I was aware that no exercises were being done and I could hear the quiet hum of a long conversation with someone. I heard her door close and footsteps retreat; then a tap at my door. Martita stepped into my room in Edwardian wig and her dressing-gown, looking very serious.

He's got no balls,' she announced.

Who hasn't?' I asked in some alarm.

Mr So-and-so.' She kept to the formalities all right.

How do you know?'

He told me. He came for a chat about sex.'

Martita was quite keen to chat about sex.

Did you verify?' I asked her.

Of course not, chéri. One doesn't ask to see a gentleman's private parts. Not unless you are Miss B.' She named a notorious man-eating actress.

What's happened to his balls?' I asked.

It's very sad, not a laughing matter. Apparently they simply *never came down.*'

Her tone implied that Nature was an untrustworthy Dame and life full of disappointments.

'Do you think I should put him on to Watty?'

'Well, she would bring down almost anything,' I said.

Leaving me rather haughtily she threw over her shoulder, 'Sometimes you are disgusting. And unfeeling.' We met again on stage and Mr So-and-so made his entrance our eyes met and we both had barely controlled giggles. By the interval she was reconciled to the poor man's plight and whispered, 'Anyway, I think Mr So-and-so is a bugger, so it probably doesn't matter much.'

The Mad Woman of Chaillot was a great personal success for Martita in New York; less so in London. I saw her in the play in Philadelphia when she was on tour. The day I arrived she had locked herself in her hotel suite. I don't recall the reason for this but it was probably the result of some quarrel with the management, with her agent and with Miss Estelle Winwood – who also had made a success and who insisted on her small dog taking a curtain call with the rest of the cast. Martita objected to Estelle, her dog, the leading man and Philadelphia. She wouldn't answer the telephone or a knock at her door. Information was passed on slips of paper pushed under the door and food left outside it, but I called out my name boldly and the door flung open. She hugged me emotionally and I accompanied her down to the theatre. The whole episode of locked rooms was over. Martita should have been, had the gods been kinder, what she yearned to be: a great actress and a great star. Unfortunately although talented, she was neither; but she was certainly a big personality and could cause hell to break loose if the mood was on her. Curiously enough she was adored by the people on whom she most depended, dressers, maids, waiters, and workmen, whom she sometimes treated abominably. On the first night of *Hotel Paradiso*, unable to find her property wedding ring she told her old, sweet-natured dresser to lend hers. The old girl refused, saying, 'Miss Hunt, my wedding ring has never left my finger. It's been there over fifty years and that's where it's staying.' Martita screamed at her, 'Margaret, you are a silly old cow! Give it to me at once!' She dived at Margaret's hand; there was a fierce tussle; the theatre resounded with their shouts and screams. Martita got the ring and her dresser collapsed in hysterics. The next day they were loving friends again, the proper ring was found and all was as if nothing untoward had happened.

One Christmas Eve I gave supper to Albert Finney, not yet a great star, in a small, chic, and excellent Soho restaurant which has now had to make way for Chinese junk. We found ourselves seated at a table opposite Martita and her constant drinking companion. I crossed the room to kiss her, whereupon she flung out her arms and brought her hands together with great force over both my ears by way of greeting. I was stunned and deafened by the blow. Back at my own table I said to Albie, 'It's no use talking – I can't hear a thing.' Three days later, my ears still ringing and feeling off-balance, I went to see a specialist. 'Lucky the blow was uneven,' he told me, 'or you'd be totally deaf for life. As things are, only the left ear is dented.' He blew the eardrum straight with an old-fashioned motor horn but I am still weak in that ear and deaf to certain registers. The specialist asked who had struck me so violently and when I told him he said, 'I have always suspected she was a dangerous woman.' I had disliked the man on meeting him but now I loathed him. 'Actually,' I said, 'she is kind, highly intelligent and very special. What is the fee for your treatment and uncalled-for comment?' I stumbled from his consulting room and erased his name from my memory. Yes, perhaps she was dangerous; but then she was always so easy to forgive.

After the first fire in her flat she managed to do it again, although not so badly. One of the last times I went to see her she had arranged for oysters and a crab dish to be sent from Prunier's for lunch. George or Harry or Les delivered them. She was sitting up in bed; her hair singed, cigarette burns the size of saucers all over the blanket, wire springs spiralling through the seats of chairs, a table with only two legs propped against a wall and a very good French clock lay face down on the stained carpet. A few books were scattered around on the bed and the whole place looked grubby but was probably fairly clean. 'Oysters or crab?' she asked. I settled for the crab. She smiled at the oysters and paid small endearments to each one before gobbling it. 'You're a fat little fellow, aren't you, darling? And you taste very fresh and good. You *were* a good fellow. Now, who else is plump and pretty and ready for Marti?' I could have wept, except that she was cheerful. She suddenly referred to the maid she employed for a few hours each week and the maid's husband.

'Isn't it disgraceful? The poor girl! Her husband doesn't take off his pyjamas when they have sex. Now that's not sportin'.' She rambled on, lit a fresh cigarette while she had one still alight and only half-smoked in her hand, pushed some books off the bed impatiently and said she needed to sleep. I took my leave, but before kissing her goodbye carried the Prunier's remains to the kitchen, removed her lit cigarette and stumped it out, and then drew the curtains against the strong daylight. She was very sweet; like a small girl being tucked up for the night.

Some time after her death a plaque was unveiled to her in St Paul's, Covent Garden; her sister and half a dozen of her friends were present. It was a sunny, summery noon and a few very brief prayers were read. The Vicar kept looking anxiously at his watch, as did Martita's good friend Caroline Ramsden (greatly given to the race track) as two expected friends looked like being too late for the little ceremony.

'I think we must consider ourselves under starter's orders,' said Miss Ramsden.

'I am the Resurrection … ' the Vicar commenced, but Caroline Ramsden halted him.

'Hold it, Vicar!' She had peered through the plate glass door of the church and saw the expected couple arriving. 'They're round the bend! They're coming up th straight! Neck and neck! Well done, well done.'

The church clock struck.

'You're off!' she said to the Vicar. If she had had a pistol I believe she would have fired it. A nice, jolly woman.

'I am the Resurrection … ' the Vicar started again. Soon he was reading a splendid passage which included the words 'death is but an horizon' and it alerted that marvellous actress Gwen Ffrangcon-Davies, who had been silent until then.

'I like that,' Gwen said. 'Death is but an horizon. Where does that come from?'

The Vicar ploughed on without enlightening her, so Gwen wandered across to the plaque, which she studied and then read aloud to us, 'Martita Hunt – Actress – 1901–1969.' The Vicar did his best.

I had invited Martita's sister, Gwen, Caroline, Stanley Hall and McGregor (both of Wig Creations) to lunch and when the service ended a vast, black limousine was waiting for us at the church entrance. We all piled in and drove in slow and stately style round St James's Park, to admire the blossom, past Buckingham Palace and up St James's Street to Prunier's. Any other restaurant would have been unthinkable; Martita had entertained all of us there, no doubt, so lavishly over the years. Menus were gazed at silently and then each one of my guests said, 'Oysters.' When the platters of oysters arrived Gwen, who is very short-sighted, looked at hers intently, murmuring, 'Death is but an horizon.' The oysters were washed down with a fine, dry Sancerre which Martita had introduced me to the first time she took me to Prunier's, and it had made a deep impression on me: cool, elegant, sophisticated and delightful. It was, I hope, a fitting remembrance, if not an epitaph.

ALEC GUINNESS, *BLESSINGS IN DISGUISE*

Although this anthology is primarily concerned with theatre, it would not be fair to leave the great monsters of Hollywood out of this chapter. It is a well-mined seam, notably by Kenneth Anger in his two *Hollywood Babylon* books, so my inclusion of the following extract is really only tokenism. In 1978 Christina Crawford brought out her autobiography *Mommie Dearest*. Her portrait of her mother Joan has an operatic grandeur, horror and sense of the ridiculous. Unsurprising that the book is a camp classic. Slightly more alarming was the Niagara of imitators that followed. It seemed for a while that Tinseltown was populated entirely by vodka-swilling, child-abusing maniacs, and that, of course, *can't* be true ...

What was so terrifying about the night raids was that they could not be predicted. They sprang full blown without warning. We were always asleep and it was always dark outside when they started. Months would go by without a night raid and then there it would be, startling you out of a sound sleep, running full speed ahead and already out of control.

What mysterious combination of external and internal events led up to my mother's volcanic behaviour? I still do not know. What I know is that they were the most dreaded of all the journeys she took us through.

Three night raids are still vividly clear in my mind and they are typical of the others.

Chris and I had already moved into Mr Terry's former room, which had

202

been redecorated for us with twin beds, new wall-paper, and new furniture. There were sliding-door closets in the bathroom that Chris used and a large walk-in closet for me right across from my bed near the door.

I was awakened out of a sound sleep one night by a crashing sound. I opened my eyes, sitting bolt upright in bed. I saw that my closet door was open, the light was on, and various pieces of clothing were flying out into the room. Inside the closet my mother was in a rage. She was swearing a blue streak and muttering to herself. I dared not move out of my bed for fear of her wrath being taken out on me directly. After the closet was totally demolished and everything in it spewed out onto my bed and the floor, Mommie emerged breathless and triumphant. She had a wild look in her eyes, and as she descended upon me I was terrified.

She grabbed me by the hair and dragged me into the closet. There before me I saw total devastation. The closet was in complete shambles. It looked as if she'd taken her arms and pushed everything off the shelves. Then she'd ripped the clothes off their hangers and thrown both clothes and hangers out into the room, where they lay sprawled over half the floor. Last to go were the shoes, which she'd thrown hard enough to hit the far wall of the bedroom. They clattered against the venetian blinds as they fell.

Shaking me by the hair of my head she screamed in my ear, 'No wire hangers! No wire hangers!' With one hand she pulled me by the hair and with the other she pounded my ears until they rang and I could hardly hear her screaming. When she finished hitting me she released my hair and dumped me on the floor. Then she ripped my bed apart down to the mattress cover, throwing the sheets and blankets across the room. When she had totally destroyed my entire part of the bedroom she stood in the doorway with her hands on her hips. 'Clean up your mess,' she growled, turning on her heel. The only other sound I heard was the double doors to her room slamming shut.

Had I bothered to look at the clock I would have seen it was well past midnight. I didn't make the effort because it was a useless waste of my strength. I did look to see if Chris was still alive in the next bed. Once he was sure that she was gone and not coming back, he turned his body slowly to face me. It was probably the first time he'd dared to stir since the beginning of the night raid. He couldn't get up because he was tied down to the bed. Mother had a barbaric device she called a 'sleep safe' with which she made sure Chris could not get out of bed. It was like a harness made of heavy canvas straps, and it fastened at the back. It was originally designed to keep babies from falling out of bed, but she had the thing modified to accommodate a growing boy. The way it worked was that the person lay face down upon the sheet and the straps that came from underneath the mattress went around his waist and across his shoulders. All four pieces were fastened together with a huge steel safety pin like the kind they use for horse blankets. From the time I can remember, we were forbidden to get out of bed at night to go to the bathroom or to get a drink of water without specific permission. Sometimes we would yell our lungs out and no one would come. There were times when my brother simply had to go to the bathroom, and I would undo the wretched sleep safe and stand guard while he raced to the bathroom and then jumped back into bed. We had it timed just like an Indianapolis pit stop because both our lives depended on expert teamwork. I would have got in more trouble than Chris if we'd ever been caught, and we both knew it. He would get beaten for getting out of bed but I would have been nearly killed for letting him out of the sleep safe.

When I was small Mommie had tried the sleep safe on me. I hated the contraption so much that I begged her to let me sleep without it, promising never to get out of bed without permission. But my brother was a very active boy and my mother got out the sleep safe once again. From the time he was a baby, she kept him tied down to the bed. As Chris grew, so did the sleep safe. Eventually it became a source of continual punishment for my brother. Every night he was pinned into this harness, even though he was way past the baby stage. There were many times he railed against the insult, against the physical evidence of mistrust his mother was bestowing upon him by forcing him to be tied down every night of his life, but he was just helpless to do anything about it. The sleep safe conspiracy my brother and I formed was just one example of how we managed to survive.

This particular night raid my brother had escaped scot-free and I didn't begrudge him that. He couldn't get up to comfort me and didn't even dare whisper for fear she would hear us and return. He looked at me sadly, and through my tears I stared back at him. My head hurt where she had grabbed my hair, and, as I gingerly rubbed the place, a few snatches of hair fell out. But the frightful ringing in my ears was beginning to subside. I was grateful the beating was over.

Slowly I pulled myself to my feet and surveyed the damage. All this, I thought, for a couple of lousy wire hangers. Something had come back from the cleaner's or the laundry downstairs on wire hangers. Mother forbade us to use them in our closets. I hadn't changed to the proper hangers right away. I guess it hadn't seemed so terribly important at the time, which I now regretted.

It took me hours to redo the closet with everything neatly folded and put back on the shelves, all the clothes returned to their proper covered hangers. I blearily mated the shoes and lined them neatly on their rack. Just as I turned out the closet light I remembered that my bed still had to be remade and seriously thought about just sleeping on the floor. But there was always the possibility that she might return, and I dared not chance a repeat performance. As I struggled to remake my bed in near exhaustion I realized that it was beginning to get light outside.

CHRISTINA CRAWFORD, MOMMIE DEAREST

ᐬ

Two fictional pieces now. The first is the end of Act Two of Noël Coward's *Hay Fever* in which the monstrous theatrical Bliss family go into their unstoppable routine, to the bemusement and fury of their non-theatrical guests. The second is a brilliant short story by Dorothy Parker.

ᐬ

SIMON. Mother – Mother, I've got something important to tell you.
JUDITH (*smiling bravely*). Very well, dear.
SIMON. Where's Sorel?
JUDITH. In the library, I'm afraid.
SIMON (*runs to the library door and shouts off*). Sorel, come out – I've got something vital to tell you. (*Returns to C.*)
DAVID (*fatherly*). You seem excited, my boy! What has happened?
SOREL (*enters with Sandy and remains down L.*). What's the matter?
SIMON. I wish you wouldn't all look so depressed – it's good news!
DAVID. Good news! I thought perhaps Jackie had been drowned –
SIMON. No, Jackie hasn't been drowned – she's been something else.
JUDITH. Simon, what *do* you mean?
SIMON (*running up C., calling off*). Jackie – Jackie!

Jackie enters coyly from the garden. Simon takes her hand and leads her down C.

She has become engaged to me!
JUDITH. (in heartfelt tones). Simon!
SOREL. Good heavens!
JUDITH. Simon, my dear! Oh, this is too much! (*She cries a little.*)
SIMON. What on earth are you crying about, Mother?
JUDITH (*picturesquely*). All my chicks leaving the nest! Now I shall only have my memories left. Jackie, come and kiss me.

(*Jackie goes to her.*
Simon goes to his Father, who congratulates him.)

You must promise to make my son happy –

JACKIE *(worried)*. But, Mrs Bliss –

JUDITH. Ssshhh! I understand. I have not been a mother for nothing.

JACKIE *(wildly)*. But it's not true – we don't –

JUDITH. You're trying to spare my feelings – I know –

MYRA *(furiously)*. Well, I'm not going to spare your feelings, or anyone else's. You're the most infuriating set of hypocrites I've ever seen. This house is a complete feather-bed of false emotions – you're posing, self-centred egotists, and I'm sick to death of you.

SIMON. Myra!

MYRA. Don't speak to me – I've been working up for this, only every time I opened my mouth I've been mowed down by theatrical effects. You haven't got once sincere or genuine feeling among the lot of you – you're artificial to the point of lunacy. It's a great pity you ever left the stage, Judith – it's your rightful home. You can rant and roar there as much as ever you like –

JUDITH. Rant and roar! May God forgive you!

MYRA. And let me tell you this –

SIMON *(interrupting)*. I'm not going to allow you to say another word to Mother –

They all try to shout each other down.

SOREL		You ought to be ashamed of yourself –
MYRA	*(together)*:	Let me speak – I will speak –
DAVID		Look here, Myra –
JUDITH		This is appaling – appaling!
SOREL		You must be stark, staring mad –
MYRA		Never again – never as long as I live –
DAVID	*(together)*:	You don't seem to grasp one thing that –
SIMON		Why are you behaving like this, anyhow?

In the middle of the pandemonium of everyone talking at once, Richard comes in from the garden. He looks extremely apprehensive, imagining that the noise is the outcome of Judith's hysterical confession of their lukewarm passion. He goes to Judith's side, summoning all his diplomatic forces. As he speaks everyone stops talking.

RICHARD *(with forced calm)*. What's happened? Is this a game?

(Judith's face gives a slight twitch; then, with a meaning look at Sorel and Simon, she answers him.)

JUDITH *(with spirit)*. Yes, and a game that must be played to the finish! *(She flings back her arm and knocks Richard up stage.)*

SIMON *(grasping the situation)*. Zara! What does this mean? *(Advancing to her.)*

JUDITH *(in bell-like tones)*. So many illusions shattered – so many dreams trodden in the dust –

DAVID *(collapsing on to the sofa in hysterics)*. Love's Whirlwind! Dear old Love's Whirlwind!

SOREL *(runs over to R., pushes Myra up stage and poses)*. I don't understand. You and Victor – My God!

JUDITH *(moves away L., listening)*. Hush! Isn't that little Pam crying –?

SIMON *(savagely)*. She'll cry more, poor mite, when she realizes her mother is a – a –

JUDITH *(shrieking and turning to Simon)*. Don't say it! Don't say it!

SOREL. Spare her that.

JUDITH. I've given you all that makes life worth living – my youth, my womanhood, and now my child. Would you tear the very heart out of me? I tell you, it's infamous that men like you should be allowed to pollute Society. You have ruined my life. I have nothing left – nothing! God in heaven, where am I to turn for help? ...

SOREL *(through clenched teeth – swings Simon round)*. Is this true? Answer me – is this true?

JUDITH *(wailing)*. Yes, yes!

SOREL *(as if to strike Simon)*. You cur! ! !

JUDITH. Don't strike! He is your father! ! ! !

(She totters and falls in a dead faint.)

(Myra, Jackie, Richard and Sandy look on, dazed and aghast.)

NOËL COWARD, *HAY FEVER*

Mr Murdock was one who carried no enthusiasm whatever for plays and their players, and that was too bad, for they meant so much to little Mrs Murdock. Always she had been in a state of devout excitement over the luminous, free, passionate elect who serve the theatre. And always she had done her wistful worshipping, along with the multitudes, at the great public altars. It is true that once, when she was a particularly little girl, love had impelled her to write Miss Maude Adams a letter beginning 'Dearest Peter', and she had received from Miss Adams a miniature thimble inscribed 'A Kiss from Peter Pan'. (That was a day!) And once, when her mother had taken her holiday shopping, a limousine door was held open and there had passed her, as close as *that*, a wonder of sable and violets and round red curls that seemed to tinkle on the air; so, forever after, she was as

207

good as certain that she had been not a foot away from Miss Billie Burke. But until some three years after her marriage, these had remained her only personal experiences with the people of the lights and the glory.

Then it turned out that Miss Noyes, new come to little Mrs Murdock's own bridge club, knew an actress. She actually knew an actress; the way you and I know collectors of recipes and members of garden clubs and amateurs of needlepoint.

The name of the actress was Lily Wynton, and it was famous. She was tall and slow and silvery; often she appeared in the role of a duchess, or of a Lady Pam or an Honourable Moira. Critics recurrently referred to her as 'that great lady of our stage'. Mrs Murdock had attended, over years, mat-inée performances of the Wynton successes. And she had no more thought that she would one day have opportunity to meet Lily Wynton face to face than she had thought – well, than she had thought of flying!

Yet it was not astounding that Miss Noyes should walk at ease among the glamorous. Miss Noyes was full of depth and mystery, and she could talk with a cigarette still between her lips. She was always doing something difficult, like designing her own pajamas, or reading Proust, or modelling torsos in Plasticine. She played excellent bridge. She liked little Mrs Murdock. 'Tiny one,' she called her.

'How's for coming to tea tomorrow, tiny one? Lily Wynton's going to drop up,' she said, at a therefore memorable meeting of the bridge club. 'You might like to meet her.'

The words fell so easily that she could not have realized their weight. Lily Wynton was coming to tea. Mrs Murdock might like to meet her. Little Mrs Murdock walked home through the early dark, and stars sang in the sky above her.

Mr Murdock was already at home when she arrived. It required but a glance to tell that for him there had been no singing star that evening in the heavens. He sat with his newspaper opened at the financial page, and bitterness had its way with his soul. It was not the time to cry happily to him of the impending hospitalities of Miss Noyes; not the time, that is, if one anticipated exclamatory sympathy. Mr Murdock did not like Miss Noyes. When pressed for a reason, he replied that he just plain didn't like her. Occasionally he added, with a sweep that might have commanded a certain admiration, that all those women made him sick. Usually, when she told him of the temperate activities of the bridge club meetings, Mrs Murdock kept any mention of Miss Noyes's name from the accounts. She had found that this omission made for a more agreeable evening. But now she was caught in such a sparkling swirl of excitement that she had scarcely kissed him before she was off on her story.

'Oh Jim,' she cried. 'Oh, what do you think! Hallie Noyes asked me to tea tomorrow to meet Lily Wynton!'

'Who's Lily Wynton?' he said.

'Ah, Jim,' she said. 'Ah, really, Jim. Who's Lily Wynton! Who's Greta Garbo, I suppose!'

'She some actress or something?' he said.

Mrs Murdock's shoulders sagged. 'Yes, Jim,' she said. 'Yes. Lily Wynton's an actress.'

She picked up her purse and started slowly toward the door. But before she had taken three steps, she was again caught up in her sparkling swirl. She turned to him, and her eyes were shining.

'Honestly,' she said, 'it was the funniest thing you ever heard in your life. We'd just finished the last rubber – oh, I forgot to tell you, I won three dollars, isn't that pretty good for me? – and Hallie Noyes said to me, "Come on in to tea tomorrow. Lily Wynton's going to drop up," she said. Just like that, she said it. Just as if it was anybody.'

'Drop up?' he said. 'How can you drop *up*?'

'Honestly, I don't know what I said when she asked me,' Mrs Murdock said. 'I suppose I said I'd love to – I guess I must have. But I was so simply – well, you know how I've always felt about Lily Wynton. Why, when I was a little girl, I used to collect her pictures. And I've seen her in, oh, everything she's ever been in, I should think, and I've read every word about her, and interviews and all. Really and truly, when I think of *meeting* her – oh, I'll simply die. What on earth shall I say to her?'

'You might ask her how she'd like to try dropping down, for a change,' Mr Murdock said.

'All right, Jim,' Mrs Murdock said. 'If that's the way you want to be.'

Wearily she went toward the door, and this time she reached it before she turned to him. There were no lights in her eyes.

'It – it isn't so awfully nice,' she said, 'to spoil somebody's pleasure in something. I was so thrilled about this. You don't see what it is to me, to meet Lily Wynton. To meet somebody like that, and see what they're like, and hear what they say, and maybe get to know them. People like that mean – well, they mean something different to me. They're not like this. They're not like me. Who do I ever see? What do I ever hear? All my whole life, I've wanted to know – I've almost prayed that some day I could meet – well. All right, Jim.'

She went out, and on to her bedroom.

Mr Murdock was left with only his newspaper and his bitterness for company. But he spoke aloud.

"Drop up!" he said. "Drop *up*, for God's sake!"

The Murdocks dined, not in silence, but in pronounced quiet. There was something straitened about Mr Murdock's stillness; but little Mrs Murdock's was the sweet, far quiet of one given over to dreams. She had forgotten her weary words to her husband, she had passed through her excitement and her disappointment. Luxuriously she floated on innocent visions of days after the morrow. She heard her own voice in future conversations ...

I saw Lily Wynton at Hallie's the other day, and she was telling me all about her new play – no, I'm terribly sorry, but it's a secret, I promised her I wouldn't tell anyone the name of it ... Lily Wynton dropped up to tea yesterday, and we just got to talking, and she told me the most interesting things about her life; she said she'd never dreamed of telling them to anyone else ... Why, I'd love to come, but I promised to have lunch with Lily Wynton ... I had a long, long letter from Lily Wynton ... Lily Wynton called me up this morning ... Whenever I feel blue, I just go and have a talk with Lily Wynton, and then I'm all right again ... Lily Wynton told me ... Lily Wynton and I ... 'Lily,' I said to her ...

The next morning, Mr Murdock had left for his office before Mrs Murdock rose. This had happened several times before, but not often. Mrs Murdock felt a little queer about it. Then she told herself that it was probably just as well. Then she forgot all about it, and gave her mind to the selection of a costume suitable to the afternoon's event. Deeply she felt that her small wardrobe included no dress adequate to the occasion; for, of course, such an occasion had never before arisen. She finally decided upon a frock of dark blue serge with fluted white muslin about the neck and wrists. It was her style, that was the most she could say for it. And that was all she could say for herself. Blue serge and little white ruffles – that was she.

The very becomingness of the dress lowered her spirits. A nobody's frock, worn by a nobody. She blushed and went hot when recalled the dreams she had woven the night before, the mad visions of intimacy of equality with Lily Wynton. Timidity turned her heart liquid, and she thought of telephoning Miss Noyes and saying she had a bad cold and could not come. She steadied, when she planned a course of conduct to pursue at teatime. She would not try to say anything; if she stayed silent, she could not sound foolish. She would listen and watch and worship and then come home, stronger, braver, better for an hour she would remember proudly all her life.

Miss Noyes's living-room was done in the early modern period. There were a great many oblique lines and acute angles, zigzags of aluminium and horizontal stretches of mirror. The colour scheme was sawdust and steel. No seat was more than twelve inches above the floor, no table was made of wood. It was, as has been said of larger places, all right for a visit.

Little Mrs Murdock was the first arrival. She was glad of that, no, maybe it would have been better to have come after Lily Wynton; no, maybe this was right. The maid motioned her toward the living-room, and Miss Noyes greeted her in the cool voice and the warm words that were her special combination. She wore black velvet trousers, a red cummerbund, and a white silk shirt, opened at the throat. A cigarette clung to her lower lip, and her eyes, as was her habit, were held narrow against its near smoke.

'Come in, come in, tiny one,' she said. 'Bless its little heart. Take off its little coat. Good lord, you look easily eleven years old in that dress. Sit ye doon, here beside of me. There'll be a spot of tea in a jiff.'

Mrs Murdock sat down on the vast, periously low, divan, and, because she was never good at reclining among cushions, held her back straight. There was room for six like her, between herself and her hostess. Miss Noyes lay back with one ankle flung upon the other knee, and looked at her.

'I'm a wreck,' Miss Noyes announced. 'I was modelling like a mad thing, all night long. It's taken everything out of me. I was like a thing bewitched.'

'Oh, what were you making?' cried Mrs Murdock.

'Oh, Eve,' Miss Noyes said. 'I always do Eve. What else is there to do? You must come pose for me some time, tiny one. You'd be nice to do. Ye-es, you'd be very nice to do. My tiny one.'

'Why, I – ' Mrs Murdock said, and stopped. 'Thank you very much, though,' she said.

'I wonder where Lily is,' Miss Noyes said. 'She said she'd be here early – well, she always says that. You'll adore her, tiny one. She's really rare. She's a real person. And she's been through perfect hell. God, what a time she's had!'

'Ah, what's been the matter?' said Mrs Murdock.

'Men,' Miss Noyes said. 'Men. She never had a man that wasn't a louse.' Gloomily she stared at the toe of her flat-heeled patent leather pump. 'A pack of lice, always. All of them. Leave her for the first little floozie that comes along.'

'But –' Mrs Murdock began. No, she couldn't have heard right. How could it be right? Lily Wynton was a great actress. A great actress meant

211

romance. Romance meant Grand Dukes and Crown Princes and diplomats touched with grey at the temples and lean, bronzed, reckless Younger Sons. It meant pearls and emeralds and chinchilla and rubies red as the blood that was shed for them. It meant a grim-faced boy sitting in the fearful Indian midnight, beneath the dreary whirring of the *punkahs*, writing a letter to the lady he had seen but once; writing his poor heart out, before he turned to the service revolver that lay beside him on the table. It meant a golden-locked poet, floating face downward in the sea, and in his pocket his last great sonnet to the lady of ivory. It meant brave, beautiful men, living and dying for the lady who was the pale bride of art, whose eyes and heart were soft with only compassion for them.

A pack of lice. Crawling after little floozies; whom Mrs Murdock swiftly and hazily pictured as rather like ants.

'But –' said little Mrs Murdock.

'She gave them all her money,' Miss Noyes said. 'She always did. Or if she didn't, they took it anyway. Took every cent she had, and then spat in her face. Well, maybe I'm teaching her a little bit of sense now. Oh, there's the bell – that'll be Lily. No, sit ye doon, tiny one. You belong there.'

Miss Noyes rose and made for the archway that separated the living-room from the hall. As she passed Mrs Murdock, she stooped suddenly, cupped her guest's round chin, and quickly, lightly kissed her mouth.

'Don't tell Lily,' she murmured, very low.

Mrs Murdock puzzled. Don't tell Lily what? Could Hallie Noyes think that she might babble to the Lily Wynton of these strange confidences about the actress's life? Or did she mean – but she had no more time for puzzling. Lily Wynton stood in the archway. There she stood, one hand resting on the wooden moulding and her body swayed towards it, exactly as she stood for her third-act entrance of her latest play, and for a like half-minute.

You would have known her anywhere, Mrs Murdock thought. Oh yes, anywhere. Or at least you should have exclaimed, 'That woman looks something like Lily Wynton.' For she was somehow different in the daylight. Her figure looked heavier, thicker, and her face – there was so much of her face that the surplus sagged from the strong, fine bones. And her eyes, those famous dark, liquid eyes. They were dark, yes, and certainly liquid, but they were set in little hammocks of folded flesh, and seemed to be set but loosely, so readily did they roll. Their whites, that were visible all around the irises, were threaded with tiny scarlet veins.

'I suppose footlights are an awful strain on their eyes,' thought little Mrs Murdock.

212

Lily Wynton wore, just as she should have, black satin and sables, and long white gloves were wrinkled luxuriously about her wrists. But there were delicate streaks of grime in the folds of her gloves, and down the shining length of her gown there were small, irregularly shaped dull patches; bits of food or drops of drink, or perhaps both, sometime must have slipped their carriers and found brief sanctuary there. Her hat – oh, her hat. It was romance, it was mystery, it was strange, sweet sorrow; it was Lily Wynton's hat, of all the world, and no other could dare it. Black it was, and tilted, and a great, soft plume drooped from it to follow her cheek and curl across her throat. Beneath it, her hair had the various hues of neglected brass. But, oh, her hat.

'Darling!' cried Miss Noyes.

'Angel,' said Lily Wynton. 'My sweet.'

It was that voice. It was that deep, soft, glowing voice. 'Like purple velvet,' someone had written. Mrs Murdock's heart beat visibly.

Lily Wynton cast herself upon the steep bosom of her hostess, and murmured there. Across Miss Noyes's shoulder she caught sight of Little Mrs Murdock.

'And who is this?' she said. She disengaged herself.

'That's my tiny one,' Miss Noyes said. 'Mrs Murdock.'

'What a clever little face,' said Lily Wynton. 'Clever, clever little face. What does she do, sweet Hallie? I'm sure she writes, doesn't she? Yes, I can feel it. She writes beautiful, beautiful words. Don't you, child?'

'Oh no, really I – ' Mrs Murdock said.

'And you must write me a play,' said Lily Wynton. 'A beautiful, beautiful play. And I will play in it, over and over the world, until I am a very, very old lady. And then I will die. But I will never be forgotten, because of the years I played in your beautiful, beautiful play.'

She moved across the room. There was a slight hesitancy, a seeming insecurity, in her step, and when she would have sunk into a chair, she began to sink two inches, perhaps, to its right. But she swayed just in time in her descent, and was safe.

'To write,' she said, smiling sadly at Mrs Murdock, 'to write. And such a little thing, for such a big gift. Oh, the privilege of it. But the anguish of it, too. The agony.'

'But, you see, I –' said little Mrs Murdock.

'Tiny one doesn't write, Lily,' Miss Noyes said. She threw herself back upon the divan. 'She's a museum piece. She's a devoted wife.'

'A wife!' Lily Wynton said. 'A wife. Your first marriage, child?'

'Oh yes,' said Mrs Murdock.

213

'How sweet,' Lily Wynton said. 'How sweet, sweet, sweet. Tell me, child, do you love him very, very much?'

'Why I –' said little Mrs Murdock and blushed. 'I've been married for ages,' she said.

'You love him,' Lily Wynton said. 'You love him. And is it sweet to go to bed with him?'

'Oh –' said Mrs Murdock, and blushed till it hurt.

'The first marriage,' Lily Wynton said. 'Youth, youth. Yes, when I was your age I used to marry, too. Oh, treasure your love, child, guard it, live in it. Laugh and dance in the love of your man. Until you find out what he's really like.'

There came a sudden visitation upon her. Her shoulders jerked upward, her cheeks puffed, her eyes sought to start from their hammocks. For a moment she sat thus, then slowly all subsided into place. She lay back in her chair, tenderly patting her chest. She shook her head sadly, and there was grieved wonder in the look with which she held Mrs Murdock.

'Gas,' said Lily Wynton, in the famous voice. 'Gas. Nobody knows what I suffer from it.'

'Oh, I'm so sorry,' Mrs Murdock said. 'Is there anything –'

'Nothing,' Lily Wynton said. 'There is nothing. There is nothing can be done for it. I've been everywhere.'

'How's for a spot of tea, perhaps?' Miss Noyes said. 'It might help.' She turned her face toward the archway and lifted up her voice. 'Mary! Where the hell's the tea?'

'You don't know,' Lily Wynton said, with her grieved eyes fixed on Mrs Murdock, 'you don't know what stomach distress is. You can never, never know, unless you're a stomach sufferer yourself. I've been one for years. Years and years and years.'

'I'm terribly sorry,' Mrs Murdock said.

'Nobody knows the anguish,' Lily Wynton said. 'The agony.'

The maid appeared, bearing a triangular tray upon which was set an heroic-sized tea service of bright white china, each piece a hectagon. She set it down on a table within the long reach of Miss Noyes and retired, as she had come, bashfully.

'Sweet Hallie,' Lily Wynton said, 'my sweet. Tea – I adore it. I worship it. But my distress turns it to gall and wormwood. For hours, I should have no peace. Let me have a little, tiny bit of your beautiful, beautiful brandy, instead.'

'You really think you should, darling?' Miss Noyes said. 'You know –'

'My angel,' said Lily Wynton, 'it's the only thing for acidity.'

'Well,' Miss Noyes said. 'But do remember you've got a performance tonight.' Again she hurled her voice at the archway. 'Mary! Bring the brandy and a lot of soda and ice and things.'

'Oh no, my saint,' Lily Wynton said. 'No, no, sweet Hallie. Soda and ice are rank poison to me. Do you want to freeze my poor, weak stomach? Do you want to kill poor, poor Lily?'

'Mary!' roared Miss Noyes. 'Just bring the brandy and a glass.' She turned to little Mrs Murdock. 'How's for your tea, tiny one? Cream? Lemon?'

'Cream, if I may, please,' Mrs Murdock said. 'And two lumps of sugar, please, if I may.'

'Oh, youth, youth,' Lily Wynton said. 'Youth and love.'

The maid returned with an octagonal tray supporting a decanter of brandy and a wide, squat, heavy glass. Her head twisted on her neck in a spasm of diffidence.

'Just pour it for me, will you, my dear?' said Lily Wynton. 'Thank you. And leave the pretty, pretty decanter here, on this enchanting little table. Thank you. You're so good to me.'

The maid vanished, fluttering. Lily Wynton lay back in her chair, holding in her gloved hand the wide, squat glass, coloured brown to the brim. Little Mrs Murdock lowered her eyes to her teacup, carefully carried it to her lips, sipped, and replaced it on its saucer. When she raised her eyes, Lily Wynton lay back in her chair, holding her gloved hand the wide, squat, colourless glass.

'My life,' Lily Wynton said, slowly, 'is a mess. A stinking mess. It always has been, and it always will be. Until I am a very, very old lady. Ah, little Clever-Face, you writers don't know what struggle is.'

'But really I'm not –' said Mrs Murdock.

'To write,' Lily Wynton said. 'To write. To set one word beautifully beside another word. The privilege of it. The blessed, blessed peace of it. Oh, for quiet, for rest. But do you think those cheap bastards would close that play while it's doing a nickel's worth of business? Oh no. Tired as I am, sick as I am, I must drag along. Oh, child, child, guard your precious gift. Give thanks for it. It is the greatest thing of all. It is the only thing. To write.'

'Darling, I told you tiny one doesn't write,' said Miss Noyes. 'How's for making more sense? She's a wife.'

'Ah, yes, she told me. She told me she had perfect, passionate love,' Lily Wynton said. 'Young love. It is the greatest thing. It is the only thing.' She grasped the decanter; and again the squat glass was brown to the brim.

'What time did you start today, darling?' said Miss Noyes.

'Oh, don't scold me, sweet love,' Lily Wynton said. 'Lily hasn't been naughty. Her wuzzunt naughty dirl't all. I didn't get up until late, late, late. And though I parched, though I burned, I didn't have a drink until after my breakfast. "It is for Hallie," I said.' She raised the glass to her mouth, tilted it, and brought it away, colourless.

'Good Lord, Lily,' Miss Noyes said. 'Watch yourself. You've got to walk on that stage tonight, my girl.'

'All the world's a stage,' said Lily Wynton. 'And all the men and women merely players. They have their entrance and their exitses, and each man in his time plays many parts, his act being seven ages. At first, the infant, mewling and puking –'

'How's the play doing?' Miss Noyes said.

'Oh, lousily,' Lily Wynton said. 'Lousily, lousily, lousily. But what isn't? What isn't, in this terrible, terrible world? Answer me that.' She reached for the decanter.

'Lily, listen,' said Miss Noyes. 'Stop that. Do you hear?'

'Please, sweet Hallie,' Lily Wynton said. 'Pretty please. Poor, poor Lily.'

'Do you want me to do what I had to do last time?' Miss Noyes said. 'Do you want me to strike you, in front of tiny one, here?'

Lily Wynton drew herself high. 'You do not realize,' she said, icily, 'what acidity is.' She filled the glass and held it, regarding it as though through a lorgnon. Suddenly her manner changed, and she looked up and smiled at little Mrs Murdock.

'You must let me read it,' she said. 'You mustn't be so modest.'

'Read – ?' said little Mrs Murdock.

'Your play,' Lily Wynton said. 'Your beautiful, beautiful play. Don't think I am too busy. I always have time. I have time for everything. Oh, my God, I have to go to the dentist tomorrow. Oh, the suffering I have gone through with my teeth. Look!' She set down her glass, inserted a gloved forefinger in the corner of her mouth, and dragged it to the side. 'Oogh!' she insisted. 'Oogh!'

Mrs Murdock craned her neck shyly, and caught a glimpse of shining gold.

'Oh, I'm so sorry,' she said.

'As wah ee id a me ass ime,' Lily Wynton said. She took away her fore-finger and let her mouth resume its shape. 'That's what he did to me last time,' she repeated. 'The anguish of it. The agony. Do you suffer with your teeth, Clever-Face?'

'Why, I'm afraid I've been awfully lucky,' Mrs Murdock said. 'I –'

'You don't know,' Lily Wynton said. 'Nobody knows what it is. You writers – you don't know.' She took up her glass, sighed over it, and drained it.

'Well,' Miss Noyes said. 'Go ahead and pass out, then, darling. You'll have time for a sleep before the theatre.'

'To sleep,' Lily Wynton said. 'To sleep, perchance to dream. The privilege of it. Oh, Hallie, sweet, sweet Hallie, poor Lily feels so terrible. Rub my head for me, angel. Help me.'

'I'll go get the eau de Cologne,' Miss Noyes said. She left the room, lightly patting Mrs Murdock's knee as she passed her. Lily Wynton lay in her chair and closed her famous eyes.

'To sleep,' she said. 'To sleep, perchance to dream.'

'I'm afraid,' little Mrs Murdock began. 'I'm afraid,' she said, 'I really must be going home. I'm afraid I didn't realize how awfully late it was.'

'Yes, go, child,' Lily Wynton said. She did not open her eyes. 'Go to him. Go to him, live in him, love him. Stay with him always. But when he starts bringing them into the house – get out.'

'I'm afraid – I'm afraid I didn't quite understand,' Mrs Murdock said.

'When he starts bringing his fancy women into the house,' Lily Wynton said. 'You must have pride, then. You must go. I always did. But it was always too late then. They'd got all my money. That's all they want, marry them or not. They say it's love, but it isn't. Love is the only thing. Treasure your love, child. Go back to him. Go to bed with him. It's the only thing. And your beautiful, beautiful play.'

'Oh dear,' said Little Mrs Murdock. 'I – I'm afraid it's really terribly late.'

There was only the sound of rhythmic breathing from the chair where Lily Wynton lay. The purple voice rolled along the air no longer.

Little Mrs Murdock stole to the chair upon which she had left her coat. Carefully she smoothed her white muslin frills, so that they would be fresh beneath the jacket. She felt a tenderness for her frock; she wanted to protect it. Blue serge and little ruffles – they were her own.

When she reached the outer door of Miss Noyes's apartment, she stopped a moment and her manners conquered her. Bravely she called in the direction of Miss Noyes's bedroom.

'Good-bye, Miss Noyes,' she said. 'I've simply got to run. I didn't realize it was so late. I had a lovely time – thank you ever so much.'

'Oh, good-bye, tiny one,' Miss Noyes called. 'Sorry Lily went by-by. Don't mind her – she's really a person. I'll call you up, tiny one. I want to see you. Now where's that damned Cologne?'

'Thank you ever so much,' Mrs Murdock said. She let herself out of the apartment.

Little Mrs Murdock walked homeward, through the clustering dark. Her mind was busy, but not with memories of Lily Wynton. She thought of Jim; Jim, who had left for his office before she had arisen that morning, Jim, whom she had not kissed good-bye. Darling Jim. There were no others born like him. Funny Jim, stiff and cross and silent; but only because he knew so much. Only because he knew the silliness of seeking afar for the glamour and beauty and romance of living. When they were right at home all the time, she thought. Like the Blue Bird, thought little Mrs Murdock.

Darling Jim. Mrs Murdock turned in her course, and entered an enormous shop where the most delicate and esoteric of foods were sold for heavy sums. Jim liked red caviar. Mrs Murdock bought a jar of the shiny, glutinous eggs. They would have cocktails that night, though they had no guests, and the red caviar would be served with them for a surprise, and it would be a little secret party to celebrate her return to contentment with her Jim, a party to mark her happy renunciation of all the glory of the world. She bought, too, a large, foreign cheese. It would give a needed touch to dinner. Mrs Murdock had not given much attention to ordering dinner, that morning. 'Oh, anything you want, Signe,' she had said to the maid. She did not want to think of that. She went on home with her packages.

Mr Murdock was already there when she arrived. He was sitting with his newspaper opened to the financial page. Little Mrs Murdock ran in to him with her eyes a-light. It is too bad that the light in a person's eyes is only the light in a person's eyes, and you cannot tell at a look what causes it. You do not know if it is excitement about you, or about something else. The evening before, Mrs Murdock had run in to Mr Murdock with her eyes a-light.

'Oh hello,' he said to her. He looked back at his paper, and kept his eyes there. 'What did you do?' Did you drop up to Hank Noyes's?'

Little Mrs Murdock stopped right where she was.

'You know perfectly well, Jim,' she said, 'that Hallie Noyes's first name is Hallie.'

'It's Hank to me,' he said. 'Hank or Bill. Did what's-her-name show up? I mean drop up. Pardon me.'

'To whom are you referring?' said Mrs Murdock, perfectly.

'What's-her-name,' Mr Murdock said. 'The movie star.'

'If you mean Lily Wynton,' Mrs Murdock said, 'she is not a movie star. She is an actress. She is a great actress.'

'Well, did she drop up?' he said.

Mrs Murdock's shoulders sagged. 'Yes,' she said. 'Yes, she was there, Jim.'

'I suppose you're going on the stage now,' he said.

'Ah, Jim,' Mrs Murdock said. 'Ah, Jim, please. I'm not sorry at all I went to Hallie Noyes's today. It was — it was a real experience to meet Lily Wynton. Something I'll remember all my life.'

'What did she do?' Mr Murdock said. 'Hang by her feet?'

'She did no such thing!' Mrs Murdock said. 'She recited Shakespeare, if you want to know.'

'Oh, my God,' Mr Murdock said. 'That must have been great.'

'All right, Jim,' Mrs Murdock said. 'If that's the way you want to be.'

Wearily she left the room and went down the hall. She stopped at the pantry door, pushed it open, and spoke to the pleasant little maid.

'Oh, Signe,' she said. 'Oh, good evening, Signe. Put these things somewhere, will you? I got them on the way home. I thought we might have them some time.'

Wearily little Mrs Murdock went on down the hall to her bedroom.

DOROTHY PARKER, GLORY IN THE DAYTIME

CHAPTER 10
OLD AGE AND BEYOND

I'M STILL HERE

Good times and bum times, I've seem 'em all,
And my dear
I'm still here.
Plush velvet sometimes, sometimes just pretzels and beer
But I'm here.
I've stuffed the dailies in my shoes,
Strummed ukuleles, sung the blues
Seen all my dreams disappear
But I'm here.
I've slept in shanties, guest of the WPA
But I'm here.
Danced in my scanties, three bucks a night was my pay
But I'm here.
I've stood on breadlines with the best,
Watched while the headlines did the rest,
In the Depression was I depressed?
Nowhere near!
I met a big financier
    And I'm here.

I've gotten through Herbert and J. Edgar Hoover –
Gee, that was fun and a half!
When you've been through Herbert and J. Edgar Hoover,
Anything else is a laugh.
I've been through Reno, I've been through Beverly Hills
And I'm here.
Reefers and vino, rest cures, religion and pills
But I'm here.
Been called a pinko, commie tool
Got through it stinko by my pool
I should have gone to an acting school, that seems clear,
Still, someone said 'She's sincere' –
So I'm here.
Black sable one day, next day it goes into hock
But I'm here.
Top billing Monday, Tuesday you're touring in stock
But I'm here.
First you are another sloe-eyed vamp
Then someone's mother, then you're camp,
Then you career from career to career
I'm almost through my memoirs
And I'm here.
I've gotten through 'Hey lady, aren't you whosit?
Wow, what a looker you were'
Or better yet – 'Sorry, I thought you were whosit –
Whatever happened to her?'
Good times and bum times, I've seen 'em all
And my dear
I'm still here.
Plush velvet sometimes, sometimes just pretzels and beer
But I'm here.
I've run the gamut – A to Zee
Three cheers and dammit, *c'est la vie*!
I got through all of last year
And I'm here.
Lord knows at least I've been There
And I'm here
Look who's here
I'm still here!

STEPHEN SONDHEIM, *FOLLIES*

Sondheim's character is undefeatable and admirable in her toughness. Toughness, however, is not always possible. In Act Four of *Trelawny of the 'Wells'* a new play is in rehearsal. The leading lady is our heroine Rose, the author a struggling actor of whom we have become fond. But instead of allowing us an unclouded happy ending, Pinero focuses in on two elderly actors in the company – erstwhile stars at Sadlers Wells.

❧

Mrs Telfer is seated upon the throne-chair in an attitude of dejection. Telfer enters from the Green-room.

TELFER *(coming to her).* Is that you, Violet?

MRS TELFER. Is the reading over?

TELFER. Almost. My part is confined to the latter 'alf of the second act; so being close to the Green-room door, *(with a sigh)* I stole away.

MRS TELFER. It affords you no opportunity, James?

TELFER *(c., shaking his head).* A mere fragment.

MRS TELFER *(rising).* Well, but a few good speeches to a man of your stamp –

TELFER. Yes, but this is so line-y, Violet; so very line-y. And what d'ye think the character is described as?

MRS TELFER. What?

TELFER. 'An old, stagey, out-of-date actor.'

[They stand looking at each other for a moment, silently.]

MRS TELFER *(falteringly)* Will you – be able – to get near it, James?

TELFER *(looking away from her).* I daresay –

MRS TELFER *(laying a hand upon his shoulder).* That's all right, then.

TELFER. And you – what have they called you for, if you're not in the play? They 'ave not dared to suggest understudy?

MRS TELFER *(playing with her fingers).* They don't ask me to act at all, James.

TELFER. Don't ask you –!

MRS TELFER. Miss Parrott offers me the position of Wardrobe-mistress.

TELFER. Violet –!

MRS TELFER. Hush!

TELFER. Let us both go home.

MRS TELFER *(restraining him).* No, let us remain. We've been idle six months, and I can't bear to see you without your watch and all your comforts about you.

TELFER *(pointing towards the Green-room).* And so this new-fangled stuff, and

223

these dandified people, are to push us, and such as us, from our stools!
MRS TELFER. Yes, James, just as some other new fashion will, in course of
time, push *them* from their stools.

ARTHUR PINERO, *TRELAWNY OF THE 'WELLS'*

ಜಾ

There being no official pension scheme for actors, the choices are limited – to retire on the millions you have made and breed chickens (a
choice alas available to but a few), to go on as long as you can learn the
lines and get from the dressing-room to the stage, or to retire with style
and hope for the best. The Victorian actor knew how to stage a retirement. In *Nicholas Nickleby*, Nicholas decides to leave the Crummles'
troupe. They go at once into overdrive, planning his farewell appearances.

ಜಾ

Mr Vincent Crummles was no sooner acquainted with the public
announcement which Nicholas had made relative to the probability of his
shortly ceasing to be a member of the company, than he evinced many
tokens of grief and consternation; and, in the extremity of his despair, even
held out certain vague promises of a speedy improvement not only in the
amount of his regular salary, but also in the contingent emoluments apper-
taining to his authorship. Finding Nicholas bent upon quitting the society
– for he had now determined that, even if no further tidings came from
Newman, he would, at all hazards, ease his mind by repairing to London
and ascertaining the exact position of his sister – Mr Crummles was fain to
content himself by calculating the chances of his coming back again, and
taking prompt and energetic measures to make the most of him before he
went away.

'Let me see,' said Mr Crummles, taking off his outlaw's wig, the better
to arrive at a cool-headed view of the whole case. 'Let me see. This is
Wednesday night. We'll have posters out the first thing in the morning,
announcing positively your last appearance for tomorrow.'

'But perhaps it may not be my last appearance, you know,' said Nicholas.
'Unless I am summoned away, I should be sorry to inconvenience you by
leaving before the end of the week.'

'So much the better,' returned Mr Crummles. 'We can have positively
your last appearance, on Thursday – re-engagement for one night more,
on Friday – and, yielding to the wishes of numerous influential patrons,
who were disappointed in obtaining seats, on Saturday. That ought to
bring three very decent houses.'

'Then I am to make three last appearances, am I?' inquired Nicholas, smiling.

'Yes,' rejoined the manager, scratching his head with an air of some vexation; 'three is not enough, and it's very bungling and irregular not to have more, but if we can't help it we can't, so there's no use in talking. A novelty would be very desirable. You couldn't sing a comic song on the pony's back, could you?'

'No,' replied Nicholas, 'I couldn't indeed.'

'It has drawn money before now,' said Mr Crummles, with a look of disappointment. 'What do you think of a brilliant display of fireworks?'

'That it would be rather expensive,' replied Nicholas, drily.

'Eighteenpence would do it,' said Mr Crummles. 'You on the top of a pair of steps with the phenomenon in an attitude; "Fare-well" on a transparency behind; and nine people at the wings with a squib in each hand – all the dozen and a half going off at once – it would be very grand – awful from the front, quite awful.'

As Nicholas appeared by no means impressed with the solemnity of the proposed effect, but, on the contrary, received the proposition in a most irreverent manner and laughed at it very heartily, Mr Crummles abandoned the project in its birth, and gloomily observed that they must make up the best bill they could with combats and hornpipes, and so stick to the legitimate drama.

For the purpose of carrying this object into instant execution, the manager at once repaired to a small dressing-room adjacent, where Mrs Crummles was then occupied in exchanging the habiliments of a melodramatic empress for the ordinary attire of matrons in the nineteenth century. And with the assistance of this lady, and the accomplished Mrs Grudden (who had quite a genius for making out bills, being a great hand at throwing in the notes of admiration, and knowing from long experience exactly where the largest capitals ought to go), he seriously applied himself to the composition of the poster.

'Heigho!' sighed Nicholas, as he threw himself back in the prompter's chair, after telegraphing the needful directions to Smike, who had been playing a meagre tailor in the interlude, with one skirt to his coat, and a little pocket handkerchief with a large hole in it, and a woollen nightcap, and a red nose, and other distinctive marks peculiar to tailors on the stage. 'Heigho! I wish all this were over.'

CHARLES DICKENS, *NICHOLAS NICKLEBY*

✌

When William Charles Macready retired, he contrived to get a tribute from Tennyson, no less. Not the most immediate or inspiring of the poet's works, but a useful tribute all the same, and worth noting for its reference to the work Macready had done in establishing theatre as a serious and respectable art form.

❧

TO W.C. MACREADY

After his farewell performance, as Macbeth, at Drury Lane, February 26, 1851

Farewell, Macready, since tonight we part;
Full-handed thunders often have confessed
Thy power, well-used to move the public breast.
We thank thee with our voice, and from the heart.
Farewell, Macready, since this night we part.
Go, take thine honours home! Rank with the best,
Garrick and statelier Kemble, and the rest
Who made a nation purer through their art,
Thine is it that our drama did not die,
Nor flicker down to brainless pantomime,
And those gilt gauds men-children swarm to see.
Farewell, Macready; moral, grave, sublime,
Our Shakespeare's bland and universal eye
Dwells pleased, through twice a hundred years, on thee.

ALFRED, LORD TENNYSON

❧

Svetlovidov, the hero of Chekhov's wonderful short play *Swan Song*, has not retired. He has got drunk and fallen asleep in his dressing-room. Waking up when everyone else, as he thinks, has left, he surveys the darkened theatre and with it his life as a provincial actor.

❧

[SVETLOVIDOV, *in the stage costume of Calchas, comes out of a dressing-room carrying a candle, and roars with laughter.*]

SVETLOVIDOV. This is the limit, it really is too much – falling asleep in my dressing-room! The play ended hours ago, the audience went home – and there's me snoring away without a care in the world. Oh, you silly old man – you are a bad lad, old boy. Got so pickled, you dozed off in your chair! Very clever! Congratulations, old boy. [*Shouts.*] George!

226

George, curse you! Peter! They're asleep, damn them, blast them and may they rot in hell! George! *[Picks up the stool, sits on it and puts a candle on the floor.]* And answer came there none – apart from the echo, that is. I tipped George and Peter three roubles each today for looking after me, and by now they must be sunk without trace. They've left. And the bastards must have locked up the theatre. *[Twists his head about.]* Ugh, I'm drunk. God, the booze I knocked back in honour of my benefit night! I feel as if I'd been kippered, my mouth's like the bottom of a parrot's cage. Disgusting! *[Pause.]* And stupid! The old codger gets drunk, but what has he to celebrate? He hasn't the foggiest! God, I've got back-ache, the old head-piece is splitting, I'm shivering all over, and I have this dark, cold feeling, as if I was in a cellar. If you won't spare your health, you might at least remember you're too old for this caper, you silly old so-and-so. *[Pause.]* Old age – whether you try to wriggle out of it or make the best of it or just act the fool, the fact is your life's over. Sixty-eight years down the drain, damn it! Gone with the wind! The cup's drained, there's just a bit left at the bottom: the dregs. That's the way of it, that's how it is, old man. Like it or not, it's time you rehearsed for the part you play in your coffin. Good old death's only just round the corner. *[Looks in front of him.]* I say, I've been on the stage for forty-five years, but this must be the first time I've seen a theatre in the middle of the night, the very first time. You know, it's weird, damn it. *[Goes up to the footlights.]* Can't see a thing. Well, I can just make out the prompter's box and that other box over there – the one with the letter on it – and that music-stand. The rest is darkness, a bottomless black pit like a tomb: the haunt of Death itself. Brrr! It's cold, there's a piercing draught from the auditorium. Just the place to call up spirits! It's eerie, blast it, it sends shudders down my spine. *[Shouts.]* George! Peter! Hell, where are you? But why do I talk of hell, God help me? Oh, why can't you stop drinking and using bad language, for God's sake, seeing you're old and it's time you were pushing up the daisies? At sixty-eight people go to church, they get ready to die, but you –. Oh Lord, you and your bad language and your drunken gargoyle's face and this damfool costume! What a sight! I'll go and change quickly. It's all so eerie. Why, if I stayed here all night, I'd die of fright at this rate. *[Makes for his dressing-room. At that moment Nikita, wearing a white dressing-gown, appears from the furthest dressing-room at the back of the stage.]*

SCENE II

SVETLOVIDOV *[seeing Nikita, gives a terrified shriek and staggers back]*. Who are you? What are you after? Who do you want? *[Stamps.]* Who are you?

NIKITA. It's me, sir.

SVETLOVIDOV. Who's me?

NIKITA [slowly approaching him]. It's me. Nikita, the prompter. It's me, Mr
Svetlovidov, sir.

SVETLOVIDOV [collapses helplessly on the stool, breathes hard and shudders all over].
God, who is it? Is it you – you, Nikita? W-w-what are you doing here?

NIKITA. I always spend the night here in the dressing-room, sir, only please
don't tell the manager. I've nowhere else to sleep, and that's God's truth.

SVETLOVIDOV. So it's you, Nikita. Hell, I had sixteen curtain-calls, three
bunches of flowers and a lot of other things – they were all quite carried
away, but no one bothered to wake the old soak up and take him home.
I'm old, Nikita. Sixty-eight, I am. I'm ill. I feel faint and weary. [Leans
over the prompter's hand and weeps.] Don't leave me, Nikita. I'm old and
weak and I've got to die. I'm frightened, so terribly frightened.

NIKITA [gently and respectfully]. It's time you went home, Mr Svetlovidov,
sir.

SVETLOVIDOV. I won't go. I haven't got any home – haven't got one, I tell
you.

NIKITA. Goodness me, the gentleman's forgotten where he lives!

SVETLOVIDOV. I don't want to go to that place, I tell you. I'm on my own
there, I haven't anyone, Nikita – no old woman, no children, neither
kith nor kin. I'm as lonely as the wind on the heath. There will be no
one to remember me when I die. I'm frightened all alone. There's no
one to comfort me, to make a fuss of me and put me to bed when I'm
drunk. Where do I belong? Who needs me? Who loves me? No one
loves me, Nikita.

NIKITA [through tears]. Your audiences love you, Mr Svetlovidov.

SVETLOVIDOV. The audience has left and gone to bed, and it's forgotten the
old clown. No, nobody needs me, no one loves me. I've neither wife
nor children.

NIKITA. Then you've nothing to worry about.

SVETLOVIDOV. I'm a man, aren't I? I'm alive. I have blood, not water, flow-
ing in my veins. I'm a gentleman, Nikita, I'm well connected, and I was
in the army before landing up in this dump. I was a gunner. And a fine,
dashing, gallant, high-spirited young officer I was. Ye gods, what's happened to all that? And what an actor I became, eh, Nikita? [Hoists himself
up and leans on the prompter's arm.] What's become of it all, where have
those days gone to? God, I just looked into this black pit and it all came
back to me! It's swallowed forty-five years of my life, this pit has – and
what a life! Looking into it now, I see everything down to the last detail

as plain as I see your face. To be gay, young, confident, fiery! And the love of women! Women, Nikita!

NIKITA. It's time you were in bed and asleep, Mr Svetlovidov, sir.

SVETLOVIDOV. When I was a young actor and just getting into my stride, there was a girl who loved me for my acting, I remember. She was elegant, graceful as a young poplar, innocent, unspoilt. And she seemed all ablaze like the sun on a May morning. Those blue eyes, that magic smile could banish the darkest night. The ocean waves dash themselves against the cliffs, but against the waves of her hair the very cliffs, icebergs and snow avalanches might dash themselves to no avail. I remember standing before her as I stand before you now. She was looking lovelier than ever, and she gave me a look I shan't forget even in the grave. There was a kind of soft, deep, velvety caress about it, and all the dazzle of youth. Drunk with joy, I fall on my knees and beg her to make me happy. *[Continues in a broken voice.]* And she – she tells me to leave the stage. Leave the stage, see? She could love an actor, but be an actor's wife? Never! I remember how I acted that same night. It was a vulgar, slapstick part, and I could feel the scales fall from my eyes as I played it. I saw then that there's no such thing as 'sacred art', that the whole thing's just a phoney racket – saw myself a slave, a toy for people's idle moments, a buffoon, a man of straw. It was then I took the public's measure. Applause, bouquets, wild enthusiasm – I've never believed in 'em since. Yes, Nikita, these people cheer me, they pay a rouble for my photograph, but to them I'm a stranger, I'm just so much dirt – an old whore, practically! They scrape up acquaintance with me to make themselves feel important, but not one would sink to letting me marry his sister or daughter. I don't trust 'em. *[Sinks on to the stool.]* Don't trust 'em.

NIKITA. You look like nothing on earth, Mr Svetlovidov, sir – you've even scared me. Have a heart and let me take you home, sir.

SVETLOVIDOV. Then my eyes were opened, but the vision cost me dear, Nikita. After that affair – with the girl – I began drifting aimlessly, living from hand to mouth with no thought for the morrow. I took cheap, slapstick parts and hammed them. I was a corrupting influence. But I'd been a true artist, you know, I was really good! I buried my talent, cheapened it. I spoke in an affected voice, I lost my dignity as a human being. This black pit swallowed me up and gobbled me down. I never felt like this before. But when I woke up tonight, I looked back – and I've sixty-eight years behind me. I've only just seen what old age means. The show is over. *[Sobs.]* You can ring down the curtain!

NIKITA. Mr Svetlovidov, sir. I say, really, old man. Do calm yourself, sir. Oh

229

goodness me! *[Shouts.]* Peter! George!

SVETLOVIDOV. And what flair, what power, what a delivery! The wealth of feeling and grace, the gamut of emotions here in this breast *[beats his breast]* – you simply can't imagine! I feel like choking. Listen, old man – wait, let me get my breath. Here's something from *Boris Godunov:*

> 'Ivan the Terrible pronounced me son.
> And from the grave his spirit named me Dmitry;
> He stirred the peoples to revolt for me
> And destined Godunov to die my victim.
> I am Tsarevich. But enough! 'Tis shame
> To cringe before a haughty Polish beauty!'

Not bad, eh? *[Eagerly.]* Wait, here's something from *King Lear.* There's a black sky, see, and rain, with thunder growling and lightning whipping across the heavens, and he says:

> 'Blow, winds, and crack your cheeks! rage! blow!
> You cataracts and hurricanoes, spout
> Till you have drench'd our steeples, drown'd the cocks!
> You sulphurous and thought-executing fires,
> Vaunt-couriers to oak-cleaving thunderbolts,
> Singe my white head! And thou, all-shaking thunder,
> Strike flat the thick rotundity o' the world!
> Crack nature's moulds, all germens spill at once
> That make ingrateful man!'

[Impatiently.] Quick, the Fool's cue! *[Stamps.]* The Fool's cue and quick about it! I'm in a hurry.

NIKITA *[playing the part of the Fool]*. 'O nuncle, court holy-water in a dry house is better than this rain-water out o' door. Good nuncle, in, and ask thy daughters' blessing; here's a night pities neither wise man nor fool.'

SVETLOVIDOV. 'Rumble thy bellyfull! Spit, fire! spout, rain!
> Nor rain, wind, thunder, fire, are my daughters:
> I tax not you, you elements, with unkindness;
> I never gave you kingdom, called you children.'

What power, what genius, what an artist! Now for something else – something else to bring back old times. Let's take something *[gives a peal of happy laughter]* from Hamlet. All right – I commence! But what shall I do? Ah, I know. *[Playing Hamlet.]* 'O! the recorders: let me see one.' *[To Nikita.]* 'Why do you go about as if you would drive me into a toil?'

NIKITA. 'O! my lord, if my duty be too bold, my love is too unmannerly.'

SVETLOVIDOV. 'I do not well understand that. Will you play upon this pipe?'

NIKITA. 'My Lord, I cannot.'

SVETLOVIDOV. 'I pray you.'

NIKITA. 'Believe me, I cannot.'

SVETLOVIDOV. 'I do beseech you.'

NIKITA. 'I know no touch of it, my lord.'

SVETLOVIDOV. ''Tis as easy as lying; govern these ventages with your finger and thumb, give it breath with your mouth, and it will discourse most eloquent music.'

NIKITA. 'I have not the skill.'

SVETLOVIDOV. 'Why, look you now, how unworthy a thing you make of me. You would play upon me; you would seem to know my stops; you would pluck out the heart of my mystery. Do you think I am easier to be played on than a pipe? Call me what instrument you will, though you can fret me, you cannot play upon me.' *[Roars with laughter and claps.]* Bravo! Encore! Bravo! Not much old age about that, was there, damn it? There's no such thing as old age, that's a lot of nonsense. I feel strength pulsing in every vein – why, this is youth, zest, the spice of life! If you're good enough, Nikita, being old doesn't count. Think I'm crazy, eh? Gone off my head, have I? Wait, let me pull myself together. Good Lord above us! Now, listen to this – how tender and subtle. Ah, the music of it! Shush, be quiet!

> 'O silent night in old Ukraine!
> The stars are bright, clear is the sky.
> All drowsy is the heavy air
> And silver poplars faintly sigh.'

[There is the sound of doors being opened.] What's that?

NIKITA. It must be George and Peter. You're good, Mr Svetlovidov, a great actor!

SVETLOVIDOV *[shouts in the direction of the noise]*. This way, lads! *[To Nikita.]* Let's go and change. There's no such thing as old age, that's all stuff and nonsense. *[Roars with happy laughter.]* So why the tears? Why so down in the mouth, you dear, silly fellow? Now this won't do, it really won't. Really, old chap, you mustn't look like that – what good does it do? There, there. *[Embraces him with tears in his eyes.]* You mustn't cry. Where art and genius are, there's no room for old age, loneliness and illness – why, death itself loses half its sting. *[Weeps.]* Ah well, Nikita, we've made our last bow. I'm no great actor, just a squeezed lemon, a miserable nonentity, a rusty old nail. And you're just an old stage hack, a prompter. Come on. *[They start to move off.]* I'm no real good – in a serious play I could just about manage a member of Fortinbras's suite, and for that I'm too old. Ah, well. Remember that bit of *Othello*, Nikita?

> 'Farewell the tranquil mind; farewell content!
> Farewell the plumed troop and the big wars
> That make ambition virtue! O, farewell!
> Farewell the neighing steed, and the shrill trump,
> The spirit-stirring drum, the ear-piercing fife,
> The royal banner, and all quality,
> Pride, pomp, and circumstance of glorious war!'

NIKITA. Terrific! Great stuff!
SVETLOVIDOV. Or take this:

> 'Away from Moscow! Never to return!
> I'll flee the place with not a backward glance,
> And scour the globe for some forgotten corner
> To nurse my wounded heart in. Get my coach!'

> *[Goes out with Nikita.]*
> THE CURTAIN SLOWLY FALLS
> ANTON CHEKHOV, *SWAN SONG*

❧

Noël Coward's *Waiting in the Wings* is set in a retirement home for aged actresses. Two of them, May and Lotta, have not been on speaking terms for years. During the play they resolve their differences and here finally allow each other glimpses of their real states of mind.

❧

The time is after lunch on a sunny afternoon in June. Beyond the french windows the solarium can be seen in all its glory.
ALMINA, ESTELLE, BONITA, CORA and MAUDIE are sitting in it enjoying the afternoon sun. MAY is in her usual chair by the fire working away at her 'petit point'.
LOTTA is seated on the sofa reading a book. After a moment or two she closes it firmly and puts it on the table.

LOTTA: Well, I plodded through it.

MAY: Poor Marion, it's a tissue of lies from beginning to end.

LOTTA: I enjoyed the first chapters about her childhood. She says that one of her earliest memories was the crunch of carriage wheels on the drive when Mummy and Daddy came home from the Opera.

MAY: She was born over a tobacconist's shop in the Wilton Road.

LOTTA: Do you think we should write our memoirs, May?

MAY: I most certainly do not.

LOTTA: At least they'd be more interesting than Marion Brodie's Think of all that we could remember!

MAY: Think of all that we can't forget.

LOTTA: Now then, May – none of that.

Cora comes in from the solarium.

CORA *(as she goes)*: I can't bear sitting under that ghastly glass another minute – it's like a Turkish bath.

(She disappears into the television room.)

MAY: Cora was always a grumbler. Even when she was doing quite well. Nothing ever satisfied her.

LOTTA: I only saw her once when she was with Hilary at the Adelphi in the 'twenties. She wore several ropes of pearls and an astrakhan hat.

MAY: She always had delusions of grandeur.

LOTTA: I suspect that she hates being here more than any of us.

MAY *(with a note of bitterness)*: I wouldn't be too sure of that.

LOTTA *(curiously)*: Do you still hate it – so very much?

MAY *(putting down her embroidery frame)*: Still hate it? Yes, Lotta, I do. I hate it with all my heart and soul. I have tried to be resigned, and even pretended to myself that I was succeeding, but it wasn't true, it's never been true for a moment. I am formally grateful for being housed and fed, but I resent every minute of every day, and every meal that is provided for me chokes me with humiliation. I was always over-proud, which was one of the reasons that I was never very popular in the theatre, but worse, far worse, than my pride was my stupid improvidence. For that I am paying a bitter price and the bitterest part of it is that I know I have only myself to blame for my contemptible destiny. *(She takes up her work again.)* And now, if you don't mind, I should like to change the subject.

LOTTA *(with a smile)*: I see you haven't entirely lost your arrogance, May. You still like to dictate terms.

MAY: What do you mean?

LOTTA: *I* might not want to change the subject. I too might wish to bare my soul a little and discuss the carelessness and the follies and the idiocies that have brought me low.

MAY *(searchingly):* Do you?

LOTTA: No, dear, I don't. I am resigned, you see, and fairly content.

MAY: I suppose it's a question of temperament.

LOTTA: Are you implying that you possess more of that dubious asset than I do?

MAY: I'm not implying anything.

LOTTA *(thoughtfully):* Perhaps it is because I always played gentler parts than you. I was always a dreadfully sweet actress. I made my début as Cordelia.

MAY: One of the most pompous and disagreeable girls Shakespeare ever wrote.

LOTTA *(laughing):* Very well, dear – you win!

NOËL COWARD, *WAITING IN THE WINGS*

When Sir Henry Irving was near death, he was visited by Ellen Terry, for many years his partner at the Lyceum theatre. She recorded the meeting in her diary.

He was taken ill at Wolverhampton in the spring of 1905.

We had not acted together for more than two years then, and times were changed indeed.

I went down to Wolverhampton then the news of his illness reached London. I arrived late and went to an hotel. It was not a good hotel, nor could I find a very good florist when I got up early the next day and went out with the intention of buying Henry some flowers. I wanted some bright-coloured ones for him – he had always like bright flowers – and this florist dealt chiefly in white flowers – *funeral* flowers.

At last I found some daffodils – my favourite flower. I bought a bunch, and the kind florist, whose heart was in the right place if his flowers were not, found me a nice simple glass to put it in. I knew the sort of vase that I should find at Henry's hotel.

I remembered, on my way to the doctor's – for I had decided to see the doctor first – that in 1892 when my dear mother died, and I did not act for a few nights, when I came back I found my room at the Lyceum filled with daffodils. 'To make it look like sunshine,' Henry said.

The doctor talked to me quite frankly.

'His heart is dangerously weak,' he said.

'Have you told him? I asked.

'I had to, because the heart being in that condition he must be careful.'

'Did he understand *really*?'

'Oh, yes. He said he quite understood.'

Yet a few minutes later when I saw Henry, and begged him to remember what the doctor had said about his heart, he exclaimed: 'Fiddle! It's not my heart at all! It's my *breath*!' (Oh the ignorance of great men about themselves!)

'I also told him,' the Wolverhampton doctor went on, 'that he must not work so hard in future.'

I said: 'He will, though, – and he's stronger than any one.'

Then I went round to the hotel.

I found him sitting up in bed, drinking his coffee.

He looked like some beautiful grey tree that I have seen in Savannah. His old dressing-gown hung about his frail yet majestic figure like some mysterious grey drapery.

We were both very much moved, and said little.

'I'm glad you've come. Two Queens have been kind to me this morning. Queen Alexandra telegraphed to say how sorry she was I was ill, and now you –'

He showed me the Queen's gracious message.

I told him he looked thin and ill, but *rested*.

'Rested! I should think so. I have plenty of time to rest. They tell me I shall be here eight weeks. Of course I sha'n't, but still – It was that rug in front of the door. I tripped over it. A commercial traveller picked me up – a kind fellow, but d—n him, he wouldn't leave me afterwards – wanted to talk to me all night.'

I remembered his having said this, when I was told by his servant, Walter Collinson, that on the night of his death at Bradford, he stumbled over the rug when he walked into the hotel corridor.

We fell to talking about work. He said he hoped that I had a good manager ... agreed very heartily with me about Frohman, saying he was always so fair – more than fair.

'What a wonderful life you've had, haven't you?' I exclaimed, thinking of it all in a flash.

'Oh, yes,' he said quietly ... 'a wonderful life – of work.'

'And there's nothing better, after all, is there?'

'Nothing.'

'What have you got out of it all ... You and I are "getting on," as they say. Do you ever think, as I do sometimes, what you have got out of life?'

'What have I got out of it?' said Henry, stroking his chin and smiling slightly. 'Let me see ... Well, a good cigar, a good glass of wine – good friends.' Here he kissed my hand with courtesy. Always he was so courteous; always his actions, like this little one of kissing my hand, were so beautifully timed. They came just before the spoken words, and gave them peculiar value.

'That's not a bad summing-up of it all,' I said. 'And the end ... How would you like that to come?'

'How would I like that to come?' He repeated my question lightly yet meditatively too. Then he was silent for some thirty seconds before he snapped his fingers – the action again before the words.

'Like that!'

I thought of the definition of inspiration – 'A calculation rapidly made.' Perhaps he had never thought of the manner of his death before. Now he had an inspiration as to how it would come.

We were silent a long time, I thinking how like some splendid Doge of Venice he looked, sitting up in bed, his beautiful mobile hand stroking his chin.

ELLEN TERRY, *DIARY*

ॐ

It is probably the dream of many actors to die on stage – indeed several have actually done so: Edmund Kean, Mary Ure and Tommy Cooper, for example. In Louis MacNeice's poem 'Death of an Actress' he remembers Florrie Ford.

ॐ

DEATH OF AN ACTRESS

I see from the paper that Florrie Forde is dead –
Collapsed after singing to wounded soldiers,
At the age of sixty-five. The American notice
Says no doubt all that need be said

About this one-time chorus girl; whose role
For more than forty stifling years was giving
Sexual, sentimental, or comic entertainment,
A gaudy posy for the popular soul.

Plush and cigars: she waddled into the lights,
Old and huge and painted, in velvet and tiara,
Her voice gone but around her head an aura
Of all her vanilla-sweet forgotten vaudeville nights.

With an elephantine shimmy and a sugared wink
She threw a trellis of Dorothy Perkins roses
Around an audience come from slum and suburb
And weary of the tea-leaves in the sink;

Who found her songs a rainbow leading west
To the home they never had, to the chocolate Sunday
Of boy and girl, to cowslip time, to the never-
Ending weekends Islands of the Blest.

In the Isle of Man before the war before
The present one she made a ragtime favourite
Of 'Tipperary', which became the swan-song
Of troop-ships on a darkened shore;

And during Munich sang her ancient quiz
Of *Where's Bill Bailey?* and the chorus answered,
Muddling through and glad to have no answer:
Where's Bill Bailey? How do we know where he is!
Now on a late and bandaged April day
In a military hospital Miss Florrie
Forde has made her positively last appearance
And taken her bow and correctly gone away.

Correctly. For she stood
For an older England, for children toddling
Hand in hand while the day was warm and bright.
   Let the wren and robin
Gently with leaves cover the Babes in the Wood.

LOUIS MACNEICE

ﾈ

But Death, as we know, shall have no dominion, especially on stage.
Dryden wrote a speech for Nell Gwynn that required her to leap from
her coffin as she was being carried off stage, dead, at the end of *Tyrannic Love.*

NELLY'S GHOST

(To the Bearer:)
Hold! Are you mad? You damned, confounded dog!
I am to rise, and speak the epilogue.
(To the Audience:)
I come, kind gentlemen, strange news to tell ye;
I am the ghost of poor departed Nelly.
Sweet ladies, be not frightened; I'll be civil;
I'm what I was, a little harmless devil.
For, after death, we sprites have just such natures,
We had, for all the world, when human creatures;
And, therefore, I, that was an actress here,
Play all my tricks in hell, a goblin there.
Gallants, look to 't, you say there are no sprites;
But I'll come dance about your beds at nights;
And faith you'll be in a sweet kind of taking,
When I surprise you between sleep and waking.
To tell you true, I walk, because I die
Out of my calling, in a tragedy.
O poet, damned dull poet, who could prove
So senseless, to make Nelly die for love!
Nay, what's yet worse, to kill me in the prime
Of Easter-term, in tart and cheese-cake time!
I'll fit the fop; for I'll not one word say,
To excuse his godly, out-of-fashion play;
A play, which, if you dare but twice sit out,
You'll all be slandered, and be thought devout.
But, farewell, gentlemen, make haste to me,
I'm sure ere long to have your company.
As for my epitaph when I am gone,
I'll trust no poet, but will write my own:

Here Nelly lies, who, though she lived a slattern,
Yet died a princess, acting in St Catherine.

JOHN DRYDEN

238

Theatre people are notoriously superstitious. Apart from the horror of quoting from *Macbeth*, whistling is deemed unlucky (especially 'I dreamed I dwelt in marble halls'), as is knitting, wearing real jewellery, or using real flowers on stage. So is peeping through the curtain at the audience, spilling face powder – though you can diffuse that by dancing on it – or playing a yellow clarinet. These go hand in hand with the age-old theatrical adages – villains must enter from the left, every joke has three parts, and so on – that exist to baffle the novice.

With all this superstition floating around there are bound to be a few ghosts. Here, to end with, is rather a sweet one, conjured up by Walter MacQueen Pope.

About 120 years ago some workmen working on the outside walls of Drury Lane Theatre in Russell Street, where the stage door is, and where those walls are very thick indeed, found a portion of them ring hollow, when it should have been solid. This intrigued them, so they broke through. They found themselves in a tiny room which had been bricked up. In that room was a skeleton and in that skeleton's ribs was a dagger. Somebody had been murdered and bricked up there, and to this day we don't know who, when, why or how. It was a male skeleton, and the bones are buried in the little graveyard at the corner of Russell Street and Drury Lane, the graveyard that Dickens mentions in *Bleak House*, on the steps of which Lady Dedlock died.

That's all we know about that man, and for all we know he is still with us, because it's from that portion of the wall that our ghost appears. He comes through the wall out into a large room. He crosses the room, goes through a door, turns left, walks right round the back of the upper circle which, according to the costume of his day, would have been the box circle, a very smart part of the theatre, then he vanishes through the wall again in the room that balances the one from which he comes on the other side of the theatre. He is perfectly clearly to be seen. He is slightly luminous; he's a man of just over middle height; he wears a three-cornered hat – it's either a powdered wig or powdered hair, you can't quite distinguish that; he has a long grey riding cloak, early eighteenth-century period, and underneath that you can see his sword and the edge of his riding boots. The general effect is all grey. He makes no fuss. There's no bother, there's no shrieks or screams or jingling of fetters. He doesn't even carry his head tucked underneath his arm or anything like that. A perfectly well-behaved ghost who doesn't mind company, often walks during matinées when the theatre's crowded with people, and has been seen many a time by people attending those matinées to see the show. He doesn't do it regularly, but quite often. You can't make him come. He won't do that for anybody. But I myself have seen him scores and scores and scores of times. There's only one curious thing about him, although there are other ghosts with similar habits, and that is that he's a daytime ghost. He only walks between the hours of 9 a.m. and 6 p.m. For all I know he belongs to a union and those are the hours.

He doesn't do any overtime because during the war – the last war – when I was Chief Air Raid Warden and about the theatre at all hours of the night I never saw him then. But during the *day* many a time and often. We like him. We're very fond of him – because in a sense he's our mascot. The curious thing is that if we see him just before a new production we have luck – and if we don't, we don't. And to my own personal knowl- edge, (I have kept records), that has held true for the past fifty-five years. We love our ghost. He is very famous. Probably the most famous ghost in the world. And he really does belong to Drury Lane.

WALTER MacQUEEN POPE, *'THE DRURY LANE GHOST'*
IN *GHOSTS AND GREASEPAINT*

EPILOGUE

Everyone knows T. S. Eliot's poem 'Gus the Theatre Cat', but I prefer this American thespian feline, from Don Marquis's charming *Archy and Mehitabel* – a series of poems typed by a cockroach, Archy, who is the reincarnation of a *vers libre* poet. They chart his adventures with the glamorous but slightly sleazy cat-with-a-past Mehitabel, who *claims* to be the reincarnation of Cleopatra.

❧

THE OLD TROUPER
i ran onto mehitabel again
last evening
she is inhabiting
a decayed trunk
which lies in an alley
in greenwich village
in company with the
most villainous tom cat
i have ever seen
but there is nothing
wrong about the association
archy she told me
it is merely a plutonic
attachment
and the thing can be
believed for the tom

looks like one of pluto s demons
it is a theatre trunk
archy mehitabel told me
and tom is an old theatre cat
he has given his life
to the theatre
he claims that richard
mansfield once
kicked him out of the way
and then cried because
he had done it and
petted him
and at another time
he says in a case
of emergency
he played a bloodhound
in a production of
uncle tom s cabin
the stage is not what it
used to be tom says
he puts his front paw
on his breast and says
they don t have it any more
they don t have it here
the old troupers are gone
there s nobody can troupe
any more
they are all amateurs nowadays
they haven t got it
here
there are only
five or six of us oldtime
troupers left
this generation does not know
what stage presence is
personality is what they lack
personality
where would they get
the training my old friends
got in the stock companics

i knew mr booth very well
says tom
and a law should be passed
preventing anybody else
from ever playing
in any play he ever
played in
there was a trouper for you
i used to sit on his knee
and purr when i was
a kitten he used to tell me
how much he valued my opinion
finish is what they lack
finish
and they haven t got it
here
and again he laid his paw
on his breast
i remember mr daly very
well too
i was with mr daly s company
for several years
there was art for you
there was team work
there was direction
they knew the theatre
and they all had it
here
for two years mr daly
would not ring up the curtain
unless i was in the
prompter s box
they are amateurs nowadays
rank amateurs all of them
for two seasons i played
the dog in joseph
jefferson s rip van winkle
it is true i never came
on the stage
but he knew i was just off

and it helped him
i would like to see
one of your modern
theatre cats
act a dog so well
that it would convince
a trouper like jo jefferson
but they haven t got it
nowadays
they haven t got it
here
jo jefferson had it he had it
here
i come of a long line
of theatre cats
my grandfather
was with forrest
he had it he was a real trouper
my grandfather said
he had a voice
that used to shake
the ferryboats
on the north river
once he lost his beard
and my grandfather
dropped from the
fly gallery and landed
under his chin
and played his beard
for the rest of the act
you don t see any theatre
cats that could do that
nowadays
they haven t got it they
haven t got it
here
once i played the owl
in modjeska s production
of macbeth
i sat above the castle gate

in the murder scene
and made my yellow
eyes shine through the dusk
like an owl s eyes
modjeska was a real
trouper she knew how to pick
her support i would like
to see any of these modern
theatre cats play the owl s eyes
to modjeska s lady macbeth
but they haven t got it nowadays
they haven t got it
here

mehitabel he says
both our professions
are being ruined
by amateurs

                              archy

DON MARQUIS, *ARCHY AND MEHITABEL*

ACKNOWLEDGEMENTS

Pavilion Books would like to thank the following for permission to reproduce copyright material. Every effort has been made to trace and contact all copyright holders but we apologize for any errors or omissions and, if informed, would be glad to make corrections in future editions.

Extract from *In My Mind's Eye* by Michael Redgrave with permission of Weidenfeld and Nicolson; extract reprinted from *My Life* by Isadora Duncan, with the permission of Liveright Publishing Corporation. Copyright 1927 by Boni & Liveright, renewed © 1955 by Liveright Publishing Corporation; extract from *Swan Song* © Ronald Hingley 1968. Reprinted from *Twelve Plays* by Anton Chekhov translated and edited by Ronald Hingley (World Classics, 1992; originally published in *The Oxford Chekhov*, vol. 1, 1968) by permission of Oxford University Press; extract reproduced from 'Her Big Chance' from *Talking Heads* by Alan Bennett with permission of BBC Enterprises Limited; extract from *The Bite of the Night* by Howard Barker with the permission of Calder Publications Limited; extract reproduced from *Index to my Days* (Cambridge University Press) by E Gordon Craig with the permission of Ellen T M Craig; extract reproduced from *Conference of the Birds* by John Heilpern (Faber & Faber Ltd) reprinted by permission of the Peters Fraser and Dunlop Group Ltd; 'A Letter to John' from *The Kenneth Williams Diaries*, edited by Russell Davies © The Estate of Kenneth Williams Davies with the permission of HarperCollins Publishers Limited; extract from 'Nativity Play' by Joyce Grenfell from *George... Don't Do That* © Joyce Grenfell, 1977, published by Macmillan reproduced with the permission of Richard Scott Simon

Limited;extract from 'My University' from *Feeling You're Behind* by Peter Nichols with the permission of Richard Scott Simon Limited; extract from *George* by Emlyn Williams reproduced with the permission of the Executors of the Estate of the late Emlyn Williams; extract from *Blessings in Disguise* by Alec Guinness (Hamish Hamilton, 1985) copyright © Alec Guinness, 1985. Reproduced by permission of Hamish Hamilton Ltd.; extract from *Our Country's Good* copyright © 1988 Timberlake Wertenbaker. By arrangement with Michael Imison Playwrights Ltd, 28 Almeida Street, London N1 1TD; extract from *Hayfever* copyright © 1925 The Estate of Noël Coward, extract from *Waiting in the Wings* copyright © 1962 The Estate of Noël Coward, extract from *Don't Put Your Daughter on the Stage Mrs Worthington* copyright © 1968 The Estate of Noël Coward, *The Boy Actor* from *Not Yet the Dodo* copyright © 1968 by the Estate of Noël Coward, by permission of Michael Imison Ltd, 28 Almeida Street London N1 1TD; extract reproduced from the interview with Fiona Shaw from *Sheer Bloody Magic* with the permission of Virago Press Limited; extract from 'Rosalind: Iconoclast in Arden' from *Clamorous Voices: Shakespeare's Women Today* by Carol Rutter et al., edited by Faith Evans, first published in Great Britain by The Women's Press Ltd, 1988, 34 Great Sutton Street, London EC1V 0DX, reprinted on pages 156-159 is used by persmission of The Women's Press Ltd; extract from *The Actor By Himself* by Lee Strasberg with the permission of Mrs Anna Strasberg.

The author and publisher are also grateful for the permission to reproduce non-copyright material of an extract from *My Double Life* by Sarah Bernhardt, published by Hutchinson and reproduced with the premission of the Estate of Sarah Bernhardt.